J

J.

JU

D0875835

Motivation in Advertising

McGRAW-HILL SERIES IN ADVERTISING AND SELLING

Steuart Henderson Britt, *Consulting Editor*

BARTON—*Advertising Agency Operations and Management*
CRISP—*Marketing Research*
DUNN—*Advertising Copy and Communication*
HAAS—*How to Develop Successful Salesmen*
LAPP—*Successful Selling Strategies: How to Climb the Ladder to Sales Success*
MARTINEAU—*Motivation in Advertising: Motives That Make People Buy*
STEBBINS—*Copy Capsules*
WOLFF—*What Makes Women Buy*

PIERRE MARTINEAU
Director of Research and Marketing, Chicago Tribune

Motivation
in Advertising

Motives that make people buy

McGRAW-HILL BOOK COMPANY, INC.
New York   Toronto   London   1957

MOTIVATION IN ADVERTISING

Library of Congress Catalog Card Number: 57-8623

II

Preface

More and more has advertising come to be one of the most effective forces of American business. Its spectacular growth and the responsibility assigned to it by corporate management are evidence that it is paying its way. It works. Furthermore it must be something wanted and used and acted upon by the consuming public, or it would have lost its effectiveness long ago. But scarcely anyone has bothered to inquire how it works, why it works.

Many excellent books have been written on advertising method. But this book goes behind the scenes to look at the way in which advertising has its influence on the consumer mind, to show how and why it is effective, and therefore how it can be much more effective. To do this, it draws upon new understandings of the consumer as a human being, which come from the social sciences.

In the past few years there has been considerable interest in motivation research. Because advertising is trying to communicate in various ways with people, it is inevitable that sooner or later it would become aware of the development of social and psychological research in the universities. If science is learning about man, isn't there the probability that some of its findings and its methods could be adapted to the purposes of advertising and marketing?

The layman, however, has difficulty with the literature of the professional scientists. The answers to his perfectly natural questions about the basic premises of motivation research as well as its uses and possible applications have been obscured by the unfamiliar jargon of the scientists. Furthermore there just are no studies generally available for him to see, inasmuch as they have been done for private use.

Here for the first time a number of actual motivation studies are discussed in sufficient detail to show the scope of the findings. In nontechnical fashion a bridge is made between advertising and the social sciences to reveal why it is so important to understand the motivational forces influencing the consumer in his buying decisions.

As a matter of fact, this understanding has vital significance for any person in marketing.

In contrast to the frequent discussions about motivation research, there is another area of learning which is just as significant for advertising and which has yet scarcely been talked about—the fields of communication and semantics. Advertising is a major form of mass communication in America. Just because so much intended communication does go off the track, here again it is essential to realize what makes the wheels go around in any communication. What are the carriers of meaning—language and what else?

In recent years a prominent advertising professional stated that all human communication was by words. Nothing could be further from the truth.

Because we live in such a highly verbal atmosphere, many professionals do look upon advertising as essentially juggling words. They are under the misconception that they are manipulating the consumer when they confront him with their slogans and themes. In actuality they are not manipulating anybody. Advertising is trying to communicate meaning to intelligent human beings, and all too often it fails in its purpose. The advertiser's meaning does not come through to the audience. The reader is unconvinced or simply fails to understand the advertiser. "I don't get it," the reader says puzzled, and goes on.

This book brings together much highly provocative thinking on the subject of what is actually taking place when humans communicate with one another. It is directly related to the process of persuasion and conviction. It will shed different light on the creative people in advertising and on the directions they have to take for successful communication.

Without detracting from the importance of copy, almost no one has come to grips with the function of the esthetic elements such as illustration, color, typography, and layout, in print advertising. Modern advertising "looks" modern because of these elements, not the words. But just exactly what is their role? There is growing awareness that these elements are not merely subservient to the copy theme, as is commonly taken for granted. Package design, color, and style have enormous sales value for products. They are entirely unrelated to the ingredient and functional qualities of the products. Nobody tries to relate them.

Why then should it be decreed that the esthetic components of advertising must be stepchildren to the copy claims? Based on communication theory and actual motivation studies, this book shows why the various esthetic elements and the nonverbal symbols are so important in their own right—how they can say things about a product or store which could never be said in words.

Also there is considerable reason to believe that the function of advertising in our economy is changing because the economy itself has changed. Now more than ever the consumer wants something else besides bare functional qualities from the products he buys and the services he employs. He wants much more than a fire-sale atmosphere.

Yet there are countless advertisers who have created no appeal for their products but the dullest utilitarian attributes. Their advertising performs at very low degrees of effectiveness because they only see advertising as bargain and technical information. Their brands have little distinction in the consumer's mind because they restrict their public relations entirely to rational claims about minute technical differences which the consumer's basic intelligence says are unimportant or nonexistent.

This book indicates other paths to product distinction which have always been important, but which are increasingly so today. They are the key to the changing function of advertising.

Acknowledgments

This book is really a synthesis of my own ideas, the ideas of many scholars in many fields, plus the ideas of my professional associates. I am indebted to the many social scientists and creative advertising people with whom it has been my privilege to work.

I am fortunate in having a staff with a diversity of backgrounds in the behavioral sciences headed by Don Klein. Their technical knowledge and brilliant insights have contributed much to the writing of this book.

Three of the chapters detail studies which were done by Social Research, Inc. of Chicago. I have used in considerable part the original studies just as they were reported. Advertising as a whole owes much to this group directed by Dr. Burleigh Gardner for introducing the concepts of product image and social class into marketing and for having made motivation research truly scientific.

Finally, it has been my extreme good fortune to have as friend and counselor one of the most creative and courageous minds in the social sciences, Prof. W. Lloyd Warner of the University of Chicago.

Pierre Martineau

Contents

Motivation in Advertising

CHAPTER I

The Illusion of Communication

"The great enemy of communication is the illusion of it." Human beings have the habit of talking and writing too much without conveying any meaning. Nowhere is this more true than in advertising, which too often ends up as the communication from one set of professionals to another set of professionals, not to the mass audience they are supposed to be reaching.

For one thing, as a middle-class, well-educated group, advertising people naturally assume that all Americans are involved with words on the same levels that they are. But in point of truth, relatively few human beings are actually skilled with words. Brought up on an intellectual diet of Grade B movies, comic books, sports pages, and electronic comedians, the average individual is not equipped to cope with the professional communicator.

As a matter of fact, he has a deep mistrust for the person who is too skilled with words. There is a term in the language—"Philadelphia lawyer"—to indicate the person who is too facile with logic. The feeling is that somehow or other he is going to overwhelm us with assertions that aren't really true. This is expressive of our profound aversion for the fast con man, the barker, the pitchman, the huckster—anyone who is too glib with words. We are repelled by him. His words have the flavor of wet cardboard. He's nobody that we can trust.

And yet this is the heart of practice and theory in advertising, a formulated strategy for persuasion which is a superstructure of words. I quote from two current advertisements addressed to the mass consumer in mass-circulation media:

1. The Bio-Flavinoids in the meat of the orange are found to affect the health of young and old in a *unique* and basic way. They have an amazing effect on the *capillary* system. . . . The Bio-Flavinoids work to keep the *capillaries functional.* Teamed with *vitamin C,* these factors in the meat of the orange help keep *capillary* walls strong, efficient. . . . A medium size orange contains a rich supply . . . about 1000 *mgs.*

1

2. Now the 3-way *Protein* dog diet adds Lecithin, a natural food substance found in egg yolk and *soya germ*,—recognized by scientists as essential to *life processes*. Furthermore this vital food element is an excellent natural source of *phosphorus* and important *B-complex vitamins*. . . . Lecithin helps increase *longevity* for your dog by aiding his *assimilation* of *Vitamins A and D*, and by more rapid *emulsification* and *absorption* of fat.

I would guess that the words and terms which I have italicized are incomprehensible to and incapable of definition for most American adults, on the basis of reading-comprehension studies.

2

However, entirely apart from this factor of word levels, there are inherent here a number of propositions which are part and parcel of our basic thinking about any advertising:

1. An overreliance on words—as if a formidable parade of words is the key to persuasion—as if words are the essence of meaning.

2. Literally, a belief in word magic—as if people are stunned and miraculously transformed by a mere flick of words. Like a witch tossing a blue powder on the flame and solemnly muttering, "Ali Kazam," some advertisers hopefully offer the consumer a diet of such meaningless words as "sensimatic," "double-torsion," "5-D," "Solium," "Gardol." Gaines dog food is better with DLM, Mobilgas with MC 4, and Alemite has CD 2. This is confusing a gimmick of communication with communication itself.

3. A straining to magnify minuscule differences between products. As if the consumer were vitally curious and impressed about minute technical superiorities.

4. Looking at the world from the eyes of the product. As if any product as a physical thing had concrete properties and superiorities which the consumer will discover and value once they are dramatized.

I have singled out these specific copy approaches only because this kind of thinking is not hard to find in advertising. Yet to me such advertising practices constitute a dead-end street which will become increasingly fruitless and barren, even though they reflect our very manner of thinking. There are two fundamental elements here which should be approached from altogether different directions: *communication* and *motivation*.

In spite of advertising's prosperity and a long history of successful campaigns, it lacks a decent body of theory as to its real purposes. It lacks an understanding of what is actually transpiring in the very process of communication, where far, far more is necessary for conviction than product claims and avalanches of words and mere information. Furthermore, advertising needs a much clearer awareness of human behavior and of the motives that move people.

The ancient Greeks, in spite of their brilliance, never developed any real science because of their weakness for building elaborate systems of reasoning on single key ideas which came from logic or common sense. It was like the child's game of building a structure of matches. If the key idea was wrong, the whole structure collapsed. Yet they never bothered to find out if these key ideas actually had any grounding in real life, which is the method of modern experimental science.

Too many advertising and marketing strategies are built on the assumption that it is always possible to single out the motives which are the key to any given sales problem merely by using logic and common sense. Just talk it over and put your finger on the motive. Again this is relying on words instead of bothering to validate the premises by studying people. For if the key motive being addressed turns out to be wrong, then the whole strategy of the campaign falls apart.

In this day and age, no manufacturer would throw his products together in the haphazard fashion that some manufacturers fashion their sales and advertising strategies. He would never toss in some grease and alcohol and raspberry jam and nails, and hopefully pray that something might come out of it. Yet this is the pattern in the conception of too many advertising strategies: your ideas and my ideas and what my wife said and what a successful competitor is doing and let's try it and see because it sounds good. Why bother to find out if people are really responsive to this appeal, so long as it makes sense on paper?

This is a critical blind spot of business and advertising—the failure to understand people for what they really are. Worse than this is the complete lack of curiosity. In absolute contradiction to the experimentation and probing and verification which are basic methods in engineering and in the physical research responsible for the never-ceasing flood of technological triumphs, business reverts from this attitude of the scientific mind to a naïve and happy ignorance as it approaches the consumer. The same manufacturer with a corps of physicists, chemists, and biologists researching his product thinks he can understand the human mind with no more equipment than any barefoot boy has.

There is every reason why motivation and communication should be systematically studied. If it is possible to probe such areas, certainly the selling strategy and the copy appeals will be infinitely more effective when they are directed toward potentially powerful motive forces instead of completely irrelevant motives; when the basic themes are not violating any underlying governing attitudes; when the overtones are consistent with the predominant social and psychological currents in our style of life; when the product personality becomes clear-cut and meaningful.

What advertising needs very badly is a fresh look at what it really is. Far too many advertisers use this powerful communication force only in a most rudimentary way—mere name identification and a claim or two which may or may not be important to people.

Insistence on product claims and economic benefits has turned far too much advertising into a dull, uninvolving chant of mechanica and ingredients which shows no awareness of how people are persuaded about anything.

"Only white Amoco-Gas passes the lead-fouling test." Does anybody know what they're talking about? Does anybody really care? Will this sort of claim make any dent on the public's deep conviction, as shown by innumerable studies, that all gasolines are the same?

One of the difficult problems that advertising is confronted with is the increasing standardization of products and services. Any actual differences in quality, price, packaging, or service have disappeared almost to the vanishing point. Bread, milk, meat, clothing, refrigerators, airline service, banks, or what have you: physically they are virtually indistinguishable. And yet more and more is it necessary for advertising to presell the product by individualizing it—making it more desirable than anything else.

In the traditional method of advertising, the only recourse is to magnify some physical difference which can be proudly held up as a product benefit. But when the actual differences are nonexistent, this technique ends up as a straining over some thoroughly unimportant feature—or as idea bankruptcy.

Furthermore the primary reliance is virtually always placed on words. Whether the features are unimportant or very important, the copy-oriented people assume there can be no communication, no persuasion, no individualization of product, no real desirability except by words. Therefore, the copy and the logic are sacred.

Yet the truth is that almost never are words the whole key to persuasion through advertising. More often than not they play a minor role in what is actually happening. Every member of American society learns to discount the words and the claims of advertising. "Oh, that's just advertising" is part of our language, typifying exaggerations which the individual should know better than to accept at face value. "The cleanest clean possible is Tide clean." "Fab gets clothes whitest-white and cleanest-clean you've ever seen." "Rinso blue washes whiter than new." "You haven't washed your cleanest wash until you've washed with Wisk." Would anybody in his right mind swallow this gem: "It's a fact that the most courteous people in the entire food industry are right here at the Red Owl Store in Winona" (Minnesota).

In the same issue of a recent newspaper were three successive full-page grocery-chain advertisements with these headings:

A store cuts your food bill more.
Save more at B store.
It's a fact you save more at C store.

Did I believe any of these? Of course not. Did anyone? I don't think so. And yet, curiously, all this advertising is apparently productive. Winston became a top-selling filter cigarette with advertising words which merely said, "Winston tastes good—like a cigarette should." But that's not enough distinction to vault Winston over the heads of well-entrenched predecessors. Something else is obviously being communicated below the word level, and the judgment to buy is apparently being formulated at this level of communication.

The advertising manager of Coca-Cola declared that in all its years of advertising, the product had never used claims—not in the "reason-why," product-benefit sense. Nothing like "50% more cola berry than other leading brands." But in a variety of ways the advertising has conveyed such attributes as "delicious" and "refreshing," though seldom saying so in words. A tremendous desirability was engendered on another level of communication than the levels of logic and language.

What are the other levels of communication which people apparently use all the time? How do people communicate when they are not using words? How important is it for advertising to use consciously these other avenues of communication?

3

The visual symbols are highly significant carriers of meaning in any advertisement. But in the enormous increase of advertising exposures which the consumer is being confronted with, the visual symbols are increasingly important in their own right. In solving the problem of how to get through to the consumer, the visual symbols communicate much faster, much more directly than any long involved argument in words. There is no work called for, no mental effort.

Any copy in advertising is an argument. It literally is throwing down a challenge to the reader or viewer and saying, "Let's argue about this." The human reaction to any statement of claim is "Wait a minute! Who says so?" Built into copy is the presupposition of rejection.

But the picture is a free gift. There is no challenge and no threat to the audience. It's a piece of decoration enjoyed without resistance. And it is communicating highly significant meaning.

Words can't even communicate anything unless they create images in our minds. Otherwise we can't conceive of the object or idea. But in so many instances other symbols, such as a gesture or picture, a tone or a mood, will create these images much faster and more adequately than words.

The average individual doesn't really like copy and words because he's been punished all his school life for not being skilled in things which are stated in words. There are punitive elements in our feelings about big new words facing us, words such as "emulsification" and "assimilation." But nobody was ever punished for not understanding pictures. And whereas we deeply distrust the propagandist and the Philadelphia lawyer because we fear they are going to overwhelm us with some phony claims that aren't true, nobody has that feeling about pictures. There is no fear that anyone is trying to overwhelm us.

In every experience I have ever had of asking people their reactions to individual advertisements, they have done much of their responding in terms of the art. Since this nonverbal communication is so important to the audience, obviously we should have insights into the communication process which go far beyond any of our present understandings. We need to overhaul our basic thinking about persuasion and product meaning and about the place of logical, highly rational appeals versus emotional appeals, which may have infinitely greater impact on motive forces. Actually what is called for is a pretty drastic fracture of our faith in the power of logic and rationality.

We are not going to accomplish anything merely by stating a logical case. We are not going to persuade anybody by winning an argument with the consumer via our logic and our words.

One of the great reawakenings of human thought has been occasioned by the rediscovery of feeling. For 300 years men have worshiped at the altar of Reason. "Know the truth and the truth shall make you free." Just present the facts, people said, and the economic man will make rational decisions. If the logic is on your side, your case is won.

Although writers, musicians, actors, parents, and salesmen have understood for centuries the primary importance of feeling in the shaping of human judgments, beliefs, and behavior, in any formal thinking no one would admit this. Feeling was pushed out of sight—buried. Man was governed only by reason and intellect. Today scientists and thinkers recognize how silly this fiction is. If we reconstruct our own lives for an hour or a day—our daydreams, our irrational actions, our behavior influenced by associations and attachments, our fondness for our children and pets, our escapes into hobbies and movies, our preference for pretty secretaries—we should be honest enough to realize that there is probably no mental action and no behavior in which feeling does not play a central role.

All of this has a very direct bearing on what we are trying to do. We have to see people as they are. We have only proceeded a few steps down the path when we construct jigsaw patterns of very sound selling argument. We have to think of the emotional appeals and the esthetic effects in advertising also—the symbolic communication and the motive appeals—or we probably shall have exactly nothing as an effective effort at persuasion.

Consider that for a human being, psychological subjective realities are just as pressing and powerful as the physical realities. A woman will sit for hours torturing herself under a permanent-wave machine. For what? For the illusion of beauty. There is no earthly reason why she has to undergo this discomfort. But try to tell her that.

Placebos in medicine are inert, inactive substances that doctors sometimes give patients who demand medicine although they really don't need it. But in study after study in specific experiments, the patients recovered just as well with the inert substance as they did with the real medicine. For example, the reduction in number of yearly colds was greater with placebos than with cold vaccine. Placebos were just as effective as any medicine in stopping coughing. Sixty per cent of subjects with chronic headaches received relief from placebos. The evidence is so overwhelming that it is stated in the *Psychological Bulletin* that "the relief of any particular complaint by a given medication is not sufficient evidence for the specific effect of the medicine on the complaint unless it can be shown that the relief is not obtained as a placebo effect."

The point is that the patients make a psychological recovery just from the contact with the doctor, which relieves their physical symptoms.

I mentioned Coca-Cola as a striking illustration of advertising success without the use of highly rational appeals. Besides the notions of "delicious" and "refreshing" and a great many other attributes which the advertising has conveyed, one piece of copy states, "Coca-Cola says you are doing the right thing." In other words, you wouldn't think of serving your guests a blackberry soda. But Coca-Cola is the fitting, proper ritual. This is a different kind of "fact" than economic benefits and physical properties, but nevertheless important.

Chevrolet has very effectively injected some meanings into its product personality with outdoor advertising picturing a car and a single word—"Perky," and in another instance "Frisky." Here again is a motive appeal which is important but which is totally unrelated to price and mechanics.

This is why the focus on all advertising has to be changed so that, instead of looking outward from the product to the consumer, we see the product from the consumer's eyes and thus can fit it into his life. It isn't important what the manufacturer thinks the consumer ought to know about his product. The important focus is: what would most appeal to the consumer as a human being?

"Schlitz outsells all other beers." So what? This is undoubtedly a source of considerable pride to the brewery, but how does it put the brand in the consumer's life?

Motivation research is rapidly taking shape as a new tool available to modern advertising in the search for understandings of people. There is every reason why we should organize and expand such new areas of research. Up to now, research in advertising has been entirely in the hands of market researchers who have essentially been supply-ing descriptive data on the size of markets and audiences. They are competent statisticians and economists, products of the schools of business, but usually with nothing in their training that would acquaint them with the disciplines involved in the study of human behavior.

The market researcher's emphasis is on measuring how many people did what. His data on national income, market potentials, character-istics of buyers, brand positions, size of audience, sales tests are all extremely important. But none of it is very helpful to the creative men on how to talk to people. Nothing in this data, for instance, gives any clues whatever to the highly significant social and psychological changes which are occurring all around us: the mass exodus to the suburbs, changing living patterns of the working class, the drift to casual living, vast shifts in our taste, such as our flair for vivid color. Why are all these things happening? What is their significance for us in advertising?

The methods of the physical sciences—the determinations of exact cause-and-effect relationships expressible in rigid quantifications—have been brilliantly successful in our technological civilization. But these same methods are completely fruitless for understanding the dynamics of human behavior—the how and why of such typical mental happenings as emotion, intuition, imagination, creativity, mood, personality structure. Illustration and music and color are integral parts of modern advertising, yet nothing from statistical research sheds any light whatever on these esthetic avenues to communication.

4

I should halt long enough to make it clear that by no means is content the only factor in advertising success. Obviously there are many other elements with highly important bearing. The mere fact of name identification has proved very profitable for many advertisers, as witness those who buy neon signs, clocks, animated spectaculars. For reasons that we don't understand, registering the name alone can do something to the consumer.

Weight of advertising is important. Big-budget advertisers are generally more successful than small-budget advertisers. Mere repetition of a message can cause it to sink into the individual's mind. Each medium of advertising also has its own individual effectiveness to contribute. And for any single advertisement, it could be pointed out that the factor of attention is vital. Before the message can persuade or even be noticed, it must have an audience.

But having said all these things, I come back to content—literally what is said and how it is conveyed. Because it is the least subject to formula, content is necessarily the most unstructured area of advertising and also the most lamentably wanting in theory. Yet in spite of the importance of content, our thinking about advertising has mostly been preoccupied with other things, as if their success would automatically solve the problem of content.

Nielsen ratings, Starch ratings, outdoor traffic counts, magazine and newspaper circulations, milline rates, pass-around readership, duplication studies are all concerned with size of audience and the factor of attention. Without derogating from their importance in any degree— because they are important—it should be stated that attention alone is no guarantee that the audience will be moved to action—or persuaded. It is a very simple thing to single out innumerable campaigns which did receive high readership or high viewership and yet which were failures from a sales standpoint. They did have an audience, and yet what was said did not move the viewers or readers to do what the advertiser hoped they would.

There shouldn't be any mystery about this. I can be attracted to look at an advertisement by many proven stoppers—by pictures of pretty girls, dogs, babies, by color, or by a good show on television. Obviously I am not going to buy girdles, office equipment, chemicals, and the long, long list of products in which I have no interest. But neither do I buy many brands in the categories where I am an active buyer, in spite of the fact that I am exposed to the advertising message on countless occasions. For me the message has no appeal, no power to activate the motive forces that make the wheels go around in me.

Such theory as there is in advertising has been almost entirely dominated by copy-oriented people who act as if the last word in advertising had been stated about thirty years ago. The one thing we don't need is a Know-Nothing movement which discourages experimentation and originality, which insists we turn back to the sacred principles of the past. All the more is this true when the sacred principles are wrong. Advertising has to move out of this hermaphroditic half-world of bargains and claims if it is to continue its constant development, if it is to move to new productivity.

As brilliantly successful and prosperous as modern advertising is, there nevertheless are whole islands where the advertiser's sights have been held so low that no one has ever experienced a fraction of what might be expected from advertising. Tire advertising in newspapers could be cited as an example of the Neanderthal approach. Every tire advertisement in newspapers is a black line drawing of a big tire, and if it isn't part of a Labor Day or a Decoration Day sale, the claims are strictly abracadabra about cords and treads. No people, no automobiles, nothing whatever in the way of an illustration into which the reader can project himself. There is no awareness whatever that the ordinary motorist acts and feels different than the professional tire buyer for a trucking company.

This lack of distinction is typical of so much retail advertising as the result of the retail counterpart of the same advertising theory. The merchandising authority E. B. Weiss has repeatedly pointed out that whereas the older chain groups started out as distinctive types of retail organizations, today they are becoming formless and faceless. Their "hard-sell" advertising gives them no individuality, no personality, a minimum of customer loyalty. Although the customer thinks of his stores from multitudinous different angles, the average merchant has one resource for talking to the customer: something on sale. "Prices slashed to the bone!"

These advertisers and those in countless other classifications are figuratively tripping over their shoelaces. And yet advertising has to be better. Mere brand identification—the feeble name-and-a-claim gesture—will have increasingly less chance to register on the consumer mind. Mediocre advertising has to compete with too much other advertising, too much highly effective advertising.

Apart from this problem of raising the advertising sights in so many fields, a much clearer articulation of advertising purpose is needed for training and teaching. Agency heads constantly mention the shortage of first-rate creative talent. How do we develop talent with originality and imagination and freshness? In the colleges, the student can get much descriptive training about method but virtually nothing on the process of creation. Knowledge of the mechanics of advertising is not knowledge of the creative process. From the elder statesmen of advertising, the fledgling hears much nostalgia and many platitudes: read the Old Masters and write a lot. But an individual could read the classics of literature and write forever without ever learning to be competent in advertising.

Apprenticeship in the actual work situation usually does not permit the youngster to come in contact with the top professionals. From others he soaks up the usual rules, which thereafter serve as his advertising conscience. He very often develops on his own and learns to pay no attention to these elementary restrictive rules in practice. But always his conscience is bothered by these ABC rules.

It is high time that advertising developed a new philosophy for itself revolving about these three factors:

1. A clear articulation of the fundamental purposes of the creative person.

2. A completely different understanding of the human process of communication which will afford entirely new insights on the attainment of meaning and persuasion.

3. A basic knowledge of motivation, reflecting a far more accurate picture of the motives that make men buy and act like people.

Such a philosophy should lift advertising's sights to new horizons of productivity, to new goals that never before seemed possible.

CHAPTER II

Advertising for Information and for Power

Well over a hundred years ago the British essayist Thomas De Quincey acutely distinguished between what he called the "literature of knowledge" and the "literature of power." The function of the first is to teach; that of the latter is to move people. One is like a rudder, the other like a sail. The first speaks to a mere discursive or rational understanding. The other must and does operate on and through, as he puts it, "that humid light which clothes itself in the mists and glittering iris of human passions, desires and emotions."

De Quincey compares a cookbook to Milton's *Paradise Lost*. "What do you learn from *Paradise Lost*? Nothing at all. What do you learn from a cookbook? Something new. But from Milton you get power." Just so, any great work of literature has the ability to move people profoundly.

The distinction De Quincey makes is fundamental for advertising. We are not just putting together information; we are not writing cookbooks and railroad timetables; we are not organizing scientific descriptions or engineering reports. On the contrary, we are using a form of mass communication which does literally have the power to move people, because it can reach them at far deeper levels than rational understanding. Modern advertising can and does reach into the emotional structure, the unconscious, the deepest sources of motivation in the individual. This is what the creative people are trying to create—a message which will incorporate this power to move human beings just because it *can* get at their primitive, fundamental, prelogical motives and impulses.

This is what is so very difficult for the practical businessman and the extremely rational mind to grasp. They see advertising only as a logical, orderly presentation of sales facts about the product which the consumer will evaluate in a logical, orderly fashion. Therefore the word is all-important. Saying the right word about the product is, to their way of thinking, the key to successful advertising. You

12

persuade the consumer—you convince him with sound selling messages which appeal logically to his self-interest.

In actuality, advertising as communication hasn't even started to accomplish its purpose if it stops here. Modern advertising is not just a posting of claims, a bare-bones statement of facts. It is far, far from being just a reliance on words and logic. It is rather a fusion of many modes of human communication, including language. Advertising as we know it today uses layout and illustration, both photography and art; it uses color and music, even choreography and drama. Actually it also uses language in a far more expressive way than just to present rational thought. Any given ad may have any number of appeals which are not openly presented. It may have esthetic appeal, entertainment value, or irrelevant but highly valuable information, as well as various psychological attractions. Besides economic self-interest, advertising leans heavily on such other psychological processes as suggestion, association, repetition, identification, fantasy, etc. The point is that the creative people are trying to achieve various effects which are just as vital to the success of the advertisement as any sales claims, and they have to convey them in a different way.

Because the entire emphasis of our educational discipline and business training is on analytical thought and cause-and-effect logic, the practical mind never gets any exposure to the workings of the artist's and the writer's mind and how they have to proceed to create anything worthwhile. In this chapter I want to bring together some material on the subject of creativity in advertising, to show how the creative person's approaches are fundamentally different from the typically analytical approach to a problem and to show why they have to be different. Neither is right and neither is wrong. They are just different.

To clarify why creative people must proceed differently, I should push all the way back to the beginning and ask the question, "What is advertising?"

I am trying to probe far beyond the long list of sophomoric definitions to the effect that "advertising is selling," "advertising is the art of persuasion," or "advertising is wants propaganda," because these are all essentially descriptive efforts, stated in oversimplified, popular terms. I am thinking more about the nature of the process itself. I should really ask the question, "How does advertising work? What is actually happening in the process of persuasion through advertising?" Approaching the problem this way should make it fairly clear that so much more is going on than just a sales argument with the consumer.

Fundamentally, advertising uses the laws of attention and association. It hopes to set off the product as something pretty wonderful by draping around it as many activating and pleasant associations as possible, by attaching to it all sorts of meanings with powerful motivation value in addition to its bare functional-use meanings. The product is no longer just a brown sweet liquid or a mechanical object for transportation. Now it carries as a part of itself a rich load of esthetic imagery, emotive meanings, and even other logical uses. All of these associations have been infused into the product personality by suggestion. Thereafter, when the consumer is in a situation of buying choice, these suggested associations come tumbling into his mind. Generally he is not aware of their source or of the exact nature of their motive power. He simply chooses the product with a feeling that "this is the best."

Our technique and objective seem so self-evident that they scarcely require elaboration. The picture of a child, the escape scene of a lake, the atmosphere of sophistication, the nuance of status, the masculinity of a ballplayer, the hearts-and-flowers musical background are clearly obvious efforts to attach these associations to a physical object. The associations are being fed in at many levels in the ideal advertisement. Virtually every ad offers the consumer some convincing "reasons why" at the rational level. There are many fairly evident nonverbal appeals, like the emotive protectiveness in the life insurance copy, the lovable animal with the so-sad eyes in the dog-food ad, the mouth-watering goodness in typical food copy. Consumers can identify these meanings.

But then also there are usually powerful meanings and desirabilities being conveyed at entirely unconscious levels, the full weight and implication of which are not fully apparent even to creative people. Who knows why the mere name-identification value of an outdoor spectacular should make a product more desirable? Who knows what color or striking layout does to people? We know next to nothing about the "why" of esthetic effects. All over the world decorative artists have used the same fundamental motifs of design, as, for example, the circle, triangle, spiral, parallels, and floral rosette. Apparently humans have a built-in esthetic capacity to enjoy these forms. Apart from various esthetic effects, however, there are many other subtleties and nuances of meaning which can come in at the unconscious, subverbal levels, communicating very clearly to the receptors of the unconscious intelligence.

In nearly every study of product images that I have seen, the advertising was saying many things entirely unsuspected by the advertiser. Some unimportant or irrelevant symbol was fastened onto by the audience, just as a limp handshake or an overbearing manner becomes a signal about the character of an individual.

Psychologists unhesitatingly state that the main appeal which advertising uses and the one on which we place our main reliance is the emotional, in the sense that we are trying to create suggested association with strong motive power. And particularly do these psychologists assert that it generally is insufficient just to convince the consumer on rational grounds.

In no sense am I minimizing the necessity for strong selling arguments. But reason-why advertising by itself just doesn't go far enough. It doesn't accomplish all that advertising could and should accomplish, if it stops short with a narrow, uninvolving statement of claims. I repeat, the literature of information and knowledge is different from the literature of power.

And that is what advertising is hoping to do—to move people as well as to present them with some claims of superiority. Advertising essentially is dealing with a primitive, prelogical process of the mind—with the compulsion to action initiated by suggestion, by a long list of conscious and unconscious motive forces, by the totally unknown power of esthetic sensibility. Yet the narrow sense of reason-why advertising would hold advertising appeal only to the adult level of rational thinking.

2

There is no need whatever for considering this an "either/or" situation. The tendency to see all things as black or white, to put everything in an "if-you're-not-for-it, you-must-be-against-it" framework is an error of reasoning strongly criticized by the semanticists. Few problems can be posed strictly in black and white. In concrete practice virtually every advertisement today is a blend of both realism and fantasy. Sometimes one emphasis dominates very strongly and sometimes the other, but both are almost always present.

Just to make the point that all advertising ranges between the extremes, let me cite some extremes.

Realism—Purely Functional Use, Economics, Mechanics

1. Announcing the new Eureka Super-Rotomatic with Zip-Clip Swivel Top and Spectacular 4-Wheel Roto Dolly.

2. Norge Washer with Dispenser Wheel Automatically makes a new kind of rinse water for up to 39% brighter, cleaner clothes. (Proof from the Laboratory. Proof at Home.)

Fantasy—Emotion, Subjective Meanings

1. It's Fun to Phone. Once upon a time there were two people who were sad and lonely and wishing they could hear a cheery word. And then a wonderful device that could send voices over wires brought them together, like a fairy wand, and they lived happily ever after. . . .

2. If you love life—you'll love France! Fall in France—how you'll love every golden moment! Paris sparkles with light and laughter from the banks of the Seine to the huddled chimney pots of old Montmartre.

But no matter how overwhelming is the logic of the product story, virtually every advertisement today utilizes both approaches. Nobody relies on a recitation of facts in a page of black type. The illustrations, the use of color, the character of the TV show, the background music and the qualities of the radio announcer's voice—even the most convincing fact story will have far greater impact if it is presented in a garb of fantasy.

The fantasy emphasis is just an overstatement of what all advertising is attempting to do in varying degree: to attach emotional or esthetic associations, or both, to a purely physical object and thereby transmute it into something other than a purely physical object. While I have cited copy examples, talking explicitly about emotion is generally awkward and makes the audience uncomfortable. Emotion is much more acceptably and meaningfully conveyed by the visual and non-verbal symbols.

The stated philosophy of the French Government Tourist Office advertising details a highly successful method. All campaigns evolved for the FGTO over a period of years have met these yardsticks:

a. The conception and execution must achieve the distinction characteristic of France.

b. They must say France immediately through the art by such well-known symbols as the Eiffel Tower.

c. They must create an emotional effect. Every ad is largely dominated by the illustration.

d. They must be sophisticated to fit the preconceptions which travelers have of France.

e. The short copy must touch a few specific things to do in France.

However, I question if we fully understand the true function of these nonrational components of modern advertising which distinguish it from a testing-laboratory report, which make it infinitely more effective. Our lifelong habits of thinking are so dominated by practicality and by the mechanistic approach to problem solving that we view such things as illustration and color and the esthetics of white space as mere incidentals, little devices to attract attention.

3

All the talking on advertising theory has been done by the copy people. As writers, it is quite natural that they would think that copy writing is the basis of advertising. They formulate the logic of the claim; they are entrusted with the care and feeding of words. But in all fairness, even if the writer did try to evaluate the other component elements of advertising from a completely objective viewpoint, it is very difficult for the average writer to grasp what the artist or the show producer is really trying to do. They just simply use different levels of expression. The literary essay on art or music is invariably too intellectualized. The writer's viewpoint is much closer to that of the man in the street.

In advertising, the typical journeyman wordsmith seems quite insensitive to the fact that illustration, color, and design can by themselves alone be powerful channels of communication to the inner man. Schwerin Research states that mood commercials are often just as effective on television as demonstration commercials. How do you best create mood in anything? Music can arouse mood faster, more effectively, and more flexibly than anything else but the very best of pictures or words can do. Most attempts to generate mood with the language of advertising jargonese end up as shallow and unconvincing. To take another example, pictures will convey ideas with a completeness and clarity that words can never attain. Try to describe a pretty girl and see how hopelessly inadequate is any word report by comparison to a picture.

In no sense am I trying to minimize copy. I am merely indicating that each of the component elements of advertising, and these include color, language in its plastic sense, and a great many nonverbal symbols, can be a channel for communicating with the audience. Communication by no means is confined to the descriptive and literal quality of the copy writer's words. Why should anyone think this is mystic speculation? Most certainly it is a different kind of meaning from rational-language thought. But what is music? Why do people everywhere enjoy it? Why does it have such tremendous power to move us? One music authority states that music reproduces the most intimate essence of our psychic life more directly and significantly than is possible in any other medium of communication.

Although the routine patterns of business life and the entire emphasis of our schooling and technical training virtually ignore the existence of esthetics and though we are actually uncomfortable with the language used in these different forms, nevertheless esthetic expression is a fundamental trait of humankind. Every one of the five senses has an esthetic capacity, as well as a survival value. We smell perfume, we like the touch of velvet, we savor the taste of good food, we hear music, we see color. Every single sensation we experience has some feeling tone in greater or less degree. It is unrealistic to overlook or minimize this powerful side of human biology.

Actually, of course, in the recognition which business management does give to package design, to styling, to color, to displays and fixtures and store windows, there is awareness, even if it is unexpressed, that the sensory, affective appeals are important avenues of influence. These are the same channels which the creative people in advertising are trying to use.

There is also an enormous amount of informative communication going on between humans at subverbal levels which is not emotional or esthetic—just informative. For instance, there are whole areas of human activity which are highly significant but which are never discussed in words. All the communication here is restricted to the nonverbal type. We never proclaim in so many words about our personality traits, where we fit on the social scale, the talents we have, the honors we might have won, what clubs we belong to. So we have to use other symbols than words. Objects tell about us. Our furniture, lodge pins, wrist watches, glasses, neckties, trophies, clothing, cars are all identifying us to others. Facial expressions, gestures, body postures, tone of voice tell others our real intentions much more accurately than words. Nonverbal cues also tell what the context of any situation is—whether it is a wedding, a fight, or a friendly discussion.

The point is that humans unconsciously but instinctively look for these nonverbal symbols as clues to the real meaning of what's going on, to the real identification of a person, to his real, underlying motives. Because they are often far more expressive and far more believable than language, the creative people have to use nonverbal levels of communication to convey many informational meanings.

What I am leading up to is that the very process of creating in this area is an entirely different one from the technical, mathematical, analytical approach to problem solving, and therefore it cannot be explained in terms of, nor can it be held accountable to, the other type of reasoning. The brilliant thinker Cassirer points out that mankind has two modes of thinking, both equally powerful and equally important, but *different*—the process of scientific thinking and that of

Beautiful Hair

B R E C K

THERE ARE THREE BRECK SHAMPOOS FOR THREE DIFFERENT HAIR CONDITIONS

The hair of a little child shines with soft, natural beauty. A Breck Shampoo helps bring out the natural beauty of your hair. There are three Breck Shampoos. One Breck Shampoo is for dry hair. Another Breck Shampoo is for oily hair. A third Breck Shampoo is for normal hair. The next time you buy a shampoo, select the Breck Shampoo for your individual hair condition. A Breck Shampoo is not drying to the hair, yet it cleans thoroughly. A Breck Shampoo leaves your hair soft, lustrous and beautiful.

The Three Breck Shampoos are available at Beauty Shops, Drug Stores, Department Stores and wherever cosmetics are sold.

JOHN H BRECK INC · MANUFACTURING CHEMISTS · SPRINGFIELD 1 MASSACHUSETTS
NEW YORK CHICAGO SAN FRANCISCO LOS ANGELES OTTAWA CANADA

Advertising grew up as a statement of product virtues and superlatives—all copy and logic. But modern advertising is something entirely different. Now it uses a wide range of esthetic effects, emotive appeals, nonrational meanings. It reaches into the motive structure of the individual by many avenues of communication.

This art style almost alone built a very desirable product personality for Breck Shampoo. The sales logic is subdued. It is the esthetic effects (color, design, the stylized women) which successfully say this is a distinctive product.

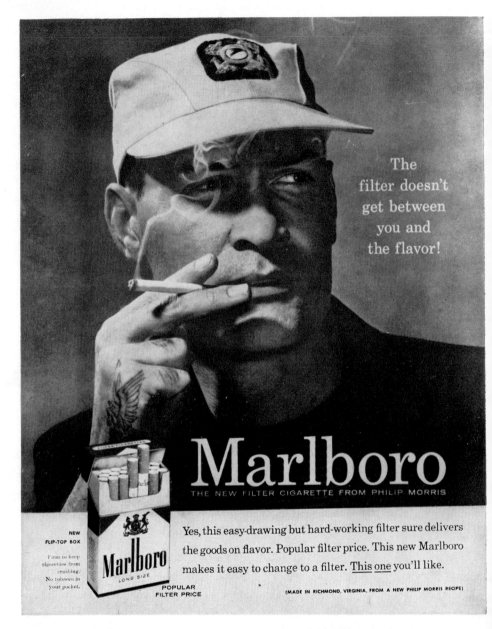

The
filter doesn't
get between
you and
the flavor!

Marlboro
THE NEW FILTER CIGARETTE FROM PHILIP MORRIS

NEW
FLIP-TOP BOX

Firm to keep
cigarettes from
crushing.
No tobacco in
your pocket.

POPULAR
FILTER PRICE

Yes, this easy-drawing but hard-working filter sure delivers the goods on flavor. Popular filter price. This new Marlboro makes it easy to change to a filter. This one you'll like.

(MADE IN RICHMOND, VIRGINIA, FROM A NEW PHILIP MORRIS RECIPE)

Writers assume that the expressive and emotive effects merely support their sales claims, calling attention to the main attraction where the persuasion will take place. This is nonsense. These other meanings can be totally unrelated to copy logic—and far more important.

Many human motive areas cannot be openly approached with words. In this very successful Marlboro advertising, the significant meanings are coming from the illustration. The copy logic is strictly after-the-fact. It merely gives the smoker a few conventional supports—after he has already made up his mind.

creative imagination. They don't come from the same sources in the mind, and they don't follow the same rules.

The word "imagination" means the process of creating images in the mind. But the imaginative way of conceiving ideas and images is not "logical" in the same sense as ordinary rational thinking. It does have its own kind of logic, however, capable of creating a stream of ideas which flash in and out of the mind instantaneously, instead of proceeding in orderly fashion from one proposition to the other as in technical, cause-and-effect reasoning. As Cassirer puts it, in creative imagination our thought is captured by the intuition which suddenly confronts it, as opposed to the methodical process of analytical reasoning. And neither can you force the imagination. Studies of the creative process indicate that almost never have great ideas or new inventions been produced by purely conscious calculation, proceeding methodically from point to point. This is why the technician, the imitator, those who faithfully follow the rules have no chance of creating anything. They are simply using the wrong thought process.

The raw material for creative ideation comes from reservoirs of the mind far below the level of intellect. In the free-and-easy flow of ideas that comes in the wake of imagination, we don't stop to reflect where they come from. Our subconscious mind just keeps pushing them on and across the stage. But a number of great creative minds in different fields who have tried to analyze where their new ideas come from have concluded that they just don't know.

The French mathematician Poincaré said that his most brilliant ideas came as sudden flashes of illumination, the fruits of his unconscious reasoning, which must have required considerable sorting, choice, and discernment. Mathematical creations cannot be tossed off without considerable power of selection. In trying to discover by what process the unconscious mind decided what ideas to present to his conscious self, he concluded that the privileged ideas were those which "directly or indirectly, affect most profoundly our emotional sensibility." While a mathematical demonstration problem absolutely must be in a certain order, nevertheless, if the mathematician has a feeling or an intuition of this order, then the various elements will operate in this order without any effort on his part in the unconscious mind.

Even if such an idea seems the very opposite of statistics and accounting theory, Ghiselin, in "The Creative Process," says that other great mathematicians agree that this is the basis of mathematical creation—not intellectual plodding. The process of great scientific discovery is exactly the same. The technician stays within a pattern of facts and routines. But the creative scientist suddenly sees a new order beyond this pattern—some departure which is flashed before his consciousness from the "underground workshop of the mind." Creative ideas in any field come from these flashes of insight, not from stumbling for years through trial-and-error mazes.

This is not to suggest that the process of creation is effortless, lazy daydreaming. Creative imagination differs from simple imagination, which does merely consist of allowing images to drift in and out of the mind. Creative imagination is a searching for new conceptions, and it does require that considerable disciplined thinking be applied to the specific problem as a preliminary. But somewhere along the line, the unconscious intelligence takes over, sifting all the available data from experience, reshuffling it in different alignments, and adding to it, from the deepest recesses of the mind and the emotional system, the raw stuff of other meanings. The unconscious intelligence literally races through the entire range of experience stored up in the individual's lifetime span, searching for images and concepts which it can grasp and present to the conscious mind.

Because all this is prelogical and preconscious, there are no guide-posts for procedure that the creative person can follow. He can't validate his symbol-making process as he goes along. He has to trust entirely to his feeling and intuition. Whenever he has moments of doubt, when something doesn't "feel right," he discards and changes.

What is intuition? It is raw, direct, immediate, preconscious, pre-logical, nonrational perception. We grasp an idea, judge a person, make a decision, size up a situation in a flash. If there is any weighing of facts, it is done entirely by the unconscious intelligence working almost instantaneously—by man's "third ear," as it has been termed, the intuitive organ which is searching for the real meaning. In the final analysis all of us trust these intuitive judgments far more than we do any words or facts or logic. We take all the facts available, we take the logic presented to us, but we still let our intuition pass the final judgment.

We say, "Somehow in spite of everything, it doesn't feel right"; "I can't say why, but it doesn't look good"; "I know everything you say is true, but I still think I'm right"; "I just feel in my bones that this is the thing to do"; "I can't argue with you, but I'm going to do it anyway"; "I just have a hunch." We put infinitely greater faith in these intuitive judgments than we do in intellection. When we go counter to these preconscious judgments, there is a disquieting feeling gnawing at us that tells without any supporting facts that we are wrong.

Actually, the educated person has spent, on the average, about sixteen years learning the discipline of rational thinking and intellection. Then it becomes so habitual to him that he completely loses sight of the fact that it was learned—that it was superimposed on the older, fundamental, more basic mental processes of biological man. He surprises himself to realize he does trust these intuitive judgments, because there is no explanation for them in the rigid, mechanistic, cause-and-effect system which has been drilled into him. Yet every time he makes a decision between choices, he is allowing this unconscious intelligence to choose. There is no logic that guarantees the financial expenditure for advertising, that guarantees the success of any campaign theme. Whenever management makes an outlay for expansion, for a new product design, somebody "feels this is the right thing to do."

The creative person, in trying to reach the otherwise unapproachable subverbal levels of the mind, has to use other means than logic. The artist expresses his meanings to his audience just because he has a high sensitivity for feeling which gives him a barometric quality of intuition. One writer described his literary apprenticeship as a discarding of all the vices of the educated man; he had to learn, think, feel, and see in a totally new fashion—in an uneducated way. Creative people just let their unconscious pour out its material in their periods of high creativity, without letting intellection hamper the flow. When a great writer or painter allows intellect to be tangled up with his symbol making, the result appears contrived, artificial, and unconvincing, no matter how technically perfect it may be.

This is why the creative person cannot really create when someone else is prescribing his approaches. Some novelists and painters in history have made tremendous achievements when they were drunk or when they were suffering badly (Freud had mouth cancer for years, Dostoevsky was epileptic, Van Gogh starved); some have even created when they were insane. (The four greatest British poets of the eighteenth century—Blake, Cowper, Collins, and Smart—all had one quality in common: they were mad.)

But no one ever created anything of significance with somebody standing at his elbow telling him what to do.

4

The mind has to work with symbols to express its meanings. We can only grasp our ideas by cloaking them in concepts for which we can design symbols. Obviously the mind doesn't operate with the concrete realities; it doesn't need them. The image or the concept will suffice. Because there are many modes of communication, there are different systems of symbols peculiar to each system of communication. The artist and the choreographer and the musician and the creative writer each have different symbol systems, all of which are, further, different from that used by the practical, logical mind.

This is the root of the creative person's difficulty in explaining his work to the sales manager or to the financial people. He is trying to plant a preference that will operate before reasoning takes place. Without this power, the advertisement is a failure, regardless of convincing sales arguments. But the management mind examines his work from the totally different framework of analytic thinking and asks, "What does it mean?"

The answer is that much of his work doesn't mean anything—not in the strict logic of everyday practicality. What does New York mean? Nothing—it just is. We don't look at a sunrise or a beautiful girl and ask, "Yes, but what do they mean?" Actually they do have a meaning, but in a different sense—they have a powerful appeal to the esthetic sensibilities. But because this is in a different form of communication, with a completely different symbol system, the meaning is simply just not expressible in the language of logic. The creative people cannot explain the real effects of their work, the meanings they are trying to capture which will appeal to these subverbal levels of the mind, because the symbols they have to use cannot be grasped, cannot be stated in words. There are no words for the subtleties of their meanings.

Because we cannot define these meanings does not in any degree detract from their power. No one can define electricity with any adequacy; we don't understand its nature at all, but that doesn't prevent us from using it. We are content to know that it exists as a force. You and I thoroughly enjoy television without any understanding of why it is.

Painters point out that the timeless element in a painting is not to be and cannot be translated into a verbal and literary form. We can only sense that a work of art concentrates into a simple formula or a few symbols a wide range of human emotions and feelings. As we stand before a painting, we are conscious that it has an ability to move us which has nothing to do with its illustrative quality and which is absolutely not expressible in language. The mood, the structural elements, the color, the shading, the rhythmic pattern are symbolic avenues capable of reflecting certain relationships between various emotions which strike us as beautiful and moving, without any verbalized message quality. Similarly, music is a sequence of tonal repetitions, a series of highly articulate, sensuous symbols in sound whose effect, which is their meaning, is totally beyond intellectual analysis or definition.

Layout in advertising, as an arrangement of mass, an obvious form of space esthetics, also has its own ability to communicate meanings totally beyond verbalization.

Language, as it is used in literature and creative writing, has a unique dual capacity. As the instrument of scientific description and rational thought, it is the most valuable tool of the human being, just because it *is* capable of precision and exactness. We can hold on to an object or an idea by means of the word. When I say "tree" or "ladder" or "yellow," these become concrete and precise concepts.

But language can also be a symbolic art form, as it is in literature. Then the arrangements of words and the created imagery, the moving thought and the emotive quality of the writing generate far more powerful meanings, which are perceivable between the lines. Although we say it aloud only occasionally, virtually always we ask the question, "I wonder what he really means?" implying our awareness that there is a different or perhaps more complete thought behind someone else's words. Literature is just as much an art form as sculpture or architecture, because of these deeper levels of language. But neither can the suggested meanings which make any literature great be adequately grasped and stated. Shakespeare is great, Keats is great, Tolstoi is great; but why? We have a vague sense that some qualitative change has happened to us in reading them. Because we can't describe it with exactness does not make the experience any less real.

Actually, literature is only great to the degree that it has these second and third levels of meaning. The story is the least important part of any novel. This is what De Quincey was talking about when he described the "literature of power." This is the source of the power —the plastic thought that we sense is embodied in the language behind the concrete meaning of the words.

If all this sounds mystical, consider the very observable sales power of package design. The good designer wants to discard all the wording possible, to create a visual image consisting almost entirely of color, space, lettering style, signature, plus any appropriate symbols or trademarks. The whole of it becomes a design that doesn't make any sense at all literally. It is purely a thing of esthetics. But it communicates meaning, which is translated into desirability by the consumer.

Archibald MacLeish, writing on why literature and poetry are taught in the universities, says that any art—and this would certainly include the arts of time as well as of space—is able to present us a direct knowledge of things, whereas scientific training deals with abstractions—with the ideas of things instead of the things themselves. The creative person in advertising is also trying to communicate with this same directness. Certainly his advertising can be informative and logical, supplying reasons for choice. But much more than this, it is also trying to evoke an instantaneous prelogical reaction so that the words flash in the consumer's mind: "This is a good company!" "This is the best kind of coffee!" "This is exactly the kind of appliance I want!" before he ever thinks of the sales arguments.

There are those who argue that the process of attaching feeling and subjective meaning to a physical object or institution is indirect and oversubtle; they prefer the direct approach of reciting product advantages. But the message with the power to evoke instantaneous preference is the direct communication. The reason-why approach in actuality is a two-step bit of logic which is the indirect avenue to this attainment of preference. The consumer has to make the closure from the claim to an attitude. "More filter traps than the next two leading brands combined"—*therefore*—"This must be a good cigarette." "Preferred for softness by three out of four women in amazing blindfold test"—*therefore*—"This must be a good facial tissue."

But there is no certainty whatever that this closure will occur. I am fully aware, intellectually, that Chesterfield is packed by Accu-ray, that Hudson cars have four Deep Coil springs, that Norge Washer has a new Dispenser Wheel. But the process stopped there. Nothing propelled it forward. The syllogism was never completed in me. No intuitive voice ever said to me *"Therefore*—this is the best product for you."

5

I said that one of the objectives of this book is to cast new light on the purposes of the creative person in advertising. He is trying to communicate meanings and associations to his audience at many levels: at the rational level, but also at evocative, esthetic, and nonrational levels. Whereas the journeyman technician is content to stop with a few common-sense claims about mechanics and economics, the really competent creative person is trying to go far beyond this ground floor of communication and persuasion. He is trying to reach the "third ear" of the audience—the area of intuitive judgment, where real persuasion and conviction will probably happen.

To accomplish this, he will have to achieve meanings which may exist entirely apart from any words, meanings which can often be far more significant than any literal language meanings. These may be emotive meanings or esthetic meanings. Or they may be just informative meanings which have to be approached by nonverbal symbols because they can't be expressed in so many words.

This is the difference between the rudimentary use of advertising and advertising of power.

CHAPTER III

Research and Motivation

My purpose in the previous chapter was to articulate the true objectives of creative people in advertising. Thereby I hoped to indicate much broader goals for advertising. Now I would like to show how the creative person himself can be helped by deeper insights into the nature of people, as advertising is learning to use the techniques and findings of the social sciences primarily through new research developments, and especially by motivation research.

When I implied that the creative people should not be fenced in by formulas and petty rules, I certainly did not mean that they should have a license to go off completely in their own directions. They have to make effort periodically to see if their meanings are actually getting through to their audiences. No matter how sensitive and brilliant the creative person may be, there is no such thing as creativity without occasional failure. The only way never to fail is never to try to be creative.

Without some systematic feedback from the audience, the creative person is relying completely on his own personal judgments, which means that in the final analysis he is being guided entirely by his own experience, his own introspections, his own hunches. He is necessarily looking at the world through only one pair of eyes, without making allowance for any differences whatever between people. The whole reason for sampling techniques in research is precisely to make certain this doesn't happen—to be sure that the problem is looked at from all representative viewpoints.

Each of us, as a human being, is walled in by his own individuality. Within this trap of my own subjectivity, I just don't see the world as a woman does, as a teen-ager does, as a person of another temperament does. My fundamental habits of perception will be colored by a number of powerful variables, including social class, age, sex, personality structure, education, occupational membership, degree of mobility, and so on. Even such a factor as religion bends a personality. There are very few Episcopalian farmers, Presbyterian farmers, or Jewish farmers. A study of the backgrounds of American scientists revealed that a disproportionately large share were of Protestant background. No one knows what there is in these backgrounds that inclines people toward this instead of some other course, but the relationship clearly exists.

Occupation is a curiously circular process. We are propelled or attracted to an occupation partly by temperament and probably also by chance. But once we are part of that group, a whole structure of viewpoints is gradually internalized to become a part of our fundamental psychic system, so that we act and see differently in many regards than do persons in other occupations. Advertising people develop many mannerisms of temperament and perception which are different from the way in which engineers, doctors, railroaders, musicians, or teachers behave. And in advertising, creative people are different in many points of outlook and personality behavior from persons in administration, account work, media sales, etc.

The point is that sometimes my introspections can be generalized outward, but more often than not I will be incorrect to assume that other people have the same motives and look at the world in the same way that I do. The fact that my hunches are right occasionally proves nothing. Even a broken watch shows the correct time twice a day. And common sense most definitely is no infallible guide. Common sense has been defined by scientists as that faculty which tells us that the world is flat. The problem is how to distinguish between common sense which gives the right answers and common sense which gives the wrong answers.

Without in any way attempting to interfere with the function of the creative people, research should be of enormous help as a source of broad guidelines and fruitful insights. I don't think that research in advertising has grown up to its real responsibilities yet. Very often it operates merely as a veto board, without making any attempt to be generative.

Besides establishing a two-way flow of communication, another primary function of the researcher in advertising should be to sensitize the creative people to make them more aware of their own creative energies. They become aware of things which are not in the research, but they only become aware of these impulses because of what the research has opened up for them.

2

Motivation research is not offered as a new religion or a way of life. It is simply a different tool for supplying a multiplicity of

"why" answers about human behavior which just are not available
from any other source. The old-time one-angle portrait photographer's
camera stereotyped the sitter in one artificial pose; motivation research
might be compared to a series of candid-camera shots. Instead of the
camera's dominating the situation, the person becomes the center
of dominant interest.

And the philosophy is different. People are not ingots or chess
pawns, and they do not behave in any mechanistic, static sense. On
the contrary, as dynamic human organisms, they are changeable, suggestible, highly nonrational, motivated far more by emotion and habit
and unconscious causes than by reason and logic. Every individual's
behavior in large part is shaped by the ideals and the pressures of his
particular society, so that a knowledge of these interrelationships and
social definitions is all-important for any real comprehension of basic
causes. I drink orange juice, hot coffee, and cow's milk instead of yerba
maté or kvass simply because I accept the patterns of the society into
which I have been born.

These are the premises on which motivation research attempts
to study the Whole Man. Each person is a dynamic individual, with
his own inner world of highly individual experiences and feelings.
The intellectual activities in his life are comparable to the skin of an
apple; the heart of the apple is his emotional system. There is a
constant interplay between his conscious and unconscious minds. In
considering him as a totality, his psychic system below the threshold
of consciousness must be included. And every individual is also tremendously influenced by the attitudes and demands of group life.
He has to conform to the conduct and viewpoints of the larger society
if he expects to lead a normal life and to be accepted by other people.

Social scientists proceed on the assumption that "human behavior is
determined by human decisions; but these human decisions to act
in some special manner, and not in another, are arrived at in an
essentially nonrational manner." This does not mean *irrational*, which
would imply that there are no cause-and-effect relationships between
the individual's needs and situations, on the one hand, and his goals
and purposes for acting, on the other. There are such relationships in
his decisions; but they are mostly not pure logic at all.

"Americans have been taught to think 'rationally,' and to insist that
they do when they don't. As a result, the ordinary individual goes out
of his way not to realize the implicit nonrational social customs and
systems in which he lives." He is mostly unaware of the basic motivational systems steering his actions and forming his preferences, and
his own reasoning on the subject generally beclouds or conceals the

real motives. It never occurs to him that his temperament is following some basic philosophy; yet this fact, whether he is strongly materialistic, idealistic, realistic, or mystic, has bearing on his decisions and motives. And actually society is striving to make his social behavior so automatic that he isn't even aware of it.

Because the root causes of anyone's behavior are often not apparent to the individual, the scientist has to develop many tests and procedures that will uncover these causes. Often he ends up in the odd position of having the individual emphatically deny the scientist's explanation of the individual's motives.

Here is the problem, then: How can advertising secure research insights into human behavior for better guidance in motivation and communication? How can our common-sense judgments be verified? How can we get out of the realm of guesswork and intuition to find out if our strategies are on the right track? How can we find out if our advertising appeals are really important to people or not?

Motivation research offers techniques and bodies of theory from the various humanistic sciences, particularly sociology, social anthropology, psychology, psychoanalysis, psychiatry, and social psychology. And I also find that semantics and various disciplines grouped under communication are extremely relevant to our problems. Because they are studying human beings, the social scientists will never be as mathematically precise as the physical scientists or even the statisticians. But they do offer tremendously helpful guidelines and insights, and after all, that is what management and creative people need.

All of the bickering about motivation research, particularly about statistical validities and psychoanalytic assumptions, is involved with the subject of tools. The controversies ignore the basic problem. Technicians are trying to understand things in terms of tools like statistics or dynamic psychology instead of recognizing what motivation research is seeking to do—which is to understand people. This is the old fallacy of trying to resolve something in the easiest terms, and obscuring the problem. After the dust from all the objectors has settled, the problem still remains unanswered—namely, how do you get at these human beings and at the real causes of their behavior?

The statistical researcher who prefers to live in his completely quantifiable world is literally ruling out any attempt to probe this all-important problem area. By insisting on a rigidly structured study governed by precise validities, he is locking out everything but his preconceptions. Great creative ideas invariably are the insights furnished by the subconscious mind. But there is no subconscious mind in an IBM machine.

One of my scientist friends tells me that this is why he prefers to work in qualitative research. With all its imperfections, it still never loses sight of the problem. By contrast, quantitative research dissects the problem into small bits and pieces, and too often loses track of the primary objective—the seeking for new insights about people's behavior. Lloyd Warner defines science as the art of sticking out one's neck, by which he means that there must continually be new hypotheses advanced to be tested. Progress in science comes from the mistakes of people who have at least tried to open up new avenues for thinking. The pioneers are followed by the verifiers and the technicians, who reduce the new hypotheses to facts and methods. But without the pioneers, there are no new ideas or generalizations.

Freud was one of the great pioneers of human thinking, and he wished to be remembered as just that: the creator of a new research tool for probing the unconscious mind. Psychoanalysis is a means to an end, not an end in itself. It is a means for explanation of the human being in much greater depth than ever before. Psychology as a science exists on two levels: the measuring level of observable and conscious behavior, and the study of the unconscious—which is by far the most important. Most motives come from the unconscious; it is the source of memory, intuitive judgment, personality structure, suggestion, imagination, attitudes, likes and dislikes. Freud fashioned a new, crude tool which opened completely different windows for peering into the psychic make-up of people, even though he fully realized that he was only rippling the surface of these dark waters.

However, psychology is only one of the approaches in motivation research. The human individual doesn't live alone. He develops as a personality through his interactions with the other people around him. It is from them also that he absorbs most of his general behavior patterns and attitudes, as well as the way he expresses himself emotionally. This is why he also has to be viewed as a member of various groups. He doesn't respond to advertising without considering the attitudes of other people around him toward the product, and even toward the store. He will be influenced in large measure by what his friends and associates think. Several sciences like sociology, social psychology, and social anthropology, are important for turning up these group attitudes, the changing currents in the society, who initiates new tastes and how, the differences in attitudes between classes.

It is also important to consider the individual is a member of a much larger society. He is an American; therefore he inherits a whole set of values—a pattern of logic, a sense of time, a moral and aspirational code, notions of the family and of the woman's place in society, a symbol system for communication, and so on. All of these are American values, not universal human laws. Often it is necessary to isolate these in proper perspective, particularly for international advertising and marketing. This is the province of anthropology.

Anthropologists also approach the problem of personality differently than the psychologists. They want to know most of all how does the individual get along with other people. The pattern and the actual mathematical rate of interaction with other people are the crucial factors in personality structure, according to them.

The point is that all of these disciplines belong in motivation research because, each in a different way and yet concurrently through a closely overlapping relationship, they contribute some light on that very obscure and complex thing we call human nature.

3

Because of the emphasis in our schooling, because of the formal attitudes of our society, we focus most of our attention on the superficial aspects of conduct—on the rational part of a person's life, on his conforming conduct, on the parts of his personality that he shows to the world when he is behaving himself. It is all-important that in advertising and marketing we develop techniques that will let us cut through these superficial aspects and give us much clearer ideas of the real person behind all the masks that he has to wear. It is high time we turned our eyes toward the nonrational, unconscious, subjective, unformal, "feeling" side of his life.

And *her* life, I should add. Because I think we have even far less understanding of the springs of a woman's psychic structure. Infinitely less of her mental life is turned over to the rationality and analytic thinking required of a man working at a job or profession. What is she really like within herself? What is she actually thinking about as she sits for hours being bored by "man talk"? In a study on the new suburban housewife, each woman was asked to define the ideal housewife. Many of them never mentioned their husbands in their definitions. They idealized themselves as either the Mother or the Good Housekeeper, not as the Wife. When asked to state the source of their greatest satisfaction, they chose the area of motherhood. They were pleased with themselves for having successfully raised children, not for being satisfactory wives to their husbands. They saw themselves as individuals, as persons, not as appendages to men.

Social scientists, philosophers, and biographers emphasize that the most revealing clues about the nature of any person are not the things he outwardly says about himself but rather the kind of questions he asks, what he daydreams and hopes about himself, and the role in which he conceives himself.

How can we get some view, some insight into the private thinking and fantasies and wishes which are hidden within people behind the barriers of reserve and incommunicability?

Our own thinking is cluttered up with excess mental baggage, too much nonsense and inaccuracy that comes to us from the ideals for behavior and the poses that we are supposed to adopt in our society to be a right-thinking citizen in good standing with the village elders. But sometimes we have to take off our Sunday suits in order to accomplish our objectives—certainly if we expect to have clearer awareness of why people act like people.

The credo of the Advertising Federation of America begins with the statement that good advertising aims to inform the consumer and to help him buy more intelligently. This is an admirable statement of principle; but if we only provided information, we would not accomplish what we set out to do—namely, to persuade people. Nowhere in the credo is expressed what every single competent advertising man is trying to achieve: the attachment of psychological associations to his product by combining emotive and esthetic appeals with the sales logic.

The point is sometimes made by ethical objectors that motivation research is wrong because it will permit advertisers to manipulate people against their wills, to sell them things they don't want and don't need. This is a rather silly argument. Wasn't advertising trying to create wants long before motivation research was ever heard of? People didn't realize they needed air conditioners, electric dishwashers, and power lawn mowers for their homes until advertising created the desires for these products. If motivation research will help us to be more efficient in our advertising appeals and techniques, certainly no one will insist that we should deliberately avoid the use of something in order to give the consumer more of a sporting chance. On the contrary, it would seem to me that the morality is all on our side if we can use our advertising expenditures more efficiently, if we can achieve more effectively what we have long since been trying to achieve.

Actually, while there may be a time and place for many little polite fictions, there also comes a time when our own thinking has to be sufficiently acute to penetrate the fog of fictions and formal attitudes. Even if the social amenities insist that everyone ignore the very existence of sex, a doctor cannot proceed unless he recognizes that it does exist. And so do we in advertising have to be intellectually and intuitively perceptive enough to distinguish between the stereotyped reasons and the actual realities. This is simply to state that whether in regard to advertising's methods and purposes or to people's behavior and motives, we should be intellectually skeptical enough to probe considerably below the level of the common-sense reasonings, the accepted popular notions, and even the individual's own report of his conduct. Motives and motivation mean all the elements in the causes, both conscious and unconscious—all the feelings and attitudes.

For the purposes of advertising, however, we are primarily interested in singling out only those motive forces which are manageable by the creative people. Many obscure and complex factors which may be important clinically are just too subtle for the creative people to reckon with. Cigarette research reveals that masochistic tendencies (deliberately hurting oneself) are important motives in smoking, but for the advertising man this leads nowhere.

We are also concerned not with any individual's peculiar motives but with forces which are common to broad groups and types of people.

Most scientists today feel that there is no such thing as a single, pure motive for anything. There are many dominant motives and subordinate motives which may be involved in people's acts. There is a tremendous interpenetration of motives also. They influence one another in considerable degree. One motive can block out another motive entirely, as happens when a person becomes angry or frightened or thirsty. Mostly, however, they exist side by side.

And actually there is no completely stable aspect to motives. What I may feel impelled to do today may be changed tomorrow by circumstances, or my own mood may be different. My motives when I feel exuberant and cheerful can be very much changed if I feel downcast or depressed. And the direction my motives finally take may be quite different, depending upon whether I am prosperous or hard up. However, in a general sense, there is a definite consistency in motives.

Attitude means the readiness of the mind to react to a situation in one given way. If anyone mentions burglary, communism, horse racing, or child labor, my mind is all prepared. An attitude can be a motive, but a motive can be many other things besides an attitude.

The word "personality" is used somewhat differently by the scientist than it is by the layman. To the scientist, personality means the sum total of any individual's whole psychic structure, conscious and unconscious, which includes all of his experiences from birth until death. Hypnosis can dig out all sorts of past experiences which apparently have been long forgotten but which still remain far below any recallable level. Yet all these long-forgotten experiences may play a part in shaping an individual's conduct.

Personality is construed to exist on at least three levels, and motivation research is trying to reveal as clearly as possible the motives involved with a product or institution from each level. There is an outer layer, which is the aspect of a person that others see. When we think of someone as amiable or morose or overbearing, this is simply the side of himself that he shows to the world. It is by far the least important. It is an abstraction of inner causes. Much of this behavior is put on and taken off like a robe as we deliberately try to make ourselves agreeable to other people. Also, we will change depending on the role we are called on to play at a particular moment. The same woman can be a stern mother to her children, a compliant lover to her husband, an unpleasant bargain hunter to her tradesmen, an ebullient companion to her friends, and a scheming striver to her country-club set.

This is why it is completely wrong to define any person by a trickle of adjectives describing a few of his or her surface aspects. "Personality" signifies the architecture of the whole person.

Within every individual is also that private conscious world where he spends 75 per cent of his mental time but which he almost never reveals to anyone else. I have carried certain daydreams with me from childhood on that I never expose to other people. My wife and I can tour happily for hours without speaking, myself enjoying my own reveries, and she, it is clear, also living with her own thoughts. My children develop their own barriers of reserve right under my nose, so that at times we are even embarrassed with each other, as strangers are.

This is much more than daydreaming, of course. I don't discuss my status ambitions and frustrations, although this is a very active thought area for middle-class Americans. I devote considerable thought time to my job strivings, to the problems of my children, to my acceptance or rejection by new friends or work associates. But conventions and, probably, an inability to articulate my real feelings operate to keep me from expressing myself on such subjects.

Then of course there is in every person that vast area of the unconscious which is so important as a source of motives and behavior but about which we know so little. The basic structure of the individual's personality is fairly well organized by the age of four or five, yet obviously it is impossible for any adult to reconstruct the infantile experiences which shaped his own blueprint. How is it possible for him to see objectively the body of social attitudes functioning in any product area—as, for instance, why men still cling to such completely useless clothing features as lapels, buttons on sleeves, cuffs on pants? Or why we Americans drink iced tea but rarely hot tea, why we forbid coffee to youngsters, why we use cough drops but not snuff (when both serve the same purpose)?

The point is, of course, how can we peer into the individual past this superficial façade which he presents to the world? How can we see in systematic form the framework of social attitudes in these product areas which the individual accepts without ever thinking about? How can we explore for the possibility of differences in these attitudes and motives existing between personality types, social classes, mobile and nonmobile persons? How can we sense the existence and the significance of the underlying currents in the society, such as the preference for brighter colors, for "lightness" in foods and beverage, for casual styles, trends, and drifts which leave some products stranded high and dry and catapult others to dizzy sales peaks?

Any competent researcher knows it is difficult to get at answers to this type of question. The ordinary consumer is generally very inarticulate about his motives, or perhaps he doesn't even recognize them himself. If you ask the typical motorist why he chooses to patronize a certain gasoline station, he generally singles out "convenience" as the dominant reason. Yet a recent gasoline motivation study indicated that "cleanliness" above all else was the primary attribute most wanted in a service station.

In this gasoline study, we probed to see if the various symbolic designs and color schemes used by the different refineries had any meanings in themselves or if they were simply pretty color and attentional devices. Certainly they play a central part in the physical totality of any station. William Henry of the University of Chicago, who conducted this research, showed very clearly that two of the color motifs and station symbols—Standard Oil of Indiana and Mobilgas— communicated very definite meanings important to gasoline sales, even when entirely divorced from any identification with their product. Standard's color motif and torch design set off a highly positive series of references to patriotism and the Olympic games which definitely contributed an important aura of high moral responsibility and good will. Mobilgas's winged horse generated associations of power and speed. Some other gasoline symbol systems had equally high recognition value but aroused no meaningful associations at all.

All of this was occurring at an *unconscious* level. The consumer was not aware that these meanings were being communicated to him. In any area there is a similar amount of unconscious impression going on. It is useless to ask a person directly for these meanings. How could the average individual accurately grasp such subtle nuances of meaning when he characteristically stumbles over gross facts? A study by the National Opinion Research Center asked people a series of questions which could be checked against official records. Of those who stated that they had library cards, 45 per cent actually did not. Nineteen per cent of those who said they had driver's licenses did not. Eleven per cent of the people with automobiles gave the wrong make or year of model.

Motivation research turns to a number of techniques in trying to understand these areas whose existence the individual does not suspect, in which he is inarticulate, or in which he is apt to give the wrong answers. "Depth interviews" are free conversations pointed in the general direction of the problem and its various component elements. The purpose is to cast as wide a net as possible to learn what is on the individual's mind, to determine the kind and quantity of feeling involved (which is not apparent in "yes-no" questioning), and to note if anything in the unguarded conversation contradicts the expressed attitudes.

Rarely does the interpreter take a person's first statement at face value. Very often it is the unsaid which is most significant. And often the point is pieced together from several different interviews.

For instance, in the study of the new suburban housewife mentioned above, almost invariably the women formally gave as their reason for moving to the suburbs the stereotyped answer about wanting more room and fresh air for the children. But as they talked further, it was crystal clear that a far more powerful motive was the wish to escape from the loneliness of anonymous big-city apartment life, the hope that they could integrate themselves into networks of friends. Repeatedly they stated that the neighborhood rather than the house was their first concern.

"Projective tests" are another revealing tool. There are numerous variations of these tests, but all of them are built on the principle of presenting the individual with some ambiguous unfinished situation which he has to complete. He unconsciously reveals the way he looks at the world by his responses. He "projects outward" his attitudes and feelings. There are no right and wrong answers, so he doesn't have to pose and give any expected response. Some of these projectives are capable of quantification by their general tone and meaning, and are relatively simple to interpret. But others require highly skilled and sensitive interpreters, and while they afford extremely revealing glimpses of the individual's psychic structure, they are much too obscure and unstructured in their fullest implications for any exactness.

The sentence-completion test presents the individual with a series of incomplete sentences, which he has to finish. Typical of this approach are these sentence stems from our gasoline study:

> A car that really has a getaway. . . .
> High octane in gasoline gives. . . .
> Rocket fuels in gasoline. . . .
> A good gasoline. . . .
> My car needs. . . .

From these and similar sentence completions, it is possible to see that most people believe that getaway is a function of the car rather than of the gasoline; that the "zoom" and power claims are received with considerable indifference or skepticism; that people really do not understand how to distinguish one brand of gasoline from another except with the use of terminology from the advertising, which they cannot precisely define, and which is not really the basis of their brand selection.

Apart from the rather obvious directions that the meanings will indicate, sometimes the rich or thin quality of the associations has considerable significance. In a motivation study of building materials, the completions of the stem, "A lumber yard is. . . ." revealed only the most meager kind of associations, such as "a place to buy lumber." In contrast to the buying pleasure and curiosity associated with other retail outlets, the lumber yard is seen as a dull, uninvolving warehouse for boards.

Another frequently used projective is to have consumers tell stories around picture situations roughly related to the problem. In a study of cigarette smoking, a picture of a young girl with an older woman was shown. People were told that the girl had asked her mother if she could start smoking, and they were requested to assume that they were the parent. What would they say? From the tenor of the answers could be derived four perfectly clear-cut attitudes which our society holds on the subject, even if they are almost never articulated:

1. Cigarette smoking is bad, with moral implications.
2. Smoking is worse for young girls.
3. Smoking is denied to immaturity.
4. Few people praise the smoking habit.

We showed a man standing against a wall with the ground littered with cigarette butts. The resulting stories revealed how closely we associate cigarettes with high tension: "The man's wife was having a baby"; "He was nerving himself to see a doctor about an operation"; "He was bracing himself to ask for a job." Almost like a medicine, cigarettes are used for relief of tension—which is purely a psychological property.

Getting people to fill in cartoon "balloons" is another helpful projective for digging out seldom expressed attitudes. In a study of toilet soaps, which are advertised almost totally to women, we wanted to know if the typical husband was happy about having to use the soap which his wife in effect bought for herself and then said to him, "You use this too." In a variety of ways we showed that the man strongly resents this situation. Over 70 per cent of the women also revealed awareness that a man resents his wife's brand of soap as being too feminine ("perfumed," "sissy," "not strong enough").

In another study we sought to determine whether the wife had any hand in initiating home-maintenance projects. We explained the cartoon as follows: "This husband and wife are talking about some decorating or home repairing. What would they be saying?" Analysis of the balloon responses from men and women indicated that both sexes believe that the woman initiates most of the projects even though all the retail advertising and merchandising of building materials is directed to men.

Frequently we can see these unexpressed feelings by asking which sharply defined types of people can be identified with a certain product or store or institution. We might specify doctors, truck drivers, movie actors, society women, bankers, grandfathers, waitresses, immigrants —types that embody popularly held notions about a definite psychological character, an age level, or even a clear-cut station in the power system of society. Or we may say that brands and companies often have a personality, as persons do, and ask the subjects to specify what traits they think apply to these given choices. We may ask them to match certain qualities with different brands, or we may present them with a forced-choice situation, such as "young–old," "masculine–feminine," "modern—old-fashioned," "active—quiet," "cigar—cigarette smoking."

"Fun-loving," "curious," and "easy-going" are consistently picked out as descriptions of the working-class woman who patronizes mass department stores. The middle-class woman, on the other hand, does not see herself as fun-loving; her self-conceptions revolve so strongly around "moral," "responsible," "serious" as to subordinate the notion of fun.

In addition to many other ingenious projective tests, there are certain scaling devices designed to measure the intensity of attitudes.

While all of these approaches are admittedly crude instruments, they are extremely illuminating and fruitful for pushing far past the barriers of inarticulation and ordinary verbal responses. Obviously the indicated course is to try to corroborate and clarify these fresh insights with more straightforward and quantifiable research wherever possible. But motivation researchers generally feel that their most useful function is that of breaking the ground on new frontiers and of supplying broad indicated directions, of advancing new assumptions, new frameworks for thinking.

To illustrate what a wealth of usable and rich insights motivation research offers to advertising and marketing, I want to detail the findings of several specific studies in succeeding chapters. Although these are necessarily dealing with concrete and therefore limiting product problems, they illustrate the potentialities of this type of approach. They show also how this research is cumulative, each study contributing some general principles which help us to a clearer understanding of human motives and human communication.

But any specific studies have to be set in a general frame of relationship to other knowledge. Drawing from the social sciences and also from a great many other specific studies, I shall try to show the psychological and communicational climate in which advertising operates.

In such a frame, the reasons for buying anything will, I hope, acquire a completely different meaning. And the workings of advertising as a communication process will take on a very different purpose.

CHAPTER IV

The Psychological Label on the Product

An advertising agency asked me to explore the possibility of a study as to how the consumer can prefer one brand of sugar over another when chemically all brands are exactly the same. To them this is a puzzling situation. The housewife continues to choose some one brand with the positive conviction that "it's better—the quality is superior. I can't explain, but I know it's better." Yet factually the brands are indistinguishable. The difference exists only in her mind.

Repeatedly we stumble across this same situation, and we usually shake our heads at such unreasonable behavior.

Any number of manufacturers put up house brands for grocery chains, so that their products end up competing with one another under different labels and invariably at tangible price differentials. And the lower-price brand isn't always the largest seller. In a year's study, twice as many families bought a certain brand of margarine in a Chicago food chain instead of the absolutely identical product under the chain label, even though the latter was cheaper.

It is easier to swallow these apparent violations of common sense if we realize that many other forces besides rationality are involved in perfectly normal human behavior. And it is perfectly normal and human for psychological overtones to become inextricably linked with products, institutions, and places, and in many instances to be the primary determinant of consumer behavior.

I would be the first to grant that functional advantages, quality differences, and price can each be the all-important factor in a buying decision. I am only highlighting the point that in very many instances, however, it is this halo of psychological meanings which is responsible for the popularity or the rejection of the product.

Take the umbrella, for instance. It performs its function in completely satisfactory fashion. There is nothing wrong with its quality or its price. But the reason most people don't buy umbrellas today is that it stamps them as ultraconservatives—old fuddy-duddies. No teen-ager, no "sports-car–butch-haircut" adult, no smart young modern carries an umbrella.

40

I don't eat oatmeal for the same reason. I can argue with myself it is a highly nutritious, low-cost food. But I still think of it as old-fashioned, plus other notions about horses and oats.

Lots of people buy auto trailers, I guess. But not me. Regardless of the wonders they may offer, I can only think of itinerant laborers, retired brakemen heading for St. Petersburg, and dubious camps at the city's edge. All these impressions, whether based on fact or not, intervene to smother any interest on my part in the auto trailer.

These, of course, happen to be negative associations for me. Obviously, just as many brands and places and institutions have as their most important asset an aura of strongly positive psychological meanings which have actually nothing to do with reality. People generally do justify their choice by insistently citing performance reasons or economic factors, and they obviously believe them. I have heard Cadillac owners spell out the low depreciation, cost of operation, safety features, and so on, of their cars—all of which may be true. But certainly one of the Cadillac's greatest sales assets is its symbolic meaning of achievement and financial success.

We tend so much to think of objects as absolutes. The manufacturer feels that his product will sell because of its innate quality and technical superiorities, as if the consumer can detect these with unfailing accuracy. Production experts, agricultural leaders, economists, and intellectuals generally believe that the task of marketing consists only of offering a good product, which somehow a discriminating public will decide to buy. Not many of these people think about the problem of investing the product with the psychological meanings which are going to play such a considerable part in his life history.

I have listened to government advisers relate their counsel to the apple growers about offering apple juice to the American family, including a lengthy rigmarole about taste tests. So it is offered, and what happens? Very little—taste tests or not. Prune juice, grape juice, apple juice, cranberry juice: none of these has had any prairie-fire success, because even in the matter of food selection, we pick and choose according to those meanings which are in our minds, not those in the products. None of these particular juices have a sufficiently desirable halo.

The truth of the matter is that, far from being absolutes with fixed sets of qualities, products and institutions and brands have almost entirely subjective definitions.

Even with so basic an item as food, what we choose becomes for the most part a problem of subjective appeals. The constant succession of new products being offered to the American table displaces other products which are seen as less desirable, although their food value, taste, and quality have not changed. Their virtues and their defects to a large extent exist in my mind, not in themselves.

So many people in blindfold tests are unable to distinguish between cigarettes. Yet few things are more personal, excite more loyalty than the individual brand. I might smoke one cigarette of my wife's brand, but not two. She refuses to take any of mine, preferring to scratch around the house in cigarette boxes and coat pockets for just a stray of her own brand. My cigarette is too masculine, too strong, too much "me" in her eyes, although in actuality the blend of tobacco is probably indistinguishable from that in her cigarette.

I have argued at length about instant coffee with the die-hards. They insist heatedly it just doesn't taste like real coffee. Time and again I have served the instant coffee in a Silex, so that these people thought they were drinking regular coffee. Then they enjoy it. I have won bets on several occasions when I demonstrated that they couldn't tell the difference in taste.

It is very apparent that their rejection stems from subjective factors which have nothing to do with taste. And it is precisely this negative set of meanings which must be modified before the unconverted start buying it.

As another direction of meaning, at my house we never serve kohlrabi, sauerkraut, cotto salami, or pumpernickel bread, because in our eyes, these are peasant foods. But my wife does offer guests such illogical dainties as vodka punch, shrimp creole, port-wine cheese, even Mexican-sunflower seeds, because these have an air of being classé and exotic.

What I have been demonstrating is that every product and service has an aura of subjective meanings over and above its utilitarian meanings which perform a very real function for the individual. Apart from its first purpose of transportation, the automobile serves also to define the individual's social importance, his ideas of his own personality, his notions of care or carelessness toward possessions, his attitude toward the relation of the individual to mechanical objects. Thus each car becomes for the individual not just a physical object costing "X" dollars with various performance qualities but an object defined by a specific aura of psychological attitudes.

Gasoline is something put in cars to make them run, and with regard to its physical properties, most people firmly believe that gasoline is gasoline. And yet they do exhibit consistent buying preference for certain brands, based on their subjective definitions. In addition to performance qualities, the gasoline becomes defined by the appearance and color scheme of the gasoline station and the behavior of the attendants, plus general notions of the moral responsibility of the company selling the product—all of which are attitudes.

A cigar, a perfume, a shaving lotion, a face powder, a lipstick have a minimum of functional use. Millions of people live just as long, are just as happy without ever using them. Physiologically they are completely unnecessary. The product areas and the brands are defined almost completely by their subjective meanings.

2

One of our primary criteria for evaluating automobiles is their appearance. We say with an air of finality that this car definitely is beautiful, that car is reasonably attractive, and another line will sell poorly because it doesn't have real beauty. Here again we are speaking of beauty as if it were an unchanging, eternal reality seen in the same likeness by everyone.

Yet nothing could be more subjective, more temporary, more illusory than car beauty. It most obviously is no fixed and permanent quality. The designs which were unveiled as breath-taking only fifteen years ago now seem ridiculously out of date—just funny. And today's beauties will appear quite as silly fifteen years hence. So this element which is such a key factor in sales success is at best only a kaleidoscopic, ephemeral quality—here today and gone tomorrow.

And in spite of a few agreements, it is actually all things to all people. One man buys a Buick, and as he and his wife admire it, they both say, "It's beautiful." The next-door neighbors are viewing their new Mercury with the same ecstatic words—"It's beautiful." What they mean, of course, is, "We like it." Appearance can exist as an independent factor. But generally it is a broad feeling summation of many, many things that people are trying to convey. We approach cars with a whole set of meanings far beyond the simple fact of how they look. Yet we telescope all these meanings into one shorthand symbol—beauty.

At the present time, we believe that sleekness in body design is expressive of smartness, raciness, power, modernity, high style. When a design, such as Nash, departs from this pattern, then we read a different set of meanings into it. Fullness of body is not the current trend of dress—we know that. A breakaway from sleekness and length might introduce the notion of dumpiness, which we interpret as inferior, not smart, clumsy.

Very often people are not certain exactly what meanings are involved with some departure, and that in itself is disturbing. This is one of the important functions of advertising: to create a set of meanings and to crystallize them so that the symbol is perfectly clear and, of course, desirable.

This whole province of product design and product beauty is almost entirely a realm of subjective meanings.

So is the concept of style, which is not unrelated to beauty. Style and obsolescence are more and more often described as the primary function of goods in our consumption economy, not utility. Almost no one wears clothes or keeps furniture around until they wear out. We get rid of them when we feel they have gone out of style.

Lest we tend to narrow the concept of style to women's clothes and perhaps cars, let me indicate how thoroughly this force has permeated many areas of consumption goods. The forests of new houses mushrooming in ever-spreading suburbia are almost entirely ranch-style and, now, split-level. Wrought-iron furniture, severely modern lamp styles, sectional davenports, and colorful draperies dominate the living rooms in the model homes "now open for exhibition." And the dining room area and dining room furniture are steadily contracting.

The carpeting industry reports more new designs in the past five years than in the previous fifty years. Refrigerators and washers have broken with the rigid tradition of operating-room white and now are paraded in gala pastel colors. Twenty years ago ginger ale was the standard mixer for drinks. Today soda sales are competing in the summer with tonic water, in the winter with the vogue for "on-the-rocks" short drinks.

But what is style?

It exists purely and simply in our minds. It is entirely subjective. No one knows how it starts, how it spreads, or how it is enforced. We used to think of it as something originated by high society, to be different, and then imitated by the lower classes. But characteristic fads for pizza, blue jeans, Dixieland jazz, and men's caps are traveling from the lower class upward.

Yet this completely subjective force that has no tangible existence is recognized as the fulcrum of economic behavior in so many areas. Without a qualm of conscience about waste or unreasonable extravagance, I consign loads of clothing to my wife's charities because they are out of style. I toss away hats with brims too wide or too narrow, an overcoat inches too short, shirts the wrong color, and suits with lapels too wide. Thousands of workers in automobile factories are thrown out of jobs because the car styling is wrong, jarring the whole economy of such cities as Toledo and Kenosha and South Bend.

The fur industry has been badly buffeted because mink is so over-sold as the fur "that leaves you breathless." Many a woman thinks that if she can't have mink, she is out of style to take anything less. And because she can't afford to buy mink, she would rather go without.

3

I hope I have established the point that a significant part of human behavior and buying is involved with purely psychological meanings that have nothing to do with engineering triumphs, chemical discoveries, or the large, economy size. And since this is so, then advertising, which is charged with the responsibility for helping to sell goods, must also concern itself with these psychological meanings.

If this is disturbing to our philosophical and moral notions of thrift and rational behavior, I can only say this is the way people are. This is the reason they buy. They are satisfying psychological "wants" which are just as real as biological wants. This is what they desire from their lives. This is what they hope to find in advertising.

Social scientists point out—and here I could quote the psychoanalyst Freud, the social anthropologist Warner, and the philosopher Langer —that all human behavior which is not purely organic is a form of self-expression.

In our gestures, in our jewelry, in our patterns of speech and dress, in a thousand subtle mannerisms, we are trying to convey to others and to ourselves exactly what we are. We don't want anyone to be mistaken about us. One woman conveys her accentuated femininity with a smart coiffure, much costume jewelry, cosmetics, and exotic cigarettes. Her next-door neighbor wears no make-up and a dowdy haircut, and refuses to smoke. One garbs herself in pirates' costumes and pixie pants, even for her housework; the other restricts herself to drab house dresses. Each is trying to say, not with flamboyant clarity, probably not even consciously, but with recognizable subtlety, exactly what she is.

I, as an individual, don't wear a beard or a beret like some avant-garde artist. And, at the other extreme, I avoid the drab brown-suit-brown-tie motif of the ultraconservative. Each and every form of behavior has to be fitting to my age group, to my social clique, and to my particular occupational niche.

In an intelligent, normal person, virtually everything is motivated by subtle reference to the individual's self-ideal—the kind of character ideal he wants to become. No reproach is worse than that you are letting yourself go, losing your self-control, going all to pieces—all of which are different ways of saying that one is not living up to his self-ideal.

When the individual buys anything, he makes the psychological decision, "This is just right." On rare occasions we do lose choice. The article is the only one of its kind, and we have to take it. At other times we do get pressured into accepting something. Then we have growing misgivings that it isn't exactly suitable.

But the purchase that I sense is entirely right fills me with feelings of satisfaction, which is an awareness that it is altogether fitting for me. Of course, there are other elements, like price. However, I wouldn't buy chewing tobacco or a derby for 90 per cent off. Unless the product fits me, unless its psychological meanings jibe with my self-conceptions and with what I want to convey about myself, you couldn't give it to me.

In addition to my practical purposes, I have various psychological goals that I am hopeful of gratifying. A man with thinning hair may grow a mustache and go bareheaded in the worst weather, not for any sensible reason, but to fulfill his own goal of conveying his vigor and potency. What practical difference does it make if he loses his hair? None. But he is concerned lest it be interpreted as a symbol of declining vigor.

We strive to cope with our feelings of inadequacy, our hunger for acceptance by others, our desire for recognition, our strivings for mobility and to break emotional dependencies. All these and a multitude of other motivations establish definite goals which become very real to the individual.

In this yearning for self-expression, we reach for products, for brands, for institutions which will be compatible with our schemes of what we think we are or want to be. Naturally we do require certain things to carry on the business of life. But there is so much latitude in our economy of abundance. We are invariably in position to select on the basis of the secondary meanings attached to the products.

Actually, I have the choice of many forms of transportation in most situations. But I do not ride the public streetcars or a motorcycle or a motor coach. Each of them has many merits. Yet they would all say the incorrect thing about me—my position, my personality, my occupational role.

There is nothing wrong with a motorcycle as a piece of machinery. What stands in my way are the unreal actualities—those eloquent reflectors of my character, of the "me." I am certain that if I drove to work on a motorcycle some bright day, my superiors would consider that I was exposing hitherto unsuspected character weaknesses, inconsistent with my role as a businessman. In your mind and my mind, the layman on a motorcycle is an arrested mental type, an irresponsible exhibitionist, a delivery boy in a silver-studded leather jacket and boots swaggering around hamburger stands.

All this has nothing to do with the piece of machinery per se. Yet this cloud of negative attitudes is a tangible, existent reality, as firmly attached to the motorcycle as the seat. The manufacturer who might hope to advertise motorcycles into a better sales position would have to wrestle with this set of negative attitudes.

Again and again in our studies we have turned up situations where similar sets of unfavorable associations were glued to a brand. But the manufacturer's advertising was wandering about in a never-never land. It didn't face up to the subjective meanings which were very significantly interfering with buyer considerations. Why give me demonstrations of smooth smoking if my real objection to cigars is a mental picture of repellent trays of butts or of the airline attitude that cigar smoking is annoying to other people?

Why tell me that "movies are better than ever" when the psychological obstacle that halts my moviegoing is the imagery of uncontrolled rowdy behavior by teen-agers in the suburban theaters?

4

This habit of attaching meanings, attitudes, feelings, even moods to inanimate objects is characteristically human. It is the mental process of symbolization, which is an integral part of the human brain's activity.

We work every day, for instance, not only for the financial returns, which of course are important, but also from numerous other motives. In a recent study, men were asked if they would stop work if it was no longer necessary financially. The great majority said that they would keep on working. Apart from a livelihood, work means friendship and contact with other people; it generates feelings of doing something worthwhile; it wards off isolation and loneliness. As nearly as we can, we choose our occupations for their prestige value, for their opportunities for self-realization, because of our own notions of physical and mental adaptation. The middle-class American wants a white-collar job, not only for its pay scales, but because of his notions of greater social prestige.

Clothing is another commonplace example of our tendency to invest things with meanings which can become active motivations. Completely apart from its functional purposes of protection, modesty, and even decoration, our clothing fulfills an enormous range of both personal and social meanings that we utilize ceaselessly.

The Christmas-necktie situation illustrates how intensely personal our clothing can become. Most of us males regularly receive gift offerings of neckties on Christmas, Father's Day, and birthdays. These are genuine expressions of feeling from our parents, our wives, our children, and our in-laws. We say "thank you" and rarely, rarely wear them. Why not? They are expensive enough; they certainly have all the quality that any tie has. But somehow, in some way they say the wrong thing about me. I try to explain my rejection by saying that they are too loud or too dull. Actually, I sense in a very vague but compelling way that they do not capture the subtleties and nuances of the personality that I think I am.

And neither can I grasp the individuality of another person. On occasion I have bought gifts of clothing and costume jewelry for my wife. Then it dawned on me that she seldom wore my selections. I can't imagine any man picking out a hat or a pair of shoes or a handbag for his wife. Because we just simply cannot penetrate the wall around another person's self, we cannot divine precisely the subtleties that he or she is trying to convey with costuming.

We even use clothing to express mood. In the evening I change into loafers and sports coat to imply relaxation and informality. If I get up in the morning feeling especially jaunty and exuberant, pleased with myself because people laughed at my jokes last evening at the party, then I toy with bow ties, high-colored shirts, and flashy handkerchiefs.

I have spoken at conventions held at summer resorts where most of the audience wore sports clothes. But the speakers had to appear in white shirts and darker suits to signify their seriousness of purpose. Driving through small towns in the summer, it is easy to single out the bank cashier or the newspaper editor—the only individual in the sea of overalls and sports shirts who is uncomfortably garbed in a white shirt and necktie.

The businessman's costume is heavily charged with moral symbolism—heavy shoes, padded coat, white shirt, drab-colored suits, constricting neckties: elements that say that he is mature, responsible, serious in purpose, with the highest moral integrity.

The men's-wear industry now hopes that men can be sold the notion of style with the same force as women. But very many retailers and manufacturers in this field cannot bring themselves to dress like style setters. Even though it would be to their financial advantage, they are much more anxious in their own choice of garb to appear as conservative and successful businessmen. The hopes of their industry run squarely into the universal American conviction that something is wrong with the man overly concerned with clothes. He may be effeminate, or conceited—or a shadowy character on the margins of society, like a gambler.

Another recent study indicates how much the meanings attached to men's clothing can influence occupational success. Contrary to the American credo that job performance should be the criterion, there is very real belief that one's mode of dress can affect his opportunities and promotions.

In response to a question asking what would happen if a foreman were promoted to an office position and then failed to dress right, 61 per cent of the men interviewed said that this person would be fired, demoted, or transferred. Another 14 per cent said that the man couldn't be promoted further in the future. And 17 per cent more figured that he would quit his job or accept a demotion. So nine-tenths of the people studied said that failure to dress correctly would have serious consequences on the man's whole future.

5

We generally start our approach to an advertising campaign by talking about sales ideas. We will create a rational, logical sales idea. But the motive force of any idea is determined by its meaning—which is all the associations that the idea represents to the individual. The richer the meaning, the more powerful the idea. And richness includes such associations as feelings, emotions, images, and symbolic meanings.

Every word, every idea can have what is called a "denotative" and a "connotative" value. "Denotative" is comparable to pointing to an object—and that's all. "Connotative" refers to the many associations it stirs up in our minds.

For instance, if I denote a mouse, I simply am saying, "That is a mouse." Period. Nothing more. But on the connotative side, the notion of "mouse" evokes an image of a gray creature running along a pipe in the basement, a memory of an experience while living in the country when you were invaded by field mice, feelings of unpleasantness, filth, curiosity that women should be so frightened about mice, notions about mousey people, wharf rats, and so on and on.

Those happen to be mostly unpleasant associations. Suppose I encounter the name "Myrtle Beach." That's all it is to me—just a name, because I don't know anything about it. It has no connotative meanings. On the other hand, "Coronado Beach" brings up a flood of associations—pleasant feelings, memories of people, beautiful grounds, picturesque old elevators, considerable emotion.

Far too much advertising is narrowly denotative. It merely points to the product and proclaims some restricted range of functional benefits. Actually, in our highly competitive system, few products are able to maintain any technical superiority for long. They must be invested with overtones to individualize them; they must be endowed with richness of associations and imagery; they must have many levels of meaning, if we expect them to be top sellers, if we hope that they will achieve the emotional attachment which shows up as brand loyalty.

Imagery plays a highly significant part in motivating our daily behavior. It is far more vivid and compelling than abstract ideas; it generates many emotional accompaniments which become translated into strong drives.

An overcoat is just an overcoat. But a trench coat conjures imagery of private detectives, foreign intrigue, handsome younger men, adventure, daring, actors, glamorous girls, spies. I want it—not because it's a protective raincoat, but because of all this associated imagery and feeling.

The semblance of truth is far more important in advertising than truth itself. We believe what we want to believe. Actually, this is true about most things. A movie star picks out a romantic name because we worship the illusion rather than the reality. Even when we know that William Holden's name is something funny-sounding and that Kirk Douglas and Cary Grant were born something else, we stubbornly hang on to the illusion. We behave toward the illusion, not the fact.

We know from any marketing experience how much package design and color can boost the sales of a product. But what does a new red package contribute to the quality of the ingredients? Nothing whatever. We aren't going to eat the package or smoke it. Yet it feeds our mental notions that, mysteriously, the product itself has become better, more desirable.

When I put on a pair of dark glasses, I feel that somehow I'm a different person. I'm not, of course, but I think I am. Wearing a homburg hat makes me a different person. A woman luxuriating in her first mink is certain that she has been completely transformed.

The product which has no other meaning except its functional uses is dull and uninteresting. Advertising which conveys only the func-

Best friends look their best
with <u>new</u> indoor-outdoor Kodacolor Film!

You use the same roll for sunlight or flash—in any popular-size snapshot camera

Now it's no trick at all to get glorious color snapshots.

This exciting new Kodacolor Film gives the best color snapshots ever—so clear, so brilliant—with all the ease of taking black-and-whites. And new Kodacolor has a great

new convenience built in. The same roll works both indoors with flash and outdoors. At the beach, zoo or amusement park, in your living room or nursery—one type of film works everywhere!

Try it this weekend. New Kodacolor Film is on sale in all popular camera sizes. It can be processed locally in many cities. Or it may be returned to Kodak for processing if you ask your dealer.

Eastman Kodak Company, Rochester 4, N.Y.

Certainly much advertising is informative, practical, built around drama-tized product advantages. But there is much more going on in human com-munication than just reason. There is always an evocative level of feeling. Mostly we are talking to the other person's feelings. This is why modern advertising is a blend of sales logic and esthetic and fantasy appeals.

This Kodacolor advertising is effectively creating emotive hooks. It is successfully attaching a halo of "feeling-meanings" to the product so that it is no longer just a physical thing.

Because our formal schooling so strongly glorifies logic, we think of product benefits generally as functional advantages expressible in rational terms: engineering, ingredients, value. We overlook that psychological satisfactions and even esthetic pleasure represent highly desirable "benefits."

This Hamm's program effectively depends on purely subjective imagery: escape, refreshment, coolness, outdoors, sky-blue waters, North woods, etc. We rarely overwhelm people with our arguments. There is infinitely greater motive power in such associations that constitute a product's "psychological label."

tional uses—that the product supposedly does only what it is supposed to do—is restrictive and static.

One of the most potent factors in the high desirability of coffee and cigarettes and clothing to Americans is precisely that they do have so many directions of meaning, that they are so self-expressive, and they are so clearly understood, at least on intuitive and implicit levels.

The orthodox traditionalists of advertising insistently advocate a convincing statement of product benefits. But what are product benefits? Who said that the concept of product benefits has to be restricted to physical factors and functional uses? Aren't the psychological meanings included in product benefits if that's what I want from the product?

I didn't choose the modern furniture in my living room just for something to sit on. I most of all want the meanings of sophistication, individuality, avant-garde styling. Why aren't these product benefits? I don't wear dark glasses just to keep sun out of my eyes. I'm much more interested in the overtones: being, for the moment, a racer, a movie star, a mountain climber, a skiing champion, an airline pilot. These are by far the most impelling product benefits to me, not some dull mumbo-jumbo about what the glasses are made of.

If style is becoming an all-important criterion in the selection of furniture and homes and automobiles, then it is imperative for advertising to crystallize the style meanings of its products. It would appear downright stupid to spend millions of dollars shouting "double-torsion, superblack picture tubes" or "automatic roto-dollies" when the goods are being rejected because of styling—which is entirely a subjective element.

Style is only one of the meanings which are encompassed in the range of psychological overtones, of course. They can go in a multitude of directions. They can be both positive and negative. They are not absolute elements; they are subjective. They can be molded. They can be crystallized, they can be modified, they can be expanded, or they can be completely submerged by a dominant set of new meanings.

But they cannot be ignored.

6

The advertiser today understands the importance of attractive packaging, attractive labels, giving the product the right name. These factors have nothing whatever to do with the contents of the product, yet all by themselves they can play a vital role in its success or rejection. Entirely by themselves they contribute desirability. Most of all, the manufacturer, or any advertiser, should realize that one of his fundamental objectives in marketing is the psychological "label" on the product or institution.

This psychological label is particularly significant today in view of the standardization of quality and the identity of service which are typically true of our market place. Besides any practical purposes, advertising must help the individual integrate the product with his psychological goals and self-conceptions. How can he use it for self-expression? What inner goals can he satisfy through its psychological overtones? What does it say about his good taste? Does it clearly define his social status? His general prestige? Does it present his personality interestingly? Does it help him to define himself as serious and responsible, as adventurous, as carefree, or as whatever he thinks himself to be?

We say that our economy is controlled by laws of supply and demand. The producer can push up the price for his goods to the limits of demand. But what is "demand"? It means that people want something. It means desirability. And desirability is a subjective factor, not an absolute quality bound up in the nature of the product. Corsets, chewing tobacco, harnesses, buggy whips, high-button shoes no longer have demand, not because of any product weakness but because their subjective desirability has entirely vanished. Demand exists in the consumer's mind, not in the product. The producer in actuality is striving for some favorable share of the consumer's mind. And in this process of building subjective desirability, the psychological label on his products plays the crucial role.

CHAPTER V

Of Men and Motives

Any advertising, any communication has far greater opportunity to influence people if it is utilizing the most important motives which are involved with that specific product area. I doubt if anyone smokes cigars to be beautiful or if anyone buys deodorants to demonstrate her self-control. Obviously advertising does hope to launch its appeals in the current of real reasons responsible for the use of things.

But what are the real reasons?

I would like to quote from a number of motivation studies done by Social Research, Inc., as concrete illustrations of how this type of study can throw a very broad searchlight beam on the personal and social motives which are most impelling. Some of these are conscious and recognizable. The majority are implicit or unconscious meanings. The point of this research is precisely that in many, many fields the dominant, powerful motives are just simply not apparent in any superficial manner.

These studies indicate the diversity of psychological problems which can exist in various areas. Sometimes these problems take the form of troublesome negative attitudes. Sometimes the problem is one of using the wrong symbols—wrong in the sense that they are ineffective or misunderstood by the audience. Or else the advertising is using appeals with comparatively little motive power and overlooking much more potent motives.

This in no sense is to imply that advertising has generally been barking up the wrong alleys. Any such implication would be silly as well as incorrect. But there is a difference between knowledge and intuitive hunches.

The whole thesis of this book is that advertising should be helped by a clearer understanding of motives involved—conscious and unconscious, positive and negative, personal and social, dominant and subordinate motives. With complete awareness that each area is peculiarly individualistic, this variety of studies is nevertheless offered to show how social and psychological research can indicate in helpful fashion the deeper, underlying, dynamic factors of human behavior.

53

A great scientist once said to me "The more we know about Man, the more we realize we don't know." Against the background of complexity which science is barely starting to unravel, it sounds astoundingly presumptuous to hear some advertiser calmly assert that he can reach right through all the forces involved to get exactly the right answer with no other tools than a little common sense.

1

Instant Coffee versus Regular Coffee. Inasmuch as instant coffee hopes to tap the same motives that sustain the use of coffee, the first set of questions has to do with the many meanings surrounding coffee itself. After all, this is only a black liquid in a cup; yet it provokes an extremely rich set of associations. When people become articulate about coffee, they go way beyond any drab thing which is on the table three times a day like a glass of water. Even those souls who don't drink much coffee are aware that it has a very special character, that it is extremely gratifying to many important human needs.

1. Coffee is stimulating. It does things to people. When one gets up in the morning, when one is tired, there is nothing in wide use which is so invigorating.

2. Coffee is strong. All kinds of people want all shadings of strength in the brew of coffee which they drink, but strength is part of its essential character.

In this range of strength, black coffee and iced coffee are at one extreme, as most appropriate for doctors, truck drivers, nurses, big shots, and movie actresses: the people who are extremely masculine, hard-working, or exotic, and legitimately in need of stimulation.

At mid-point on the range is coffee with cream and sugar, the most conventional drink for adults who are up to date, mature, and hard-working, in and out of the home.

Instant coffee is still considered to be on the weak side. It is not thought of as being what doctors or truck drivers would want. It is more narrowly feminine—but it is growing in popularity—something for the most modern people.

The weakest beverages are caffeinless coffee and Postum, suitable for grandfathers, children, athletes, doctors, and nurses. Doctors and nurses symbolize both overwork and health consciousness, requiring therefore both the strongest and weakest coffee.

3. Coffee is a sedative, even though it is also a stimulant. It is like many products or activities that people use to renew their energies—

soft and hard drinks, cigarettes, and vacations—both relaxing and invigorating.

4. Coffee is a sign of vigorous, busy effectiveness. When subjects are asked to describe heavy coffee drinkers, they pictured them as dynamic, nervous businessmen—hard workers. The light coffee drinker is thought of as much less effective—a placid person.

The personality of coffee is mature and active. Drinking coffee can make a person feel identified with solid and serious ideas, and therefore more effective and forceful as an individual.

5. Coffee has multitudinous social meanings. People can drink coffee alone, but it especially serves as a universal sign of graciousness, sociability, hospitality, friendliness, equality. In any social scene, coffee can be served as an acceptable gesture, as an expression of good will, and without apology. It is equally at home in a lunch-counter mug or a fancy demitasse cup because it belongs everywhere.

6. Coffee is an important ritual, a part of American life, a habit adhered to, like eating three meals a day.

Because it does have these meanings of friendliness and hospitality, it requires care and pains in preparation. Even though her finished product may taste like battery acid, it is a cornerstone of the middle-class American woman's notion of a good housewife that she take time and effort in making coffee. The woman who fails to do so is considered a poor housekeeper and an indifferent hostess.

Although instant coffee has made considerable progress, there is still a tremendous difference in psychological meaning between it and regular coffee.

a. Regular coffee very sharply emerges as a hearty, tasty, clear, full-bodied, hot, dark, fragrant liquid. It signifies stimulation and strength, personal comfort, vigor and activity. It is a broad symbol of sociability, universally suitable for hospitality, a gesture of friendliness and graciousness.

b. Instant coffee goes counter to virtually all these ideal qualities. In spite of its increased popularity, it is still considered an inferior substitute which can only suffer by comparison with the real thing.

When people were asked to sum up the character of coffee in three words, they said:

- Satisfying, flavorful, invigorating.
- Fresh, priceless, stimulating.
- Delicious, satisfying drink.
- Strong, hot drink.
- Rich, full flavor.

These words were almost never used in describing instant coffee. Typical comments were:

— Not very useful.
— Weak, flat taste.
— Just too sweet.
— Very poor substitute.
— Easy, no aroma, flat-tasting.

c. Instant coffee stigmatizes and typifies a certain type of housewife. The housewife can serve it on occasion, of course. But any woman who goes contrary to the ideal housewife's dedication to her home and her family is neglecting her duty. If she consistently uses a product whose main claims to fame are the time and effort they save her rather than flavor and quality, she is bound to be stigmatized. She is seen as a lazy and indifferent housekeeper, not really a devoted wife.

The women who were considered to use instant coffee the least were described thus:

— She's always baking.
— The best cook of all.
— She cooks heavy meals.
— She uses recipes all the time.

d. Nevertheless the devoted housekeeper can properly use instant coffee on occasion, for example, when she is hurried, when she only wants a cup, or when she is simply at her personal leisure and wants some refreshment. When presented with the incomplete sentence, "A good homemaker uses instant coffee to . . . ," typical answers were

— Save time and money.
— Drink when in a rush.
— Get a fast cup of coffee.
— Make small quantities.

e. The ideal cup of instant coffee really belongs to a busy housewife having herself a cup during her morning or afternoon break. It is for the working wife getting a fast breakfast before rushing out. And it is for the young housewife who is hurried, harassed, or on a tight budget. The types who received the most votes for using instant coffee were

(1) The working woman.
(2) The beginner.

f. But instant coffee is a social insult. Its main drawback is that it is unaccepted for sociability. Serving it to guests is somewhat insulting, because it means that the hostess doesn't care to take the trouble to prepare "the correct thing."

g. Instant coffee's advantages are mostly practical. It does serve very important functions for many, readily summed up in these three-word definitions:

— Convenient, quick substitute.
— Economical, fresh, speedy.
— Good economical drink.
— Speedy, fast, cheaper.
— Speedy, time and money saver.

Actually, these descriptions occur more often among housewives than do derogatory words. These advantages make instant coffee especially desirable for people who want only one cup or who are under pressure of work and time. There is considerable usage among older people using only small quantities.

h. And of course the position of instant coffee is changing. Its popularity is growing, which makes people believe that the product is improved. Although it is still considered a substitute, most people feel that it is getting closer to the real thing. And it is becoming more respectable socially. It definitely has these psychological assets:

(1) It is recognized as a coming thing.
(2) It is economical when you want only a cup or two.
(3) It is time-saving and convenient.
(4) It is modern.
(5) It is suited to young people, rushing to get to work, progressive. This means that they are youthful, busy, hard-working, up to date, smart, clever enough to use modern innovations.

Undoubtedly much of the inferior reputation of instant coffee came from the advertising, which primarily emphasized it as a cheap substitute. The other thematic approaches, revolving around ingredients and processes (in spite of the success of flavor buds), necessarily build a mechanical, nonsocial character.

Coffee most strikingly is not consumed in a vacuum. It goes with things and people. When asked to complete "The thing that goes best with coffee is . . ." people do not say "a saucer" or "a mouth and throat" or "a big glass jar in buckeye art treatment." They mention such human and enjoyable associations as

— Chewy cookies.
— Toast.

— Sweet rolls.
— A cigarette.
— Good conversation.

As long as instant coffee stresses purely impersonal uses of speed, economy, and convenience, which are emergency uses only, it will never acquire the rich meanings of sociability, effective activity, and stimulation that still belong to regular coffee.

2

Cigarettes—Their Role and Function. With just the most cursory probing, the most general set of meanings emerging as our society's attitude toward cigarettes is their badness. There is practically unanimous consent that cigarette smoking is in some degree immoral, unhealthy, dangerous, and dirty. People can become quite vocal about setting fires, cigarette burns, the filthiness of smelly rooms, stained fingers, spilled ashes; and of course the range of organic disturbances, especially lung cancer and various respiratory troubles. We don't allow children to smoke, although actually there is no physical reason why they shouldn't. Smoking, however, signifies moral looseness. Nonsmokers regard the habit-forming quality of smoking as highly objectionable.

To overcome all these negative attitudes, the real reasons for cigarette smoking must be very powerful and gratifying. And they are entirely subjective reasons. Almost the only positive reason that people can cite is that smoking relieves tension, that it relaxes and calms them. But this is only a fraction of the cause, and generally it is not the real explanation. The person smoking a pack a day couldn't possibly have twenty different emotional or physical crises. He would be a raving lunatic by the third day if this were so.

Actually, the enormous variety of meanings that cigarettes actually do have is striking.

1. Effectiveness. Americans smoke to prove that they are virile—to demonstrate their energy, vigor, and potency. Cigarette smoking means physical strength, masculinity, competency, activity, and successful accomplishment. When people were asked to characterize a heavy smoker, he was thought of as "busy and doing," a terrific worker, entitled to some relief of the strains he is under.

One consequence of this idea is that smoking is still traditionally a man's activity. Our notions of delicate and "good" women do not quite yet jibe with these manly attributes. The mere fact of a woman smoking means that she is borrowing some masculine prerogatives:

self-assertion, activity, freedom, worldliness. The emancipation of women proceeds slowly. A girl under eighteen is the last person who should be smoking. And we still criticize any woman who would walk down the street smoking. There is a definite feeling of aversion about older women smoking.

Older women smoke to imply their youth. Younger people smoke to prove that they are older. Cigarette smoking symbolizes prime-of-life, productive maturity, sexual potency.

2. Oral indulgence, or mouth pleasure. The lips and other tissues of the mouth are delicate and sensitive zones, the first experiencing part of the body in infancy. Through the basic satisfactions in feeding, oral sensations develop great significance. They are realized in such diverse pleasures as chewing gum, sucking cough drops or mints, overeating, or even just talking.

The stimulation which smoking affords the oral zone is one of its most deep-seated satisfactions. The closeness between smoking and eating is readily apparent in their substitutive relationship. Again and again I have heard people justify their overweight by the fact that they had given up smoking, as if we should understand that they necessarily required a substitute mouth activity.

3. Possessiveness. This is a very important satisfaction: having a particular brand, which becomes highly personal property. There is an intense intimacy about one's cigarette. It becomes virtually an extension of oneself.

4. Self-expression. The mere fact of smoking itself, all the mannerisms of smoking, and the individual character of each brand all help people to define themselves.

5. Poise. It was repeatedly pointed out that cigarettes help composure by occupying the hands. Like a cocktail glass, a cigarette in the fingers makes people more sure of themselves in a gathering.

6. Reward for effort. We feel that we have earned a cigarette by any difficult accomplishment, whether a good golf shot, a conference completed, or an operation just finished. Or, as in theater intermissions, we are fortifying ourselves for more effort.

7. Proof of daring. The youngster learning to smoke, the elderly woman, and the woman asserting herself are all indicating their daring.

8. Social meanings. Cigarettes are almost synonymous with sociability. Offering a cigarette is universally understood as a gesture of friendliness.

9. Symbol of sophistication, of worldliness, of having been everywhere.

10. Informality and relaxation. Cigarettes are involved in countless daily habits that give satisfaction, such as taking a break or the marked sense of pulling a meal together with that "after-dinner cigarette."

These are among the principal reasons for smoking. Of course, they don't explain brand preference. And every smoker does distinguish between brands. What exists is a set of attitudes, a pattern of implicit attributes which create a product personality. These become stereotypes. Like a political cartoonist abstracting some particular feature, this is the way we generally think of people and things. Once these attitudes are crystallized, they are difficult to change by sensible argument.

These stereotyped notions about individual brands range along four principal lines of meaning:

1. Masculinity–Femininity. Some cigarettes are typed as very masculine, some as feminine, some as acceptable to either group. Camel is by widespread agreement the "he-man" cigarette, particularly of the athletic and working-class male. Chesterfield is for both men and women, but for a different sort of male—the white-collar type.

2. Strong–Mild. Each cigarette acquires its own shade of character along this range. Smokers want to strike a balance between being too unhealthy and evil (the strongest cigarette) and being too innocuous and prudish (the mildest).

3. Economical–Expensive. A cheap cigarette may actually cost less, or it may be rated as cheap because it is considered inferior. The brands that give coupons suffer much contempt. Cost doesn't stop the average smoker. People can think of more reasons why they shouldn't smoke than why they should. So there is no point in making matters worse by smoking a cheap cigarette. But of course, a cigarette may be economical without being cheap, as are long cigarettes.

4. Ordinary–Classy. These meanings also contribute to a cigarette personality. "Classy" means all kinds of things—glamour, money, status, sophistication.

For all of the ranges of meaning, it is significant that the four top sellers—Camel, Lucky Strike, Chesterfield, and Pall Mall—had the sharpest, clearest image. In choosing a brand, the individual has to feel that the cigarette, in terms of these subjective definitions, is worthwhile or suitable according to his own personality needs. Also, when he switches from one cigarette to another, it isn't just haphazard. Almost always it is within a confined group of other brands more or less congenial, saying much the same things about himself, satisfying similar needs.

The question to be answered in evaluating advertising themes is whether or not they activate any psychological needs sufficiently to make us do something—or at least include the brand among those we might smoke. Knowing whether people like the theme is not enough. The different brands are so widely advertised that there naturally is much awarenes of the major catch phrases and claims. But in this study, there was little relationship between this awareness and the brand smoked. Smokers often admire the advertising of some brand and go right on smoking something else.

Each of the themes has an effectiveness or lack of it peculiar to the category of motives involved with smoking and cigarettes. The competitive theme fails to take into account the close attachment which smokers feel toward their brand, unlike many other product areas, where they don't care. But when their cigarette is openly attacked by such references as "these five major brands," etc., they become defensive and are driven to support their own choice more than ever.

The cigarette-properties theme likewise is not particularly forceful, although "properties" themes are effective in other fields. The indifference of most people here to technical claims is due to the fact that they don't think there is really any more to a cigarette than tobacco and paper. Smokers are really interested in the properties from a psychological point of view—how do they help to define a cigarette as milder, more exciting, classier, or whatever the meanings?

Who cares whether the cigarette is an eighth of an inch longer or not?

But is it an exotic cigarette? Is it ruggedly masculine? Will it attract attention, appear sophisticated, and still alleviate my health worries?

3

Attitudes toward Shaving. It is easily apparent that men have contradictory feelings toward the whole subject of shaving. They complain much about the time consumed; there is the notion of wasting so much effort every day so pointlessly, the feeling that this is something they have to do. We know these negatives.

However, the much more interesting fact is that shaving is also pleasurable in itself. From the various approaches used to get through the cloud of stereotyped responses and various screens, it is obvious that men do enjoy the act of shaving for definitely positive reasons. As an indication that much of the complaints are overexaggeration, 150 men were asked to rate various statements. These are typical:

	Usually	Sometimes	Not Especially
Shaving tunes me up	87	35	34
It's fun to see your face come clean	78	22	46
I like to shave leisurely	85	30	35
Shaving is messy	18	31	95

When men were asked to complete the sentence, "When I have had a good shave, my face usually feels . . . ," only one-fourth said "clean." The rest said "smooth," "fine," "comfortable," "refreshed," etc., indicating definite degrees of pleasure. The satisfaction stems from four principal sources.

1. Shaving, for one thing, permits much sensuous gratification, offering a range of stimulations. More of these feelings are satisfied by the use of brush, lather, and safety-razor shaving, but they are still present with electric shaving. Sample quotations from more articulate men clearly point up the wealth of pleasure incident to hot and cold wettings, rough towels, creams and powders, and astringent pre- and aftershaves. This is virtually the only occasion when a normal man can indulge in toilet waters and scents. After all, the male is the decorative sex among both primitives and animals. Yet our particular society rigidly forbids him any other access to lotions and scents.

When men were asked what qualities the ideal shaving cream should have, invariably they mentioned scent. And when they were asked to prescribe the scent which should be used, they didn't mention any medicated odors. On the contrary, they suggested such possibilities as "lilac," "apple blossom," "sweet," "dry and light," "mild and masculine."

2. Shaving affords a tremendous amount of self-awareness. A woman can stare at herself in every shop window and not be criticized for studying and admiring herself. But not a man. Again, he cannot be self-admiring without being suspect.

In shaving, however, he can indulge himself, stripped to the waist or even naked, facing himself in the mirror, learning about himself more intimately. He studies the way his hairline is holding up; he discovers the curious swirls in which his beard grows, the way his eyes look in the morning. In fantasy he sees himself physically handsome, muscular, and therefore powerful.

Shaving is a wonderful few minutes for vanity, self-contemplation, daydreaming, and self-criticism of his physical being.

3. Shaving is a man's daily transformation. Where a woman puts on her make-up, a man "takes off" his face to achieve the same result —the sense of newness and transformation. It is much more than merely removing his beard. A man wakes up unkempt, disorganized, harried by his anxieties. It is this "face" that he takes off as he prepares himself for his family and for his social and occupational responsibilities. This is the way he reorganizes himself, reestablishes his identity and sense of security.

4. Shaving means masculine strength. No matter if the individual shaves once a week or once a day, he still insists that he has a tough beard. The basic wish to have a beard is typical of every male. The beardless youth is callow and immature; the beardless adult is presumably a eunuch. A man with strong masculine strivings wants a full beard. Shaving is a daily affirmation of masculinity. Men today are required to demonstrate their maleness by removing one of its very obvious signs—the beard.

Even though the basic shaving process is the same, the way a man shaves permits him to some extent to say what kind of a person he is, if only to himself. Shaving definitely is an expressive behavior. Seven main dimensions of character meanings are quite evident. From somewhere along these ranges men borrow nuances of self-revelation:

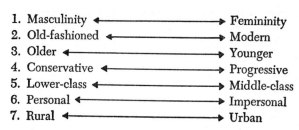

1. Masculinity ◄————————► Femininity
2. Old-fashioned ◄————————► Modern
3. Older ◄————————► Younger
4. Conservative ◄————————► Progressive
5. Lower-class ◄————————► Middle-class
6. Personal ◄————————► Impersonal
7. Rural ◄————————► Urban

Most men have tried most methods, looking for the procedure that best satisfies their needs, their notions of what they are. In digging out some of these deeper meanings, researchers used various character types. People gave clues to their own definitions of the methods by designating in turn the character types who would use them.

1. The "folk" methods, most used by such types as grandfathers, farmers, and longshoremen. Grandfather typifies "Old-fashioned" and "Older," the farmer is "Rural" and "Conservative," the longshoreman is "Masculine" and "Lower-class." They are the outstanding selections for

a. Brush and shaving soap or cream.
b. Plain toilet soap.
c. Straight-edge razor.

This is the most "primitive" method of shaving, for men who don't want to get mixed up with the new-fangled gadgets that they believe are less masculine than their own harder ways. Very few men in the study used a straight-edge razor, but it defines the character of this group.

2. The "ordinary" method. The people who shave this way are the plainest kind of people, not especially progressive or conservative, both lower- and middle-class, young and mature, etc. They are typified by such persons as high school boy, policeman, foreman, clerk, salesman. These men represent the middle-of-the-road use of

a. Tube brushless shave cream.

b. Safety razor.

A man who shaves this way has accepted the generally established values of his society, neither lingering in the past nor lured by the future.

3. The "advanced" method, ascribed to such people as the movie actor, college student, company president. These are the most modern people, the most urban and sophisticated; they mainly use

a. Aerated pressure-type lather.

b. Electric shaver.

This is the newest way, the most up to date. It has a particular appeal for people who want to express their individuality, in part, by moving ahead of the established way of doing things, by taking quick advantage of what modern technology offers.

None of these methods are hard and fast because personality is not rigidly cut and dried. The various methods may even be combined. Many men use more than one way of shaving. But it is evident that the shaving situation allows a certain variety of self-expression within the framework of a general conformity. And the various brands involved in each step continue this expression of personal needs according to the particular series of ideas, the individual character attached to each well-known product.

4

I cannot see how any of this material is restrictive to the creative people, except that it does indicate that certain copy approaches are much less fruitful than others. Shouldn't every creative person be helped by this awareness, regardless of how he uses it?

Such a major amount of cigarette advertising in the past has emphasized health appeals. But no one actually ever smoked to protect his nose or throat. If he sincerely wanted this protection, the most sensible course in the world would be not to smoke at all. These negative appeals are overlooking completely the underlying basic meanings that cause people to smoke in the first place. They may capture momentary competitive advantages, and they may offer some reassurance to the inveterate smoker. But they do utterly nothing to widen the market, to tap the driving force of the real psychological satisfactions.

Consider why people do smoke. In spite of a whole beehive of unpleasant associations about sinus trouble, etc., and a knowledge that this is a cost which is absolutely wasteful in that it provides not one earthly tangible good, about one-half of the urban adult population goes right on smoking cigarettes.

The psychological satisfactions, however, are intrinsic justifications for smoking. They are, consequently, the best material for advertising themes and appeals, because they carry their own reassurance. They are the emotional supports which have developed in American society to make smoking seem completely reasonable, justifiable, and highly desirable. They obviously cannot be thrown in people's faces in their bare essence; but when they are implied, when they are communicated, they are understandable and satisfying.

The study on shaving points to a very definite reservoir of masculine interest in toiletries, which is a potential sales aid if the appeals are skillfully handled. Sensuousness is an important source of both physical and psychological satisfaction, but it is a private pleasure. If it is made too outspoken, it signifies unmanly vanity. The advertising should capture some of the sensory aspects of shaving (the air of intimacy about the bathroom, the odors and smoothness of the lotions and the creams, the refreshed feeling afterward). But advertising cannot tackle these things head on.

In one way or another, the basic referen e of shaving is masculinity. A beard is vigorous, adult maleness, and removing it is part of proclaiming it. Advertising should take account of this factor of masculinity somehow. Besides sports and men winning girls, there are many other possible angles for introducing masculinity on an implied, believable, and unobjectionable basis.

The assumption that now underlies most advertising related to shaving is that all men are alike, that they all have tough beards and tender skins, and that the advertising should only be concerned with these issues. There are many more meanings than these and far more powerful motives.

CHAPTER VI

An Automobile for Every Personality

Year after year the automobile moves farther out to a center-stage position in the minds of most Americans as virtually the most exciting thing in their lives. The cost of purchase and upkeep ranks second or third in the average family's budget, yet no one ever raises an eyebrow about the wisdom of such an expenditure. In our national thinking, we assume that automobile ownership is as vitally necessary to decent living as indoor plumbing and adequate shelter. It actually startles us when we occasionally encounter middle-class families without a car.

And the sales curves for the industry testify that this desirability is becoming more intense all the time, to the point where the automobile seriously interferes with the prosperity of any number of unsuspecting industries. Whether they know it or not, almost all retailers and manufacturers selling the consumer are competing with this American passion for dazzling new cars. When the family reaches out for more and more fascinating extras, for sporty convertibles and station wagons which are more expensive than the less exciting conventional models, then it has less to spend on other things like jewelry, apparel, entertainment, and furniture.

Why is this so? Why does the car mean so much? What intense gratifications does it provide to create this remarkable desirability? Why is it assuming still greater desirability?

Of course, it is a means of transportation. This is perfectly obvious, and it is a practical reason that no one can minimize. But the automobile represents so much more than transportation. If that were all it stood for, we would buy inexpensive cars and drive them for 150,000 miles. This mere factor of transportation sheds no light whatever on the public mouth-watering for brilliant colors, for two-tones and three-tones, for rear-fender esthetics and chrome side strips and lush interiors. Nearly all cars today are mechanical achievements, yet the individual decides that he wants a Ford, or a Buick, instead of some other car. Why?

To show the potentialities offered by competent qualitative research for revealing insights into the dynamics of behavior and to show how it opens up new directions for thinking, this chapter will discuss in some detail our automobile study (which was also done by Social Research, Inc.), touching these specific points:

1. The car is pretty close to being the most desirable product in our economy, and it is worth examining the motive elements in this desirability just to see how any product can climb so high.

2. Although it is essentially a complicated piece of machinery, the car has attracted to itself a wealth of other meanings far, far beyond its functional qualities.

3. The car has intruded itself very successfully into the currents of change in our national system of values.

4. This study throws significant light on the whole process of decision making in any field, although it is clearer to see in the case of the automobile.

5. Some highlights on the basic objectives of advertising itself are given.

6. This study documents the birth of an entirely new dimension in advertising and marketing: that of a product seeking to sell itself to various personality types, each of which may have different goals and different self-conceptions.

Occasionally some penetrating mind calls attention to the fact that the American market, or any other market for that matter, is not composed of millions of people exactly alike. Rather there exists a multitude of markets—different age groups, the two sexes, racial and religious groups, social classes, urban and rural distinctions, income and occupational levels, geographic viewpoints, and probably many other factors generate different wants and different standards of taste.

Personality is certainly not the least important of these distinguishing factors. Again and again in my experience, the ordinary criteria for separating buyers could give no explanation for product successes and failures. The buyers and the nonbuyers were indistinguishable except on a personality basis.

Extensive studies of sales abilities of department store clerks indicate that the crucial factor is one of basic personality components. Another study of unsuccessful business executives established that their failure was attributable, not to knowledge deficiencies, but to personality problems.

Our automobile study very clearly shows that the market for a Plymouth or a Pontiac is not composed, actually, of all the people in a certain income group or a certain locality, but rather of distinctive personality types. Neither does this mean, however, that personality is the only factor. But it is a dimension which should not be overlooked. Many a product can carve out its own segment of the market by creating a specific appeal to a definite personality type, instead of trying to be all things to all people.

Smirnoff vodka, Parliament cigarettes, and Schweppes tonic water are concrete illustrations of this achievement: they have become meaningful and important to a definite group, small percentagewise but large enough in number to constitute a profitable market.

2

The practical, social, and personal meanings which the automobile embodies are grouped around five central ideas.

First, of course, the car is a mechanical object with important practical uses. The car as a means of transportation does satisfy many practical goals and needs which are motives in themselves. These are the sensible reasons why people want cars. We have become such a physically mobile people that transportation is literally a key factor in our physical and social life. However, this element of transportation is so obvious that it isn't necessary to labor it.

Much the same is true about the technical features. The car certainly is an extremely complex machine with an appeal to our national passion for technology and gadgetry. Nevertheless it is highly important to indicate that the number of persons with a really overwhelming mechanical interest is definitely in the minority. Cars have become so complex and so mechanically perfect that the average driver understands very little of the intricacies of operation.

In this study, people were asked to tell a story about a picture of a car with the hood raised and a man peering under it. There were two women in the back seat. The stories all identified the situation as a breakdown on the highway. But a general helplessness was indicated in the responses as to how the man would fix his car. The consensus was that he should look for a garage or a service station and not tinker with it himself. The average motorist today rarely if ever raises the hood of his own car. He has only the barest notion of car mechanics.

Of course, we do like to talk about the spectacular new engineering triumphs, particularly the well-advertised features. They are conversation pieces on the American scene. The individual betrays that he is out of touch with things if he cannot at least identify such wizardry as power steering and hydramatic drives. But our interest is much more in the gimmicks and latest innovations, not the complexities. And we are far more interested in what they will do rather than in how they operate.

A second group of meanings revolves around the automobile as a sizable investment with an important place in family economics. The individual has to think about it often and seriously. It never gets pushed out of mind by other things. It is important to point out how these economic factors work, so that they don't muddy other ideas which parallel them. Cost is only one of several considerations, and usually is not the determinant in the choice of one make instead of another. All of us are exposed to an avalanche of spectacular bargain claims from less popular cars. But we yawn them off. Unless the make is appealing to us, we aren't particularly interested.

The automobile retailer probably would disagree with this. He knows in one sense the power of excessive dealing. But today the car dealer does little to sell the individual make. The fortunes of any car over the country, the upcurves and downcurves of its sales graph, are pretty uniform regardless of dealers. When the prospect arrives at the retail showroom, he has already been presold on the make he prefers. Naturally he wants the best offer he can get on that car. But the point is, he has done more thinking, both consciously and unconsciously, about the make than about the deal he might get.

Actually, people in this study spent more active thought about cost of upkeep and gas mileage than about the price of cars. This was true in any price class. Regardless of income level, every American fancies himself a shrewd and careful manager. So he nods his head owlishly about low gas mileage and frequently tries to convince himself and his friends that this was the reason for his car choice.

Almost every person I know with a European sports car has tried to justify it by describing how much gasoline he saves. He is obviously screening other motives. His gasoline savings would have to be fantastic to compensate for the difference in car price for some of these cars. Cost of upkeep is not a powerful motivating idea. It is not likely to be the important reason for buying some particular make.

The third general field—the social meanings surrounding the car—should in large part be apparent: how much the car is involved with people being together—family vacations, driving to work with a friend. Social companionship is a powerful motive, and this factor is quite obvious. Yet it is important to detail how much the automobile in American life has come to be used as an indicator of the individual's social status, his position, his place in the scheme of things.

Regardless of whether this is utterly illogical, we unconsciously classify every car and use it as a yardstick for determining how important a person is in our society. When we observe a stranger getting out of his car, our behavior in considerable part is determined by the make and the age of his car. We go to college reunions and assess a classmate's lifetime as a success or failure just by taking a look at his car.

Furthermore, the automobile is a portable symbol of status. Only a handful of people can be aware of my bank balance, my investments, my wife's fur coat, my country-club membership. But the car is a useful device for carrying my position and accomplishments with me for all to be aware of, wherever I may go.

Price is one more indicator of a car's status, not a cause of it. They do match up very closely, however. It is permissible for any American to buy whatever car he chooses. The car is really a prestige object, like a fur coat or a Florida vacation, that anyone can help himself to if he can afford it.

Nevertheless, car selection is very much influenced by its own status with other cars and by the status and personal wishes of the buyer. Some people, of course, overreach themselves, because the individual's dreams, his hopes, his wishes, and his own notions about himself play an extremely vital role in the automobile's meaning.

The average man can buy a classy car and still be wishing. He can enjoy all his daydreams about wealth, importance, sophistication everytime he steps into his car, and yet he hasn't tipped his hand, as he would if he tried moving into a neighborhood too far up the ladder. He can leave all his dreams in his car with no one being the wiser.

The halos of different cars vary considerably; some are chic, sporty, flashy, whereas others are more down to earth, less pushy. Some low-price cars are most acceptable as second cars; others are definitely not.

In the fourth set of meanings, the automobile emerges as a powerful symbol of self-control. It clearly signifies personal mastery and control of basic human impulses. The car is a mass of enormous energy, and because the driver is controlling all this power, he knows the pleasures and fears of handling major drives.

Self-assertiveness is a basic impulse expressed in many motives. Competition, rivalry, the individual's desire for authority and self-importance are manifestations of this urge. The car provides deep emotional stimulation by satisfying this drive through a sense of power, with the thrill of speeding, by offering many opportunities for showing personal superiorities.

Affiliation is the expression of the need for human companionship, such as sex, friendship, or anything that pulls people together. The auto plays an important part, obviously, in our mating and dating habits.

A major part of the car's desirability is that it provides socially acceptable outlets for these basic human drives, affiliation and aggression, while at the same time it is a massive, concrete symbol of our self-control, to which we attach a high premium. Any driver senses that he is directing potentially powerful forces.

Because of this, cars are very much able to satisfy the important desires of Americans wanting to "be somebody." I am somebody by the specific way in which I individualize self-control. This is far more than social recognition. Every person wants to be important and effective in ways that other people recognize. I want to be a good bridge player, or a good dialect-story teller, or a standout in my work field. Most child and adult games allow each person in turn to be "it," which provides an importance, if only momentary. We crave spoken and unspoken praise, if only from imaginary audiences.

For many reasons and in many ways, having a car gives us the feeling of "being somebody." The man who owns a car, or even the youngster who is driving a borrowed car, feels more important, more substantial, more achieving, more masculine than the man without a car.

The fifth area of meanings has to do with the car as an extremely important avenue of self-expression. The automobile is one of the most clearly understood ways in our society of conveying characteristics and feelings and motives that typify a particular individual. The car tells what we want to be as persons—or what we think we are.

Because these personality differences in people do have so very much to do with the way they express themselves in car selection, this study indicated some of the broad areas of what essentially different people want to be. These dimensions were drawn to cover a normal range, instead of trying to examine clinical types. People were construed to vary along these lines:

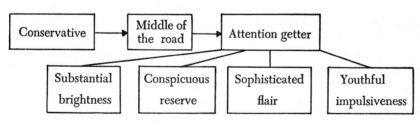

In general terms, the wish to be conservative or reserved is recognizable in the solid citizen who emphasizes conformity, wants to be considered reliable and stable, draws back from anything conspicuous or drastically new, and doesn't want to experiment with fads and fancies. In automobiles, his conservative tastes very definitely weight his preferences in makes, models, and car qualities.

The conservative prefers the less flamboyant colors and has been the last to accept lighter colors and two tones. He hangs back on each new innovation; he walks a middle road on chrome and extras; he wants a neat-looking new car rather than a high-styled or extreme design. Certainly he thinks his new car is exciting and shining, but he definitely doesn't want a jet-plane or an all-white car. In all his buying, he stresses money values—in this case real economy, trade-in value, and dependability. These factors are more important to him than appearance or power.

The next broad group of personality types is composed of people who emphasize the wish to be sociable, who don't want to be either extreme conservatives or too advanced. They are the ones anxious to be up to date, to be popular, to do the fashionable thing. If many people are moving toward glamour and sportiness in their tastes, this group wants to be on the bandwagon. Consequently, this attitude is the most suggestible, and the easiest to influence. It is essential to establishing a new fashion.

In cars these people will generally prefer what is currently thought smart without being extreme. They want new styling, and they worry less about mechanics and more about appearance than the conservative.

The third personality type stresses the wish for attention. This is a perfectly normal human trait which everybody possesses to some degree, but in this group it becomes very important. These people especially want to be different and outstanding; they enjoy being talked about. Consequently, they are the innovators and the style setters, just because they are looking for the newest things. They don't hesitate to try some novelty.

All these people of the third group would like to be noticed, but how they express this wish will vary. There are four main directions of this attention-getting wish:

1. Substantial brightness means big, ornate costliness in cars; loud, impressive display; everything the best and most expensive. Especially do these people want the widely recognized high-status symbols. This could be the car owner who wants to cut an important figure by having everything the best and most expensive, who is anxious for others to realize that he has arrived. But this group also includes many people who feel denied in certain areas of living, for instance, Negroes

who are overly anxious to prove that they are equally as good as anyone else by driving big, shining cars.

2. Conspicuous reserve characterizes a type that want others to be aware of their status, but at the same time they would like to express modesty. They go in usually for dignified display or deliberate downgrading. This is a familiar technique among people perfectly certain of their higher social standing. They assume indifference to position by purposely buying less expensive cars than might be expected—dilapidated station wagons, old cars, lower-price lines. The upper middle class is in too precarious a struggle for status to take any such chances.

3. Sophisticated flair describes young intellectuals, sophisticates, professionals, creative people, and others who lean toward avant-garde living. They especially prize individuality in car styling and colors; they seek smartness rather than gaudiness; they want bright colors just as they shun drabness. Being in the forefront of the style setters is extremely important, and consequently they will try anything—foreign cars, white convertibles, estate wagons. They are the people who introduce pizza, turtleneck sweaters, moccasins, and exotic-sounding vodka mixtures. They think of themselves as being very individualistic, considerably ahead of the generality of people in taste, intellect, and colorful personality.

4. Youthful impulsiveness is characteristic not only of youngsters sighing for gadgets and hot rods but also of the eternal sophomores of any age, who express their youthful yearnings through automobiles. The sixty-year-old driving a convertible with the top down, wearing his trench coat, a crew cut, and no hat, is very much expressing his eternal youthfulness. For these people a car is a means of demonstrating their daring and their youth, by the way it looks and by how they drive it.

3

This is only one very elemental scheme for classifying personality. And it should be made clear that probably most persons are a mixture of many of these characteristics. Furthermore, all of this is vastly oversimplified. But it was purposely done so in order to point up this factor of personality.

On the basis of this and many other studies, it is apparent that any buying process is an interaction between the personality of the individual and the so-called "personality" of the product itself. They are not the same thing, of course. Product personality can be called its character, its reputation, its image. Essentially, it is the whole set of attitudes that people hold toward it.

A car or any product has to accomplish certain purposes. But my decision as to which particular auto can best fulfill the job becomes a personal expression of me. In any price class there is a wide range of choice. The car or the brand I pick out expresses what I think I am —or what I want to be. To decide anything as a choice is actually to express the self. Any person who makes a decision among alternative choices is actually stating, "This is the kind of individual I want to be. This is me."

What is a self but a permanent mode of selection?

It is important to realize that cars in exactly the same price class can be appealing to very different people. For instance, the lines of models in the fine-car field are actually appealing to quite different markets—different kinds of people.

Cadillac has become the outstanding status car, with a very wonderful set of favorable attitudes haloed around it. It is considered the most luxurious, the finest-engineered, and the most impressive car. It has been transformed in recent years from the "high-society" car to the symbol for the man of achievement, the realization of our American dream of business success.

Almost more than any other symbol, the Cadillac signifies the end of the rainbow for the man who has with his own two hands carved out his own road to financial achievement. Curiously, in many companies the president drives another, less expensive car because he has had his position and money for a generation or so. He doesn't have to convince the world. It is the sales manager or the New York State Division manager who drives the Cadillac.

Because of its extreme status, a Cadillac also holds magnetic attraction for people deprived in other areas of living. On the other hand, there are some members of its former high-status market who resent it for this specific attraction, because it is now too common for them.

In research studies, the other cars in the fine-car field didn't have these overtones in any degree at all. Lincoln had a sporty aura, a luxury elegance. Chrysler Imperial was an expensive, modern car. But they were not the rainbow's end of the Horatio Alger dream like Cadillac.

Each car has its own distinct image which sets it off from the others. In addition to many other favorable attributes, Buick is seen as the car for successful people moving upward. It is an especially popular car among small-town lawyers, bankers, and doctors, who for policy reasons wish to avoid any criticism for owning the highest-price cars.

[The car purchase is comparable psychologically to building a house, in the sense that it is a composite of many things. One element, such as color, may be balanced or combined with the model lines to produce a particular self-satisfying totality. Price, performance, styling, any number of factors are offered, and the buyer selects this, rejects that, establishing a composition of elements especially suitable to him.]

There is no simple relationship between kinds of buyers and kinds of cars, however. Any human is a complex of many motives—his practical aims, his economic limitations, his personal characteristics, his own particular social pressures. All these motives should be seen as patterns, with predominant and subsidiary meanings which may vary in countless combinations.

Nevertheless the different makes and models are seen as helping people give expression to their own personality dimensions. The conservative in car choice and behavior wishes to convey such ideas as dignity, reserve, maturity, seriousness about work and family matters. He will emphasize practicality and dependability. Such features as the four-door sedan, restrained colors, minimal accessories and gadgets, as well as certain makes, help him express his personality. He will generally drive his car longer than average, and his purchase is governed in great degree by high trade-in value.

Another definite series of car personalities is selected by the people wanting to make known their middle-of-the-road moderation, their being fashionable. They are anxious to be known as not too stodgy and not too flashy, very much up to date and yet not ahead of the times. Such features as two-door models, lighter colors which are yet not breath-taking, the current fad for gadgets, and a combination of practicality and looks—any and all of these—give expression to what this type is trying to say about themselves.

Further along the range of personalities are the innovators and ultramoderns, reaching out to select car personalities which will imply their individuality and modernity. The cars, the models, the features that they buy because they do mirror the self-conceptions of this group contain consistent elements—the most striking colors, accessories which are certain to be talked about, always something excitingly new in models, such as hardtops and ranch wagons.

The steady trend of sales in this direction also reveals the shifting base of the whole society. The conservative wants to reach out for color and two tones to escape his stodginess in some degree. And as he moves to accept chrome strips and sporty models, the other types shift with him. The individualist, for example, is never happy when the majority of people adopt his tastes because then he isn't modern and different. He is constantly adjusting his buying patterns to keep ahead of the style current.

4

Of course, this basic set of motive appeals existed fifteen years ago. This does not explain the enhanced desirability of the car, nor the recognizable swing to brighter colors and sporty models, nor why design has become the primary component in sales appeal. These elements are directly related to a visible change in our American style of life, to the underlying social and psychological currents which are causing such other drifts as the pronounced shift to informal living and the vast increase in hobbies and participation sports.

Since 1939, our tremendous economic gains have spurted family income far past the subsistence level. Historically, periods of widespread leisure and prosperity have very often led to

1. A considerable increase in self-indulgent behavior.
2. A greater seeking for new thrills and stimulation.
3. A desire for much more self-expression.

Whereas in other such periods of history the favored ones indulged themselves in art, magnificent estates with fountains and formal gardens, stables of fine horses, today the automobile is the instrument best fitted for our whole society to give form to these motives. Although twenty years ago your conservative neighbor would never have dared to drive a lavender-flamingo ranch wagon, today the drifts in our living styles have made it conventional to use vivid colors as an outlet for self-expression.

This does not mean any increase in the number of attention getters in the population nor any decrease in the number of conservatives. It simply indicates that more people in all groups and types now seek opportunity for self-expression and that, besides such outlets as do-it-yourself activities around the house and new participation sports such as skiing, sailing, and pheasant shooting, there are many elements about the automobile which permit the greatest number of people the greatest opportunity for self-expression, such as color, special models, plush interiors, and extra gadgets.

And as we moved out of the 1930s, with their emphasis on the depression and subsistence values of price, economy, and dependability, we began to look for products and services which embody these other motive areas of more individuation, exciting new stimulation, more glamour and color. The functional factors of comfort and sturdiness are far less appealing than designs which permit people to identify all these new values with themselves. Hence the competitive battles are won, not by gearshifts and more head room, but rather by exciting designs and new color combinations.

And the automobile itself elbows other products aside because it is the most self-expressive thing we have in this era when a premium is placed on self-expression, being acceptably different, being a colorful person within a framework of conformity.

5

In the light of these study findings, it seems obvious that the most effective automobile advertising should utilize two basic sets of motivations, which by and large could apply to any product:

1. The basic wish for ownership of the product.

2. The personality of the particular brand.

These are two different concepts, but they both offer fertile fields for creative minds to harness. As a matter of fact, both levels of appeal can be in the same advertisement.

In spite of the automobile's tremendous hold on the public imagination, the copy can and should try to channel some of the motives which induced the buyer to go shopping for a new car. After all, there were certain motives causing him to make such a considerable expenditure.

So much car advertising falls into the "name-and-a-claim-and-a-price" category, taking no recognition of this area of motives. Whatever impact this advertising has is purely an underscoring of the attraction of the car's present character. It concentrates on attributing to the car certain mechanical or stylistic features which the consumer is supposed to value, with no regard for the pressures which caused him to want to spend several thousand dollars.

These are typical of the practical and expressive motivations which exist as potential copy areas in this particular field:

1. To "be somebody"—to convey to others that we individually have interesting, colorful, effective personalities.

2. To acquire a sense of financial power and importance. The auto is one of the most easily recognizable signs of financial success—one of the most important goals in the life of the American male.

3. To accomplish transportation. Unlike many products such as beer or cigarettes, the automobile does have tangible practical purposes.

4. To convey a sense of strength and capability, a feeling of personal power, a command over one's environment.

5. To provide socially acceptable outlets for basic emotional forces, at the same time symbolizing self-control.

6. To show that one is adult and entitled to the privileges of adulthood. Not only does this seem important to teen-agers, but also to various grownups who always feel that they must prove their right to be considered adults—for instance, short people.

7. To extend one's boundaries—having freedom of action at least subjectively, being independent at least in one's mind.

8. To show social standing—the group or the rung on the ladder that one belongs to, or secretly hopes to belong to.

9. To show some personal superiority. Competitive rivalry underlies so many of our actions; we continually try subtly to show how we excel. Car ownership permits us in a variety of ways to impress our friends and work associates. "My car has a better performance record"; "The model I'm driving is absolutely exciting"; "The new push-button gearshift I have is wonderful, and you don't have it."

10. To express one's own individual personality and style of living.

11. To celebrate the important personal changes in our lives. The car is a concrete means of making others aware that something significant has happened: getting married, an important promotion, a change in our circumstances from nose on the grindstone to easy comfort, achieving maturity, etc.

6

Turning to the other facet of the advertising problem—selling any particular make—the advertising has to reckon with the broad attitudes which exist toward the car and which comprise its product personality. The advertising is most effective when it is in terms of this product personality and when it is expanding it to make it more desirable to more different kinds of people.

The dimensions of these objectives can be stated this way:

1. What is the current character of the brand in the mind of the general public?

What does the advertising do to build, modify, or contradict this character?

2. What is the long-run character that the advertiser wants to establish?

How does the campaign contribute to this desired character?

It is highly important to stress—and this applies to any product or institution—that the advertising must come close to fitting the existent product personality. Of course, this can be widened, but in the case of a well-known product, the process has to be done gradually, in acceptable steps. A complete contradiction of the public image of any product is simply rejected.

People believe the advertising that fits their preconceptions. Again and again in this study, the persons interviewed about certain car advertising would sound off their opinions of the car first and then transfer these likes and dislikes into their judgment of the advertising. A certain car that was considered rather stodgy, unexciting, for the Casper Milquetoasts of this world, in one advertisement was portrayed arriving at Sun Valley. It was a ludicrous situation to the people interviewed—being asked to believe that the mousey, ultra-reserved buyers of this car would ever venture to a sophisticated, gay resort.

In the broadest sense, the optimum objective is to endow the car with the widest possible range of appeal. Unlike some products which are content with a thin segment of the population, the automobile aspires to mass appeal. Those cars with narrow personalities, either because of extreme features or single-track advertising, definitely limit themselves. This does not mean that each single ad should be loaded with a multiplicity of appeals, but rather, by using different campaigns with different themes, entirely different audiences come to view this particular product as best expressive of them.

Ford retains from its Tin Lizzie past a recognizable market which values it as the most economical, the best for rugged wear, a plain farm car. At the other extreme, it is intensely attractive to youngsters and sophisticates for its flair, its power, its speed. It is very popular with high-income families wanting a second car. The choice it offers in ranch wagons and convertibles and station wagons has particular attraction for the smart set. Its range of color combinations constitutes an appeal for another type of individual. Each of these highly distinct personality groupings sees some facet of the Ford personality as reflecting itself.

As biological organisms, all men are similar. But multiple pressures operate to differentiate us, so that we look at the world through different eyes, with different values and beliefs, and with different tastes. In the final analysis, advertising is the one means the manufacturer possesses which he can consciously control to represent his car in many ways to these many different people. The car is only a mechanical object with certain mechanical features for a price. Its success or failure in this day of technological near perfection will result from its subjective desirabilities, which are essentially unrelated to the mechanics.

Advertising is the multiplier of symbols. Like a prism, it can present many different facets of the car's factual and subjective character, so that fundamentally different people each see it as their car. "This is me—for me"; they make this unconscious closure of decision. Then—and then only—does buying occur.

CHAPTER VII

Women Are People

In contrast to the rich meanings that coffee, clothing, cigarettes, and cars hold for people, there are many product areas which are thin and colorless—almost devoid of any associations except their utilitarian uses. Packaged soaps and gasoline, for instance, are typical areas where the brands are mostly blurred and without distinction in the consumer's mind.

It might be argued that such products by nature do not lend themselves to rich imagery. On the other hand, our studies would seem to indicate that some of this paucity of feeling results from the predominant type of advertising in the classification. Much packaged-soap advertising has pounded product claims entirely at the functional level. Constant repetition of chemical jargon, cliché situations, coined words, and stereotyped claims actually does little to create any depth of overtones or emotional involvement.

This approach does not offer the consumer many meanings which could be self-expressive, either to others or to herself. It is difficult to form really profound brand loyalties when the brands themselves are not trying very hard to create a distinguishable identity with many shadings of meaning. Much of the advertising is addressed only to a very superficial part of a woman's life. It overlooks entirely that she is a human being with a wide range of emotions, feelings, and interests.

As a basis for discussing this phase of advertising, I want to cover in detail the study done by Social Research, Inc., on packaged soaps and chemical detergents. I would like also to use it as a springboard for delving into the subject of the woman consumer. This is the creature whom we hope to influence in such a large part of our advertising effort. Yet as men, we mostly have little insight into her goals, her daydreams and anxieties, the avenues she uses for self-fulfillment.

With characteristic egocentricity, we assume that our wives and daughters are intensely interested in the same purposes, the same subjects which preoccupy our mental energies: politics, sports, hobbies, business achievement, the mechanics of our cars.

They aren't. Although they listen politely to our animated discussions about these masculine areas, it is because they are forced by our own society's definition of the feminine role to be passive. A man generally becomes irritated whenever he is exposed to "housewife chatter," as he calls it—babies, sickness, forthcoming weddings, club work. Unless he is exceptionally henpecked, he very shortly breaks it up. But a woman can't interrupt a similar session of masculine talk. She can't afford to risk offending her economic overlord. She resigns herself to being bored. Nevertheless, this is no excuse for us men not to sense that her real interests veer off in entirely different directions.

The modern educated girl does not have a free choice between her career and housework. She has no choice at all—it's housework, period. Why wouldn't she feel purposeless and disappointed if she has a talent and many years of study invested in science or music or writing but nevertheless has to bow to the dictate of our society that the only goals for a woman are marriage, having babies, and doing housework? There is no alternative. Some women, of course, are intensely happy in this role. On the other hand, there are multitudes who feel that the definition of a woman's role is narrow and constricting.

In this soap study, among the projective tests, women were asked to complete this unfinished sentence: "The job of a housewife. . . ."

There was no reason at all why the completions should be loaded in any direction. But these were characteristic:

- Is a million things.
- Is never done.
- Is to keep her temper.
- Stinks.
- Is never through when you have small children.
- Is drudgery.
- Is twelve to fifteen hours a day.

With half an opportunity, women are quick to express their view that being a housewife is arduous, irritating, and unending. What can they do about it? Nothing.

Furthermore, technology's inexhaustible procession of work-saving appliances and prepared foods (even prepared meals), steadily minimizes her opportunities to be creative. Her tiny realm is the only possibility she has for being ingenious, for displaying her intelligence,

Soap dries your skin, but
DOVE <u>creams</u> your skin while you bathe

Sensational new bath and toilet bar is one-quarter cleansing cream

DOVE is a completely *new* formula – DOVE actually creams your skin while you wash! Because DOVE is one-quarter rich cleansing cream, it leaves your skin feeling soft and smooth – with none of that dry tight feeling you get from soap. DOVE makes soap old-fashioned! Lever Brothers guarantees that DOVE is better for your face, your hands *all* of you – than any toilet soap. Or your money back!

Research shows the most important impact of this Dove ad is an over-all impression of wonderful feeling: an aura of refreshment, relaxation in the tub, the luxuriousness of creams and rich lather, the notion that such self-indulgence and youthful carefreeness is acceptable.

Advertising is a subtle and complex form of human communication. The best modern advertising goes far beyond any rudimentary name-and-a-claim approach. Besides the rational advantages, it must create important psycho-logical overtones appealing and acceptable to the consumer's self-ideal.

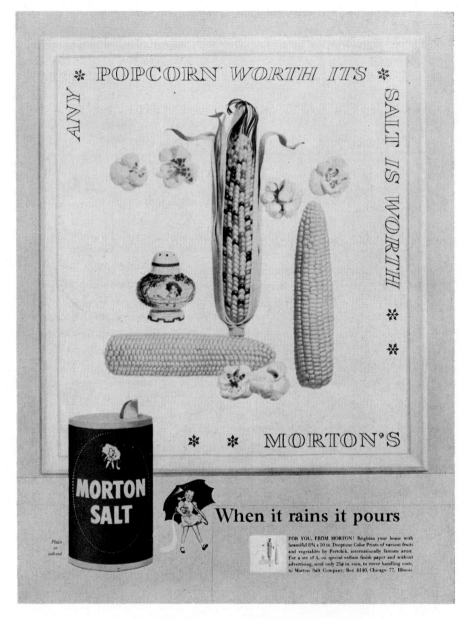

Communication includes all the ways by which people convey meaning to each other. There are many nonverbal "languages" such as painting, music, architecture. Much human communication occurs through gesture, facial expression, voice modulation, symbols of identification and expression such as clothing, hair style.

Modern advertising has learned that esthetic values communicate in their own way. They don't need words. The art meanings of this Morton ad—design, subdued tone, the Mexican corn—are saying very significant things at the prerational levels in men.

for creating anything. Why wouldn't she feel empty and frustrated when these avenues are cut off, when she is bent more and more to the slavey's chores?

Actually she resists many new products that could save her time and effort. She unconsciously senses that they cut into her role as the effective woman performing important tasks. The person who still bakes her own bread and cake is considered the nearest to the ideal mother.

And the woman in today's big city is lonely. While she is in school or working, she thrives on companionship. Every human being craves the society of others. But as soon as she marries, she is committed to being alone all day. Her husband departs at dawn, her children leave the house, her father or her aunt living with them come and go when they want to. But she can't. Just on the chance that one of the children might get hurt or be sent home sick from school, she is anchored to the house, like a stand-by night watchman.

Why should it be necessary to reiterate that she is a complex creature, compounded of yearnings, daydreams, unfulfillments, buried hopes, satisfactions and frustrations both, eager for affection and praise? Probably even more than a man, apart from her everyday duties she moves in a world of emotions and feelings and moods and hopes.

The modern woman, with all her kitchen gadgets and much smaller family, doesn't have to work nearly as hard as her grandmother. But she is still wrestling with the emotional adjustments consequent to being chained to many chores for which she was never trained, which no one thinks are worthy of an intelligent person, and which isolate her from other people.

2

Inasmuch as this soap study was attempting to shed light on one small phase of the homemaker's job, a bird's-eye view of her whole task would make clearer how cleaning fits into place. She has four main spheres of activity:

1. Being a wife. This of course is the number-one goal for a woman in our society—securing and holding a husband. If a girl has made a good marriage, she is considered a success. If she has made a bad one, there is nothing she can do except try to adjust to it.

On the other hand, if she has made no marriage, she is sentenced to a life of frustration and loneliness. In everyone's eyes she is tagged a failure. Therefore, being loved is not only part of a woman's life;

it has to be her occupation. Making herself attractive is imperative for purposes of economic security.

Once upon a time a woman could relax after marriage and quit worrying about her figure and her looks. This isn't true today, as simple as divorce is. So she has to spend all her life keeping herself attractive, not only as to her clothes and her appearance, but as to her personality as well.

2. Raising the children. She is charged with the discipline, the clothing, the music lessons, taking them to the dentist and the barber, conferring with teachers.

3. Feeding the family.

4. General housekeeping and cleaning.

There are, of course, a sizable number of working wives, with outside interests. But this study purposely concentrates on the stay-at-home wife, especially in the average, mass-market family. In pursuing her four major areas of activity, she is governed by a central set of feelings and aims, which largely determine whether she is satisfied or anxious.

These are her primary motives:

1. Maintaining family unity. This is an intense wish to hold her husband, to hold her children to her, to hold the family together. This set of motives emphasizes her desire for security and her practicality. She wants a home that is stable, held together by her personal effort—by her tenderness, by her work. And she wants to be a copartner in the operation of the home, recognized for her indispensability. She feels that her husband is expendable—that the home could go on without him—because his contribution is economic. But no home could exist without her, because she is tenderness and practicality.

2. Maintaining self-esteem. Every human being periodically needs to prop up his feelings of importance and effectiveness. A girl child is just as egoistic and hungry for flattery as any male. Yet when she marries, she has to fit into a routine of drudgery, in which it is difficult to fulfill this sense of self-esteem.

In the first place, every husband thinks that a moron could accomplish the work to which she is mostly committed—making beds, counting the laundry, feeding the dog. One doesn't have to be bright to do these things.

Also, her opportunities for recognition are almost nil. A man gets promoted, he gets more salary, he wins at golf, he brings home strings of fish. But his wife, day in and day out, labors over the same monotonous treadmill, within four narrow walls.

And furthermore, she is expected to carry out her housework as a duty and matter of course. She scrubs and mops all day long, and not one soul in the world ever notices it. Occasionally my wife, after waiting hopefully for me to praise some chore such as defrosting the refrigerator, will prod me with a question: "Do you notice anything different?" So I look around and ask, "No, what's different?" There isn't any husband who says, "Thank you, darling, for washing the dishes today." But we feel infuriated when she doesn't keep up her dismal, always-the-same routines.

To prove to herself that she is doing something worthwhile and that her family relationships are secure, she looks for reassurance in these principal directions:

1. Pleasure in the doing. She has to spend hours and hours at home alone carrying out her duties. When she is first married, she frequently complains, but she soon learns that her husband is bored with and irritated at her griping.

So she becomes a seasoned veteran; she tries to get satisfaction in what she is doing, a pleasure in her housewifely skills. Even if the male population is unimpressed with the intelligence required for her work, she convinces herself that it is important. She has to. However, she does periodically require—

2. Approval from the outer world. She is very anxious that she be considered a devoted wife and mother. She has submerged herself in a routine of dull tasks; she is willing to sacrifice herself to her family's welfare. But it is only natural that she is hungry for some recognition of this. Mostly, however, she looks for—

3. Affection and appreciation from her family. Her biggest rewards are going to come from her husband and children. Her daily effort is primarily directed toward having a grateful family.

Nevertheless she is still a person, beset with yearnings, daydreams, insecurities, and disappointments. I overheard a woman justify her purchase of a new dress, explaining to her own mother: "Every woman regularly needs a red dress to pick up her morale." Which was her way of reaffirming her own belief that her charms were still existent, in spite of kids and drudgery. Secretly she still believes herself an irresistible sex machine, fascinating to scores of men, regardless of the veneer of respectability.

A woman loves to go shopping for hats because she doesn't have to satisfy 95 per cent of the people she ordinarily has to please. By general agreement, women's hats don't make sense anyway. So she can just be herself. One woman explained to me that whenever she feels particularly depressed and purposeless, there is no tonic comparable to shopping for hats. Then she is entirely on her own, she cares naught for the world and its judgments, she is simply being a person.

3

Although there is a strong negative flavor to the notion of housework, feeding her family does offer a real satisfaction. This is the path to closeness and affection with her family, the sure reminder of her indispensability, a means of displaying her skill and intelligence.

The women in this study were asked to complete the sentence, "My family most appreciates me when . . ." Ninety-five per cent of the completions had to do with cooking:

- — I cook a good meal.
- — I have a hot meal on the table.
- — I'm cooking.
- — I give them a good dinner.

Cooking is the daily opportunity for a woman to feel important and loved. Whenever she wants to bask in her family's obvious admiration, she can riffle through some recipes and concoct something new and amazing. On occasion, when my wife has committed some blunder with the car, the dinner that night will be particularly wonderful. This is her reminder that she is very expert in her own department and that I certainly cannot get along without her.

No housewife wants to let this task get out of her hands, either. If she is sick or baby-tending, so that her husband does the shopping, she patronizingly belittles his performance as a grocery shopper. Almost no women teach their grown daughters how to cook.

But in contrast to all these positive feelings about cooking, practically no one in the study was enthusiastic about house cleaning. Emotionally it is quickly associated with unpleasant feelings. It is hard, thankless work, it involves dirt, it presents a woman's worst side to her family—when she is being the disciplinarian; and all of it makes her feel isolated, angry, and punishing.

This is why she craves some awareness of her efforts. When this is absent, she feels like a drudge, an unpaid servant, alone and meaningless. But if she does glean some acknowledgment from other people, from her reading or entertainment, from advertising, it makes her feel important and worthwhile—a successful person.

She is resigned to the fact she probably isn't going to get much open thanks from her family, since they regard what she is doing as a duty. Usually she has to create a satisfaction by the pleasure she finds in the exhibition of her cleaning effort. Women want the cleanliness of their homes, children, clothes, etc., to be admired, imitated, discussed; they want to surpass other people in this area.

But the other side of the problem is probably even more important. Cleaning involves so many negative, disciplining feelings that part of the central problem is avoidance of criticism. Being clean means winning approval, but more profoundly it means avoiding censure. Her in-laws, her own mother will pass severe moral judgments on her if she lags in her cleaning.

4

Cleaning products are good technically—she knows that. But she can't allow them to be perfect in her eyes, because they never can achieve the grand wish of no house cleaning at all. Also, she has to protect her own importance and necessity by fighting off the notion that they are as good as all that, just as she regularly asserts how busy she is no matter how many appliances she has and how much dilly-dallying she may be guilty of.

A woman finds very little distinctiveness for herself in using any particular brand of detergent or packaged soap. Her family furthermore shows little interest in what brand she uses, so that her ideas and judgments are few and thin. She spends little mental energy trying to distinguish between the brands. At some time or other she has tried most of them, and the differences are not clear at all.

The brands have not been imbued with many secondary meanings. There is little social prestige or opportunity for self-expression in using any particular brand, and the consumer has little emotional attachment. Her loyalty to any brand or any product rests on her inner sense of conviction. But there are few feeling connotations in this area which can create really deep preferences. Although she generally identifies with a particular brand, she will try something else with almost any incentive, which isn't true of other areas where she has developed much more intense loyalties.

Each brand has an individual advertising problem resulting from the strengths and weaknesses of its product personality. But in a larger sense, the advertising has a fundamental task of satisfying the housewife's motives and wishes, inasmuch as it hopes to influence her. Practical technical considerations are important, of course. However, the housewife is calloused about advertising claims proclaiming superiority in the light of her common-sense experience. The net result is that she somehow comes to her own decision to use certain products, and then she attributes to them any claims that she feels are necessary to justify her choice.

This process was strikingly clear in the research. A list of widely advertised claims, appeals, and themes were offered for identification and evaluation. While certain ones were unmistakably recognized, the most favored claims were generally attributed to Tide, the most popular seller. In fact, one slogan was invented: "Test after test proves no detergent under the sun gets out more dirt than. . . ." Forty-six per cent of the women ascribed this orphan claim to Tide, their favorite.

When the women were asked to evaluate the significance of many widely used claims, mostly these were rated as not particularly important. On the basis of these tests, it is evident that to a large extent the competitive claims lack distinction, they are discounted in the woman's mind, and they don't help her really to distinguish brands. It is not the usual run of claims that establishes the significant differences between products.

The basic criteria of successful advertising are how creative is the presentation of product claims and to what extent the advertising helps the consumer in nontechnical ways. Advertising themes and techniques should be regarded as avenues for messages appealing to the housewife's real goals rather than as mere product claims.

Advertising could so meaningfully contribute to her positive emotions. It could make her feel much better about the drudgery and the thanklessness of her job. It could help her experience feelings of downright pleasure in keeping house. It could foster her hunger for self-esteem and worth. It could exalt the role of housekeeper by letting it be known, through believable indirection, what an important, valued, and proud thing it is to be a housewife, fulfilling a task unrewarded, unappreciated. So much advertising in this area shows little awareness that a woman has any other motives for using products except to be clean, to protect herself and the objects cleaned.

On the contrary, essentially she wants satisfaction and pleasure at four levels:

1. In the product she is using.
2. In the results she gets.
3. In what she is doing as a house cleaner.
4. In her relations with other people.

Most advertising concentrates on the first two—especially the second. It bypasses or overshadows the importance of the last two, and very often the critical determinants are here—the psychological overtones, the associations which will activate behavior.

Logic cannot persuade her to believe what she doesn't want to believe. In cases where the products are extremely similar in many respects and where her intelligence tells her that this is true, words alone cannot persuade her to a deep brand preference. But she can establish this conviction very often for products which have persuaded her in other ways.

Sometimes advertising does this very well. However, much advertising in this particular category definitely fails to say anything outside the area of soap. Too many print ads are basically pictures of pretty women holding boxes, surrounded by more and more claims. Much of the copy is impersonal, saying the same things within a narrow range of ideas. And much of it presents irrelevant claims that run counter to the housewife's own real goals. Over and over, the product themes assert that she will get speedy, incredible results using a pleasant and gentle new discovery. Actually, when so many brands have shouted the identical virtues, then cleanliness—whiteness—and brightness become indistinctive words that hide rather than build product character. The housewife would have to be a chemist to straighten out the convolutions of all the conflicting claims. The result is a certain immunity to this waterfall of assertions. She happily confuses them, or borrows them at will to justify her own product. These interview comments are typical:

> I don't know what to think about how they advertise. Seems they all say the same thing.
> You'd go crazy if you paid attention to all of them telling you the same things like a broken record.
> They have to say something about the soap, but the women don't pay much attention to it.

In no sense am I arguing for the complete abandonment of product claims. But they should be presented in a fresh, convincing way, and they should support other motives which are usually far more responsible for the buyer's behavior.

Too little of the advertising in this field recognizes that a woman has a much wider household than the washing machine or kitchen—that she has many things to do, many interests in life besides washing dishes or clothes. The advertising too often overlooks the fact that she has feelings of frustration, achievement, irritation, hopefulness, pride, ambition, etc. The women in the print ads are too often nonentities playing a very secondary role to the product.

On the other hand, advertising which does take cognizance of her humanness and of the wide range of her perfectly human emotions, will make it much easier for her to feel that the product is for her—not for some abstract woman.

The contrast between reactions to the impersonal ads and to those which show even some slight sign of more believable interest in the housewife as a person is immediately noticeable. The impersonal ads are often quickly stripped down to the specific claims. On the other hand, ads which suggest a real human situation evoke lively associations and cause the woman to see the brand and the product as something she might use.

Advertising should show awareness of her problems. She hungers for a respect for her devotion, her achievement. So much advertising irritates her by implying that the products will do all the work. Regardless of their magic, she knows she still has to supply effort and hours.

Furthermore the constant drilling on the economy and bargain themes in this field of merchandising does not really contribute much to personal satisfaction. Economy is an important motive in housekeeping, of course. But economy usually means that money is saved where it is of least importance. The soap industry has created the impression in considerable degree that soaps and detergents are of little importance in the scheme of things.

In general, instead of attempting to build distinctive character that will lead to unshakable brand loyalty, the emphasis has been to move merchandise with short-term hypodermics. The housewife responds to these offers precisely because she has no profound inner convictions. But she doesn't stay with the "special-offer" brand unless it is obviously superior or unless the advertising does create a meaningful character. Since this very often is not the case, she wanders back to something else which she just "knows" is best for her and which has the advantage of being familiar.

Besides this area of themes involving her personal satisfaction, there are the copy approaches relating to her involvement with other people. The fact that cleaning is an isolating, irritating activity, that it doesn't generate much feeling from other people, is an extremely irksome problem for the housewife. Her dishes are done alone in the kitchen. The washing goes on all alone in the basement or utility room, with clammy floors and dripping pipes. Her husband is gone, her children are away, and she is washing walls, swabbing toilet bowls, mopping up dog tracks. Nobody will thank her; no one will even be aware of her effort.

Advertising should help her reduce this feeling of isolation. But it rarely does. It seldom tries to help her believe that her activity is importantly related to other people. Mostly it adds to her feelings of isolation by showing women alone in their basements or bathrooms or kitchens, rejoicing over boxes, admiring clothes without people in them, happy about dishes that don't look as if they ever had asparagus or potatoes or sliced tomatoes served on them.

Soap advertising especially needs the implications, through copy appeals and artwork, that involve this housewife with other people, that make her feel that she is doing something for which they do appreciate and esteem her, in spite of their seeming indifference. It could assuage her emptiness by reminding her that her household performance has wider meaning, important functions. It could stress to her in believable fashion that she is significantly related to others—via admiration, love, appreciation, competition, giving, receiving.

In this study one ad was used which portrayed a husband with his arm affectionately around his wife, both of them admiring his clean shirts. It wasn't a literal situation. Probably few husbands do this. But it had considerable emotional loading. It aroused considerable warm feeling because it did include another person—an affectionate husband admiring his shirts and his smart, capable wife. Repeatedly in the interviews it made women think of their own husbands, it made them like the ad, and it led them to praise of the product, as in this typical comment:

That's an attractive ad. I like Tide. I always get good results from it. It's a very attractive picture. Don't put this down, but I never get Earl's shirts white like that [laughs]. I like the box, but I like the picture best.

Obviously this ad did entangle her feelings.

When it's all said and done, the housewife is involved with many, many people—her husband, her children, her neighbors, and her in-laws, and much that she does is in terms of them. She wants her husband to recall her thoughtfulness when he puts on a clean shirt. She hopes that the Sunday school class will notice her youngster's fresh dress. She scrubs and mops valiantly to prove to her own mother that she is a competent, devoted helpmate. Her behavior is conditioned infinitely more by her relations to these people than by washcloths in the box, coupons worth a nickel, or blue granules.

5

To restate the essential point of this chapter, much advertising in this field has overlooked the woman's personal satisfactions and her relationships with other people. By overwhelmingly stressing a narrow area of product claims, which at best touches only a few of her goals, brands mostly have not attained the richness of meaning, the distinctive product personalities which exist in many other areas. Granted that the product class has inherent problems stemming from the housewife's aversion to cleaning, nevertheless it should be possible for advertising to say much more to her.

For example, all of the following are pools of copy approaches that could create positive feelings on her part.

The advertising could

1. Make her feel better about her routine of duties.
2. Arouse feelings of pleasure in keeping house.
3. Give her more sense of achievement in getting things done.
4. Generate feelings of self-esteem and worthwhileness.
5. Alleviate her feelings of solitude in cleaning.
6. Recognize her feelings about her effort and her accomplishment.
7. Imply that the products are for real housewives with real feelings who have many other activities and goals besides cleaning.

CHAPTER VIII

Product Jargon

The results of many years of circulation research indicate that when the typical housewife is queried as to why she doesn't read our particular newspaper, most generally she replies, "We can't afford it." Her kitchen may have many expensive new appliances, a nicely polished car may be in the driveway—in fact, everything about the home may exude prosperity. But she firmly insists that she has no objection to the newspaper; she really likes it, and only a question of budget is involved.

On the other hand, when we undertake research as to why people do read a newspaper, they stress its key role for them as the source of world events, political news, public affairs. It is educational—very much so—in keeping the individual abreast and well informed on the major public issues. This is the story from the man's viewpoint.

But then, as we dig into his reading patterns, it turns out that the sports pages, the financial pages, Dick Tracy, Dennis the Menace, the crossword puzzle, and various human-interest stories regularly score as the high points of his reading.

It is very clear that in both cases we are getting not the actuality but something else. The woman, contrary to her denial, obviously can afford the newspaper; and the man reads the newspaper, not to be a good citizen, but very definitely from other motives.

These aren't falsehoods, because these people honestly do believe their own statements. They are simply stereotyped rationalizations.

In this chapter I want to explore the very human habit of consciously or unconsciously screening our real motives with sets of standard rationalizations. In virtually every product area that I have studied, there are reasons employed by the consuming public to justify product use and brand preference which generally have little relationship to actual causes.

I think it is quite important to realize the function and the nature of this product jargon. It is certainly necessary, in the first place, to realize that there can be a wide gulf between real motives and these standard reasons which are given in good faith by the consumer.

Because it is so deeply ingrained into our way of thinking that people ought to know their own minds, that they should be able to describe the causes of their actions, I am going to document at some length how much more is going on beneath the rational explanations.

2

In daily experience, when the average individual is asked why he prefers some one brand of beer instead of another, he uses two principal reasons: "It tastes better" and "It's a nice, light, dry beer."

But when he starts to explain about the taste, it turns out that he isn't talking about taste at all. The stimulation is not something which affects the taste buds, but rather the nerve ends in his throat. He mentions "feel," "smooth-bodied," "richness," and other sensations of feeling, not taste.

When he is pressed to explain what he means by a "dry beer," he flounders. It doesn't make his mouth dry—he realizes that. He can't adequately explain how a liquid can be dry. But in spite of his floundering puzzlement, he goes right on mentioning "dryness" with a feeling that somehow people understand him.

Similarly in the cigarette field, "taste" and "mildness" are two overworked attributes which the smoker employs as explanation for his brand preference. Any number of persons smoking filter-tip brands have each stated that their cigarette allows the taste to come through the filter. But here again, no one is exactly certain what a cigarette tastes like as a taste. It is not a well-defined flavor in our minds like, say, coffee or peppermint or wintergreen or sugar or salt or licorice. We can clearly envision these as "taste." However, to speak of cigarette taste mostly evokes notions of acidity, burning, sharpness. Or we say, "It tastes strong," which is not taste, but feeling. Certainly the aftertaste from too much smoking is not a pleasant taste, a sought-after flavor. You wouldn't go looking for this taste.

In spite of its nearly universal appearance in cigarette advertising, no one except a few women wants the mildest cigarette. A completely mild cigarette evokes images of the most effeminate brands, the medicated or nicotineless brands, not far from children's imitation cigarettes. It would be something without strength, and therefore completely effeminate—or something the doctor would prescribe during illness. In our research, Kool was characterized as the mildest, followed by several highly feminine brands.

When the strength-factor disappears for the average smoker, so does the satisfaction. One person being interviewed stated: "A completely mild cigarette would be like drinking a cocktail with no alcohol. Why bother with it in the first place?"

I have already indicated how the car buyer so often leans on three crutches as principal justification for his choice: "I got a good deal"; "It's a beautiful car"; and/or "You really save on the gasoline." Car beauty, as I pointed out, is almost entirely a subjective factor, summing up many, many attitudes. Trade-in arrangements are important, but only if the car is thoroughly acceptable on many scores. And low maintenance costs are almost never the real determinant of purchase. If they were, the Willys jeep would be the top seller.

These areas of explanation give no clues whatever to the car's desirability for its sweeping chrome strips, its exotic color combinations, its value as a thermometric indicator of social status and as an expression of the individual's personality wishes. What I am saying is that the commonest explanations are not only *not* the full explanations generally, but they also operate to screen much more significant motive forces.

The woman who explains her conviction that instant coffee is not the real coffee bases her contention mostly on taste. Then, as she elaborates her criticism, she also accuses the product of being creamy, filmy, cloudy; sweet, bitter, and weak—lacking in body and flavor. But these are attitudes, not necessarily facts. I have heard the instant-coffee manufacturers demonstrate that none of them are true.

Almost none of the terms in the consumer's coffee lingo are ever used with clarity of knowledge, or even consistency. Usually they are simply ways of indicating good and bad. When pressed for more precise delineation of these terminologies—the grinds, blends, weakness and strength, aroma, flavor and texture—the consumer becomes vague, repetitive, or amused, or simply gives up.

The middle-class housewife very knowingly explains that luncheon meats are all right to serve at times but that they are not really the same as meat. Somehow they are not as nutritious. So if you demonstrate to her they are just as nutritious, that there is absolutely nothing substitutive in luncheon meats, what happens? Nothing. She still doesn't serve these products except on occasion. She wouldn't dare tell her husband as he leaves for the train on the average morning that tonight for dinner he gets pimento loaf or sliced baloney—not unless she wants to discard her reputation as the devoted mother. Meat is the center of the meal. And that means hot meat. She isn't a "good wife" if she trifles with that notion, if she palms off something else on her hard-working husband and her growing children just because it saves her some time. She most definitely wouldn't offer such a meal in a company-dinner situation, when meat and potatoes are unquestionably called for.

So all the business about nutrition and substitutes means something else. The words have another meaning besides their literal meaning.

Women speak of packaged soaps and detergents as "heavy-duty," "medium-duty," "light-duty," and "all-purpose" products, repeating the manufacturer's jargon. But they stumble helplessly when they try to explain what the differences are in any exact technical sense. Products which are substantially the same chemically are classified differently, according to their product personalities. When a woman categorizes a product as "medium-duty," she means actually that she doesn't know much about it or that it is inferior. A "heavy-duty" product means that it is adequate for difficult cleaning tasks, but this also has overtones that she doesn't like because they are contrary to her feminine standards—such implications as ingrained dirt, scrubbing, physically hard work.

3

Isn't it clear what is actually happening in all my illustrations? All these conventional, much used reasons are actually emotional symbols. They are shorthand summaries of much deeper feelings and attitudes which in most instances are totally unrelated to their surface meanings.

When the beer drinker attributes to his favorite beer some of the words from the advertising, he isn't sure at all what these terms mean. But they are emotional symbols expressing pleasure in beer drinking. "Smooth," "light," and "dry" are just positive, admiring characteristics applied to the beer he likes—and are qualities missing in the brands he doesn't like.

On the other hand, the common negative descriptions applied to the beers he doesn't like—"bitter," watery," "sharp," "flat," "sour," "acid-tasting," "biting"—are simply words that might be applied to anything unpleasant.

The housewife categorizing package soaps as "light," "medium," "heavy," and "all-purpose" is expressing her wishes for what she thinks they ought to be and ought to do for her. Over and over again she looks for a set of characteristics somewhere between pleasant and unpleasant.

The smoker wants to choose his cigarette from somewhere along a continuum of strength to mildness, depending on his own psychological needs and on the conception of himself which he wishes to express. He doesn't want to think that his cigarette is the strongest. Some other cigarette must always stand between him and being a lost soul. The strongest cigarette is unhealthy and evil. At the opposite pole, extreme mildness is too "feminine"—or not even feminine, but totally lacking in vigor and stimulation. When the smoker describes his cigarette as "mild," he means that there are stronger ones. After all, masculinity, strength, and irritation tend to go together in the definition of a cigarette; but how much of this should he take?

Somewhere on this arc of meanings is precisely what he needs in a cigarette. Yet this transpires beneath the commonplace words that the strongest cigarette must be avoided as too irritating and that the mildest cigarette is tasteless.

Over and over again in our research as to why people prefer this brand or that brand, they first start by stating that it does the job for which it is intended better. In other words, it has better functional use. Of course, the point is that this becomes entirely a subjective matter. When ten different women each state that ten different soaps get clothes whiter, brighter, and cleaner, somebody has to be wrong. What each woman is actually saying is, "I *think* my brand is best. I *believe* it is best because it suits me. It does best what I want it to do —for me." And she develops her definite convictions of superiority, although in many instances the products are identical.

Naturally people attempt to support their convictions with some rational justifications. They employ the terms from the advertising or the popular jargon as their support. They use them literally, they believe them literally; but actually, it is the deeper meanings that they are using. And it is the deeper meanings which almost invariably determine their buying behavior.

4

But we all prize rationality so much that we cannot admit lack of rationality. Both the advertiser and the consumer are defensive about any nonrationality, because of the way our society has trained us. As rational creatures, we feel we must always be able to give a connected, logical, and coherent account of ourselves, and all of our mental processes are unconsciously manipulated to give this impression. We aren't supposed to admit that we ever deliberately do nonrational things. Anything that might seem nonrational is explained away by wrong reasons that somehow sound convincing, both to ourselves and to other people.

This is the human mental process of rationalization—where we try to justify our economic behavior—and, in fact, all our behavior—on grounds of plausible rationality. It is perfectly natural that we should search for some logical supports for our brand preferences, whether they are the actual causes or not.

I have heard some persons insist that they have never committed an irrational or nonrational act in their lives. They would simply not be living up to their self-ideal if they were to recognize that there are cracks in their armor of logic. Because of this self-concept, they have so surrounded themselves with outright rationalizations as to be incapable of any self-understanding.

An enormous part of our behavior stems from causes buried so deep in our unconscious minds that we couldn't possibly know the real reasons. Apart from our individual personalities, we have imbibed the ethical, political, hygienic, and religious beliefs and the daily routine habits of our society so completely that we are not even aware of them. We eat three meals a day, we tip our hats to women, we shake hands for greeting, and we shave—not because these are eternal laws, but because our society tells us to.

On a personal basis, we may change our brands because someone we admire is using them, although we aren't aware of any imitation. But we want our own reasons. Neither do we have the slightest idea why we are introverts or avant-gardes or strivers.

But then, there are also many other things we do which it just wouldn't sound right to reveal in the light of day to our associates, for one reason or another, although we might know the causes of our actions. We aren't really prevaricating when we offer more acceptable justifications. We firmly believe our rationalizations.

For example, no girl ever admitted that she picked out her husband because he represents economic security, he'll take care of her, or because he has social position. We would consider her cold-blooded, a calculating schemer. So she sends out rhapsodic telegrams on her honeymoon: "Divinely happy. Never knew love could be so thrilling. He's wonderful."

Most people accept the religion of their parents. But it doesn't sound very rational for an adult to admit this. So he sells himself on the proposition that his belief rests on completely logical grounds. He has examined, he says, numerous faiths, but his own is the one that makes the most sense to him. He would angrily deny the actual reason.

So would the attention getter deny heatedly that he was telling off-color jokes and serving vodka and wearing a back-yard chef's costume so that he could occupy the center of the stage. So does the social striver deny the true but not acceptable reasons why he has changed churches, changed friends, and changed neighborhoods.

All of this is by way of explaining how and why the consumer has no trouble justifying his buying decisions with rationalizations which just are not the real motive forces. It is important to grasp this so that the advertising and the marketing strategy are not aimed entirely at the rationalizations and the product jargon, especially when the activation for buying can stem from some other source entirely.

To develop this point, let me recall how each and every one of us regularly turns off salesmen with whatever excuse is handy if we are not yet entirely convinced that we want what he is selling. Rather than provoke endless argument, which could require too much of our mental energy, we grope for some reason that will terminate the discussion politely. At the same time, to avoid any self-accusation that we are story-telling and also to maintain our illusion of logical behavior, we come to believe the reasoning we use.

We probably have masked our real objection, which often is the fact that we just don't have enough desire. But the salesman, if he reports his call, is reporting our rationalizations, not what actually is the problem.

I have been on exactly the other side of this sales situation, too. We would take the person's objections and arguments, and methodically show them to be incorrect. But then the buyer came up with a new set of objections. We were always struggling with his rationalizations —never coming to grips with the root cause of his refusals. We were unable to solve the problem because we never really knew what it was.

All this parallels the consumer buying situation in the many instances where the advertising blunts itself altogether on such issues as taste, dryness, mildness, appearance, and what have you, which are in reality screens for the much deeper motive forces. Why should the instant-coffee advertiser concern himself with the literal meanings of "taste" and "substitute products" when it is not really the dictionary meanings that are the problem? The problem is rather the underlying feelings and attitudes for which these literal words are only symbols.

There is nothing mysterious here. After all, words are only sounds which stand for certain meanings. They do not have fixed, eternal, absolute, single meanings. Actually, the meaning of any word is determined entirely by the context of the situation. Such sounds as "cut," "rat," "mean," and "stake" have many meanings. A "light dash" could be several things. "Bare" and "bear" are the same sound; the context determines which is which. "Mother" can refer to a female parent or to mother of vinegar.

Even these dictionary meanings may change through time, as we realize when reading Shakespeare. Many of his words have lost all meaning for us. And on the other hand, slang is constantly creating new meanings. "Pitch" is not only a turpentine source; now it also means a solicitation. "Heel" now describes a despicable person. Language is always shifting. Regularly we assign different meanings to the same sound.

What I am trying to make clear about this product jargon is that people constantly reach out for words—any words—to express their feelings in intangible areas. Naturally it is better to use acceptable, stereotyped terms. This is exactly what is happening when the consumer talks about "lightness" and "dryness" in beer, "mildness" in cigarettes, "beauty" in cars, "taste" in instant coffee, "fluffiness" in rice.

This is the very essence of metaphor. When I say, "I'm going crazy," "My feet are killing me," or "I'm getting away with murder," I am just grasping at ways to express my feelings, my attitude more clearly, more adequately by using words completely out of their literal meaning. Everyone adjusts his behavior to the attitudes being expressed, not the surface meanings. This happens all the time in life—the real meaning is intelligible behind the surface meaning of the words, and it is on the real meaning that we base our response.

Ruesch and Kees state that Americans are particularly prone to use words, and communication generally, not for their surface meaning, but for their real essence. If a group is asked to define words, rarely will their definitions be exactly the same. For instance, in an experiment, "provocative" was defined variously as "stimulating," "annoying," "meaningful," "stirring," "exciting," "spiritual," "teasing," "alluring," "uncommon," and "argumentative." Yet there is a vague agreement behind all these, and it is this vague essence toward which we act. If I ask for a "mild" cigarette or a "beautiful" car, while I can't define these attributes literally, I still know that they indicate something desirable—and so do my listeners. The average motorist isn't sure at all what "octane" in gasoline actually is. He doesn't know if there is peppermint octane or chocolate octane. But he does know vaguely that it is something good. So he orders "high-octane" gasoline, because he wants this essence quality behind the meaningless surface jargon.

5

We rationalize so many of our decisions in terms of money, which conceals our real motives. We decide that we want or we reject things for whatever cause, and then we explain our decisions by saying, "We can't afford" or "It's a very fine value." In a report from the MacFadden Wage Earner Forum on the desirability of mutual funds as investments, the negative comments so consistently stated lack of interest or lack of money that they could be seen as equating expressions. What the individual does not know enough about, what he is not sold on, what he does not desire, he rejects with the feeling that he can't afford.

The American worker does believe that he needs a car, fishing trips, a TV set, electric refrigerators and washers. They are requisite to his standard of living. He has no problem justifying his purchase of any of these things to himself or to his associates, rather than saving their cost. He wants them, he desires them—although, of course, he cloaks all this with rationalizations.

I am trying to indicate that price and value can be blind alleys. When the consumer says that the product is not a good value, this can be his shorthand way of saying that it is not desirable from many standpoints. There is no point in arguing out this value factor if it is merely concealing some other attitudes.

The president of the advertising agency for an automobile having a very poor sales year attributed this entirely to the fact that the car was a poor value. Therefore, his primary advertising theme was devoted to convincing the public that it was a good value. But in our research at the same time, which cut through these consumer rationalizations, it was obvious that the car buyer was really objecting to something else—not value per se, but a radically different styling.

In a study of department store personalities in an upper-middle-class neighborhood, we asked women shoppers to rate the stores for style, selection, color, quality, price, bargains, and values. The stores were rated "very good," "good," "so-so," "poor," and "very poor." It was quite significant that the store with the most energetic promotion, hammering at low prices, was not rated first for values and bargains. The two highest-price stores of the city were adjudged to have the best values and the best bargains. The shopper has no trouble rationalizing her choice—which was really determined here by the over-all store personalities.

One of the most successful beers started out as a popular-priced beer in its own market. When it decided to expand its distribution, it raised its price to become a premium beer. The price jump also permitted much larger advertising funds, which were used very skillfully to create much greater desire on the part of the consumer.

The beer has infinitely better sales success with the higher price. In the consumer's mind, it has more value today because it has more desirability.

6

Where is all this going? In no sense am I arguing that the advertiser should abandon the use of this product lingo, even if it is not the real activation for buying. On the contrary, it plays quite a necessary role in the fact that it helps the consumer find articulation for his conviction. He wants to justify his choice in terminology which sounds reasonable to himself and to others, terminology which is understandable and acceptable. He is looking for some rationality to support his lack of rationality.

It is not rational to develop deep brand loyalties for a cigarette which is indistinguishable in taste tests from other cigarettes, for detergents which chemically are the same as other detergents, for a brand of margarine which is identical with other brands put out by the same manufacturer under different labels, for a lipstick that comes from the same laboratory turning out many, many brands—for any product with a trivial advantage, or an attractive package which has nothing to do with its content.

The manufacturer profoundly hopes that this irrationality will occur. Even though his product is identical with countless others, he hopes that the customer will fall in love with his product and keep on buying it regardless of lower-price come-ons, coupon offers, and advertising blandishments from his competitors. By advertising, by packaging, by word of mouth he tries to create this blind conviction which will be manifested as brand loyalty.

But apparently it is also necessary that he provide some word labels to help the consumer substantiate this loyalty. The advertiser literally resorts to logic in the hope that he will achieve an illogical effect. This is one of the very definite purposes of advertising: to help the consumer become articulate about his buying choices, to put words in his mouth which sound convincing, even if they are not the right words.

David Riesman says that the reason a person reads a Ford ad is to find out why he bought a Ford. In part, this is what I am saying. Several automobile companies have told me that their readership studies reveal that the best reader of their advertising is not the man getting ready to buy their car but the man who has already bought one. He is looking for support of his judgment. He is also trying to find acceptable reasons that he can use in his explanation to others. He would be not only mystified but uncomfortable if the advertiser nakedly discussed the motives involved—his strivings for power, masculinity, rivalry, or status. The product jargon provides him with the handy and acceptable rationalizations he is looking for.

I bought a Packard car. I wanted a Packard. It was my choice. When I tried some honest self-analysis for this choice, the only fact that turned up was that Packard began with the letter "P" and so did my first name. This is consistent with my other lifelong interests in things and places that begin with the letter "P," such as the Philadelphia Phillies.

Now, obviously I couldn't make this explanation to other people. It was utterly irrational and would make me appear very silly in their eyes. So I groped for more acceptable causes, because I felt vaguely uncomfortable when my friends asked me how I liked the car and I was inarticulate about its mechanical qualities.

Then I encountered in the advertising many proclamations about "torsion ride." I didn't have the slightest idea whether this was something on the antenna or the rear bumper. But this was my face saver. Now I could articulate to other people why I bought a Packard. I felt much better. My choice rested on logical foundations.

When the housewife is queried as to why she likes Uncle Ben's rice, she says that it's fluffy. The word "fluffy" evokes imagery of whipped cream, soap suds, something light and airy. Cooked rice is anything but this. Yet the housewife is happy because the advertising did provide her with a term which serves as a rational, acceptable support for her choice.

7

Again and again we have noted how the temporary sales peaks caused by free deals, coupons, and other forms of sampling flatten out as the consumer wanders back to her regular choice. She has tried the product, but she doesn't develop any liking for it because she doesn't know what she is supposed to like, in the absence of effective advertising.

Unless the product has some salient advantages which would be plain to a blind man, nothing crystallizes her preferences. It would help her to frame her feelings if she could lean on some familiar terminology, especially if it is presented in fresh and interesting fashion—something about product benefits, quality, value, taste, aroma. These will provide her with the material for her rationalizations. They will prop up her conception of herself as a completely logical person, a competent manager, a shrewd bargainer.

But the trouble is that far, far too much advertising is built solely around this jargon.

The advertising approach most certainly should support the more powerful motives. The ideal campaign probably does both. There are thousands of campaigns which consciously or unwittingly do this, combining the product lingo and the appeals to the real motivating forces.

Camel cigarettes straight-facedly mention "mildness." But in our research it developed that nobody believes that Camels are mild. They are universally considered one of the strongest cigarettes. At the same time the really powerful message which the advertising is communicating with its symbols is that Camel is the brand for rugged masculinity, particularly for the mass-audience male.

James Adams, who was so instrumental in creating the halo of wonderful desirabilities which Cadillac enjoys, told me that his method was to combine the dream and the rationality in each ad. He utilized the symbols of success, aspiration, achievement, prestige, luxury—all the key meanings which Cadillac represents. But he also gave the buyer several practical reasons. Ideally, the owner can feed on the dream, probably at the never-stated level, while at the same time he knowingly talks about safety of construction or some other functional quality.

8

I have tried to throw a different light on the very complex process of choice-making and the axles of meaning on which people lean as explanation for swinging their whole decision. These axles of meaning invariably are rational and tolerable, dealing with economics, surely, such other acceptable familiarities as convenience and taste, and from there on going into the jargon idiomatic to each product area.

But somewhere the marketer has to realize that these terms are in reality merely symbols for an infinitely greater range of feelings and attitudes and that there is much more in the choice-process than meets the eye. The familiar words are actually the consumer's rationalizations. If the marketer accepts them at face value for their literal meanings, then he can't understand the real process of what's going on.

Generally there are several levels of meaning. Besides that of the acceptable social lubricants, there are levels of attitude and feeling that we won't talk about or just don't understand—or aren't even aware of.

I have heard manufacturers complain on occasion that when they tried to ascertain why people bought their products, all that they secured in consumer interviews was a playback from their own advertising. If a chewing gum features flavor in Maine advertising, then people in Maine will insist that they chew gum for flavor. At the same time, people in Texas will assert that they chew gum to relieve tension, if this is the theme of the Texas copy. This isn't bad—it's good. Advertising does put words in people's mouths. They want to think in conventional terms, and advertising supplies them with acceptable, conventional terms. Each person can say to himself, in effect, "Okay, mister, you're rational," and then go on behaving from nonrational causes.

However, the advertiser shouldn't fall into his own trap. If he furnishes some words which serve as articulations of consumer attitudes, then he shouldn't end up trying to cope with his own words as the consumer parrots them back to him.

To submit an extreme case, a bleaching powder was advertised in Chicago as "the new pink magic made from wonder earth." If the advertiser succeeded in creating desirabilities for his product, certainly it would have been the apex of insanity to research "pink magic" and "wonder earth," no matter if the housewife did mention these words. The advertiser invested his brand with affective meanings by involving her feelings, by employing imagery and color and loaded words. He has built attitudes, preference, and desirability from these elements.

It is important to realize what actually is transpiring so that we, as advertisers, don't bog down before the consumer's dictionary meanings, which can be completely misleading. Sometime, somewhere it is necessary to come to grips with the deeper feelings which the person is really signifying.

CHAPTER IX

The Distaff Side of Persuasion

Advertising as a form of communication is attempting to influence an incredibly intricate organism—the human being, who is a complex interplay of physiological, psychological, and social forces. I hope that this book will have the effect of establishing that advertising, just because it is a communication process, involves infinitely more than a straight-faced recital of facts and barefooted claims about trivia such as magic bottle tops that now screw on and free coupons worth a dime.

I am always puzzled at the number of checklists and sets of rules for successful advertising, which grossly oversimplify. Many fundamental components in the communication process are brushed aside, or lost in a swamp of banalities. Here, for instance, is a set of so-called "basic points" for copy writers by a veteran department store advertising manager.

1. Think before you write.
2. Have your facts at hand.
3. Write the ad in its entirety.
4. Write a selling headline.
5. Write adequate descriptive copy.
6. Make a layout that serves the reader.
7. Know how to calculate the space required by type.
8. In art fight for clarity.
9. Read your own advertisements.
10. Be a prolific writer and reader of good literature.

This sort of advice puts advertising down on the level of how to build your own back-yard barbecue pit. There is not even the slightest recognition here of the whole area of feeling, of affectivity, of emotion, of esthetics, except by pointing a little finger toward the word "art." Yet there is virtually no advertising today which does not utilize affectivity in rich degree—art, color, photography, layout, metaphor, entertainment, humor, fantasy, announcers with personality, emotional arousals. In any analysis of advertising, in any how-to-do-it formula, the field of affectivity has to be established as one of the primary components. I think that it is the all-important primary component.

Every creative man knows this. Every practicing advertising man uses some elements of affectivity in virtually everything he prepares. Why then do the teachers and the high priests of advertising ignore it so completely in their pronouncements? Here again is the curious phenomenon of people displaying a certain behavior and yet refusing to acknowledge that such behavior exists when it is formally stated.

It has been said that when the myth of the Economic Man was exploded, we immediately started bowing to his fellow myth in the next seat—the Logical Man. We are doing just this when we attempt to brush the whole subject of affectivity under the rug in our formal thinking.

Metropolitan department stores utilize magnificent window displays, Christmas parades, Santa Claus, toylands, foreign fairs, beautiful interiors—a thousand avenues for creating atmosphere and desirability along with mere showcases of goods. Yet whenever department store executives speak formally about their function, they go right back into their act about furnishing the right merchandise at the right price. "Merchants—that's what we are. Best quality, best value." When they are confronted with this atmosphere, this store personality, they deprecate the whole area: "Oh, yes, we pretty up the store." Obviously it is far more important than they formally admit.

The traditionalists who do acknowledge the factor of emotion in advertising handle it as something awkward which they don't exactly know how to handle. Like a family skeleton, they concede that it does exist, but they wish that they could keep it in the closet so that it wouldn't reappear at embarrassing moments to upset their airtight schemes of cause and effect. The business mind generally feels uncomfortable in any discussion of emotion. It is something that is not to be talked about. Just look the other way and pretend it isn't there.

I suppose that Americans back off from formal recognition of emotion in behavior because they are afraid that it will necessarily invoke the raw passions like hatred and fear. But there are all shades and degrees of emotion. Humor, enjoyment of golf or music, pride in a job well done, friendly warmth, admiration of somebody, pleasure in our families—these are milder emotions.

When I speak of the affective components of advertising, I don't only mean emotion, however. They may be any coloration, any feeling

tone, any esthetic effect, any atmosphere. In the broadest sense, I suppose affectivity can be summed up as all of the feeling and esthetic
effects as distinct from the logical sales message itself. "Affective" is
an awkward word, but there is no other term which will convey that
this concern is much broader than what we ordinarily describe as
emotion.

Esthetic effects can be achieved by striking color, by satisfying tone
sequence, by movement, by the arrangement of masses in layout, by
moving thought. Men blowing smoke in big outdoor spectaculars, or
beautiful patterns of lights—these are affective from the impact of
esthetic elements.

It almost seems unnecessary to insist that these affective components
of communication are part of the very fabric of modern advertising,
except that in too many fields of marketing, such as household appliances, gasoline, and retailing, they are almost elbowed out of the
picture. They are subordinated out of all proportion to their potential
powers to influence. Therefore, I want to put this area in a proper
focus of importance and to discuss how and why these particular
meanings are engendered.

But first, because I realize that this is an uncharted subject and that
some people may not be exactly certain yet what I am trying to en-
compass, let me point to the affective meanings in a good many areas
beside advertising. Then I think it will be immediately clearer how
much force they do exert in human behavior and why they should
never be pushed aside or unnecessarily subordinated.

2

Western Airlines tripled its business and became a formidable
competitor by introducing "Champagne Flights." United Airlines
operates "Executive Flights" with an extra special assortment of
atmosphere: free slippers, cigars, favors, filet mignon, no women
allowed on the flight, and a red carpet as the passengers leave the
plane, plus the name itself—a flight for executives. Northwest Airlines
inaugurated its New York–Chicago flights with a "Fujiyama Room"
in its ships, replete with Japanese atmosphere.

Travel agents in their promotion literature dwell on ghost towns,
pirates' caves, legends, hayrides, native dances, music festivals. This
is what the traveler seeks—the pageantry of Williamsburg, the ante-
bellum South at the Natchez Garden Festivals, the flavor of the
halcyon mining days of the nineties at Central City, Colo. San Francisco to the visitor stands for the Golden Gate Bridge, the cable cars,

Fishermen's Wharf, Chinatown, sunset as seen from the "Top of the Mark" Hopkins Hotel. New Orleans means the French Quarter, Antoine's Restaurant, Mardi Gras.

Some flavor of color, of atmosphere, of reputation—these are paramount to the traveler. Nobody bothers to visit the dull places which can offer only oil refineries, factories, office buildings, and chamber-of-commerce statistics. But people will travel halfway around the world to the Oberammergau Passion Play, ski resorts in the Alps, the Folies Bergère, voodoo dances in Haiti.

The same principle is operating when we use our imaginations to endow our products and institutions with some extra desirabilities in the very names we give them. Automobile models become El Dorado (status), Caribbean (status and adventure), Thunderbird (power), Skylark and Starfire (gaiety), Holiday (gaiety, sportiness), Safari (adventure), Riviera (status).

The Safeway grocery chain conceived these names for its private brands: Bel Air frozen foods, Sky-lark bread, Old Mill vinegar, Oven Glo crackers, Nob Hill coffee, and canned goods with such names as Honeybird, Lalani, Gardenside, Country Home. There obviously is greater sales appeal in these names than there is in such a dry-as-dust label as "Grade A soda crackers." The product in the consumer's mind in some manner becomes different with the mere flick of a name.

Any hotel owner employs the force of affectivity when he builds his dining rooms and cocktail lounges. He doesn't just set up a bar and some plain tables with a sign that says "Drinks." On the contrary, he goes to great lengths to manufacture atmosphere. If his hostelry is very expensive, it stresses austere color and names of such restrained character as the Camellia Room, the Mayfair Room, or the Peacock Room. On a broader base, imaginative night club owners may dim the lights, dress up their waiters in smocks, create Hawaiian motifs, feature singers called Johnny Pineapple, and charge outrageous prices for rum concoctions dubbed "Suffering Bastard" or "Regretful Virgin."

And the customers happily enjoy it and come back for more. What do they get for their money? Almost entirely, color—atmosphere—"feeling tones."

The proprietor of the famous Pump Room in Chicago commented about serving food on flaming skewers: "The people like it and it doesn't hurt the food—much."

The same principles of affectivity are very much in evidence in advertising. Heinz ketchup calls itself "red magic, made from aristocrat tomatoes." Chevrolet introduces its new models by proclaiming,

"The hot one's even hotter." Storz beer in Omaha is the "Orchid of Beer," and Miller is the "Champagne of Bottled Beer." Ethyl Gasoline and Jell-O create a special symbolism of birds and animals.

Coors beer from Denver plays this central theme: "Brewed with pure Rocky Mountain spring water"—thereby evoking a rich imagery of coolness, snow-covered mountains, icy spring water, incredible refreshment for a parched throat. Mere water has here been transformed into something wonderful.

One of the frequent complaints leveled at advertising by the intellectual is that it confuses the consumer's ordinary rational processes of judgment by injecting affective values into the situation. This was one of the principal arguments for grade labeling; it is the thesis of the Consumer's Union. The intellectual feels that something very wrong is going on when the imaginative advertiser creates desirabilities through the use of mood; jingles; artwork of orchids, dogs, babies, pine trees; shows which generate feeling effects; colorful writing about "red magic," "blue magic," "spring water." He believes that the advertiser should stick to barebone statements of fact about product functions.

It becomes doubly astonishing to hear the dispensers of advertising theory who formally are apathetic about this phase of communication or who deliberately minimize it. Not only are they overlooking one of the most potent weapons in the armory of advertising—as the intellectual points out—but they are just simply forgetting what makes people behave like people. This is what the consumer apparently wants. This is what moves him the most.

3

It is extremely important to realize that there is far more occurring in any communication than rational thought. Even in the most intellectual conversation, there are still several sets of attitudes operating simultaneously—not only rational, but social and emotional attitudes as well. Scientists point out that to regard language only as a means of expressing thought is to take a one-sided view stressing a very specialized function of language. Certainly language is the wonderful instrument by which humans exchange knowledge and information. But it is also the means by which we express our feelings and intentions.

Of course, we can do this directly. By far the most often, we convey feeling by indirect means. Profanity is an explosion of raw feeling. A strongly emotional tone indicating fear or sorrow or laughter is much more significant than words. Ordinarily it is the subtle nuances of voice tone and manner, emphasized by gesture and facial expression, which tell the other individual in a conversation what our real feelings are behind the façade of words. These are the cues speaking to the other person's third ear; these are the signals he is searching for in order to evaluate the literal content of our words.

We use loaded words which have the ability to express feeling. Their feeling meaning has nothing to do with their literal meaning. If we call a person an "idiot" or an "ass" or an "angel," we don't mean that he is any of these things literally. But they express feeling. The man who calls his wife "baby" is expressing tenderness. "Fox and Hounds Restaurant," "Sarah Siddons Walk," "Gingerbread House Nursery School," "The House of Vision"—in each case the words act to create an imagery, a set of feelings attached to an otherwise inanimate thing.

The jingles and slogans that we use in advertising have another affective purpose. "Be Specific—Go Union Pacific" generates rhythmic echoes which are much harder to forget than ordinary statements. In a study of Pepsodent advertising, as soon as women saw the first half of the jingle, "You'll wonder where the yellow went," they had an unconscious compulsion to finish it—". . . when you brush your teeth with Pepsodent." The total couplet was fixed in their minds like an unforgettable tune.

Semanticists point out that when communication becomes affective, it takes on a power, an impact, a force. This is why, apart from our factual meanings, we have to give our communication efforts some affective meanings. If we expect the audience to be involved, to be moved, to feel about our products and ideas and institutions the way we do, it becomes imperative to heighten as much as possible the force of these affective elements.

By the very nature of what advertising as communication is trying to do, this is important. Much human communication has for its purpose the conveyance of information. The largest part of conversation is for sociability—pulling people together, developing friendliness and warmth. But advertising isn't trying to do either of these things, essentially.

As pointed out by S. I. Hayakawa in *Language in Thought and Action*, advertising falls into another category of communication, classified as "directive." When I tell my youngster, "Pick up your things and come in the house," I am neither being informative, expressive of feelings, nor sociable. I am directing someone what to do. That's the purpose of advertising—to persuade someone either to adopt a new habit or to keep on doing what he is already doing. We are trying to influence somebody else—which is why editors pontificate, politicians orate, ministers preach, why parents and teachers criticize. All of them are attempting to direct, control, or influence the behavior of other persons. This is directive communication.

As these experts in semantics point out, if directive communication is going to direct, there must be affective elements and they must be built up as much as possible. Such communication cannot be impersonal or dull, a bare statement of fact, any more than you could sell bulk butter today minus any packaging, any coloring, any attractive labeling. Don't ever find yourself with a lawyer who expects to win your case merely by monotonously reciting the pertinent facts. A good trial lawyer hopes to have the law on his side, but he sways the jury by garnishing his arguments with as many affective devices as possible—dramatic highs and lows in his voice, reference to sacred symbols (innocence, justice, freedom, liberty), vivid demonstrations, gestures, open emotional appeals.

Society itself loads its rituals with these affective meanings when it wants them to be long-remembered. We don't let a young boy and girl just say a few words to be married. Now they are adult members of the society, heads of a new family, with responsibilities and obligations. So we have evolved the marriage ceremony, with all sorts of trappings—music, a service, a beautiful setting, the ritual of presents, costumes, a honeymoon, bridesmaids—all with the purpose of engendering profound affective meaning which will forever influence their behavior.

Processions, bands, flags, invocations, speaker's tables, patriotic and group singing—these are the color and solemnity and atmosphere injected on other occasions to make them more moving and more memorable. They reflect the profound wisdom of the race that people mostly think with their feelings, act from their feelings, and remember according to the degree of feeling involved.

These are exact parallels to advertising and illuminate how it is operative as a process capable of moving people, of investing products with tremendous attraction. I have elaborated this material from the field of semantics because it indicates in plain English that unless advertising has high affectivity content, it is useless. It isn't going to direct behavior; it isn't going to accomplish anything. Even the greatest sales ideas, the most obvious technical advantages need to be invested with affective hooks of some kind—some coloration, some shadings of feeling meaning, something besides the naked sales argument.

4

It is essential to bring these principles out in the open and establish them once and for all as realities, even though most good creative people intuitively utilize them. In the constant disagreements as to whether the advertising should strive for more affective power or stick to product claims, the creative people are too often overruled by policy makers because they have no articulated argument to cope with the "common-sense logic" of the client mentalities from the sales and production departments. As matters now stand in advertising theory and copy research, our eyes are fixed in one direction only.

In the playback technique, the researchers strip and strain to improve the memorability of the logical sales message. They toss overboard so-called "left-field" ideas. But the evidence from psychology and semantics indicates that by far the greatest memorability is achieved for the product by its affective qualities, by its nuances of feeling, by any traces of emotional meanings.

The creative people complain that there is no concrete evidence that copy research has produced better advertising, more productive advertising. How can it if it concentrates on factors not really responsible for memorability, factors which do not generate the most motive power?

In a weighting of the affective versus the logical elements for achieving memorability, I should think that our own personal experience would make the answer self-evident. Our pattern for remembering people and places is to encapsulate them into associations of feeling and color. We telescope the years of our lives into a handful of high moments, dropping out almost everything else. Try to remember what you did in some period ten years ago. What you recall is a funeral, a big party, some triumph, a child born, a fishing trip, some exceptional dose of color and heightened experience. For any number of older men I know, their war service, their golden days of freedom at college, or some particularly colorful trip are the Matterhorns of their lives. They have lost all the intervening years of mundane, practical, rational existence; these have faded out to nothing.

The systems which teach better memory to people advise using imagery to the fullest possible extent—to get vivid and even ridiculous associations to act as hooks, as a means of fishing up the memory from beneath the surface of the mind. Some systems insist that the more ridiculous the associations, the better—which certainly points in the direction of affectivity.

All that the "playback" techniques can establish is an improvement in the memorability of the logical message, the product claims. So what—if the real motive power is coming from the other direction and, worse still, is being overlooked, minimized, or even sacrificed as a result of such research?

When Procter & Gamble introduced Cheer with adequate advertising proclaiming it as "good for tough-job washing," it was just another detergent going no particular place in sales, according to our research. Then it was given a blue color, and in the housewife's mind it acquired a completely different character, making it seemingly capable of functional wonders totally uncalled for by anything in the mere color. Thereupon it became a tremendous national success. The advertising very carefully avoided any untrue implications of bluing; the housewife reads that character into it herself. The very competent advertising merely talks about the "blue magic." What magic could there be in the bare fact of blueness? Yet it was the affective power of this blue color in the product and the advertising imagery which set it apart from competitive products—not the logical claims.

5

If in advertising theory we are now willing to concede the existence and even the force of these affective elements, it is still customary to say that all of these components are meant to reinforce the impact of the product claims—to make them more attention-getting, more memorable, more interesting. But is this true? I think that they add a meaning and a feeling all their own which may have nothing to do with the product claims. Consider our use of animated bears and giraffes; peculiar voices; beautiful girls; whistles; singing rhymes, devices for movement; such fanciful characters as pixies, Chessie the Cat and Elsie the Cow; musical backgrounds; artwork showing a grateful husband kissing a smart wife; and collie dogs nursing their puppies.

Highly rational people can't bring themselves to admit that advertising may generate some loose feeling or emotion, floating in space and not necessarily related to any product claims at all. Even though in multitudinous cases the affective meanings apparently outweigh the product claims in what they contribute, the traditionalists consider it heresy to suggest that the affective meanings could go it alone. An Eastern railroad ran copy showing only a cute baby on a Pullman seat, with no signature except the railroad's initials on a towel. The

Symbols are shorthand summaries of meaning and feeling. The advertiser packs into his character, trademark, package or name a freight of desirabilities and associations. He creates a conditioned reflex. Thereafter when the consumer sees his symbol, bells start ringing and these associations come tumbling out.

This nonverbal symbol telescopes an immensity of meaning. It evokes the logical ideas about South Africa just as well as a map or statistics. Also it bathes the idea with feeling. And it communicates quickly and effortlessly.

Any product is defined partly by its functional attributes, but also by subjective attributes and attitudes which exist only in people's minds. Both sets of meanings constitute its brand image. This is why the idioms of advertising style are so important. The meanings coming from the visual dramatics contribute significantly to the product character.

Here the magnificent photographic effects are the most important factor in building product desirability and distinction. These mannerisms of style—the aesthetic and emotive meanings endow this brand with its "something-special" character.

copy critics in the advertising trade press excoriated it as cheap and smart-alecky.

But I think advertisements which are virtually pure feeling—pure affectivity—occur more often than we let ourselves recognize in formal theory. I don't mean only the institutional advertising run on holidays. I am talking about campaigns completely dominated by great art ideas, whose few words go almost unnoticed; about great shows that say far more about the sponsor than the trite commercials; about campaigns which create mood just as does mood music.

I still think that the Ford two-hour anniversary spectacular was one of the best commercial shows ever done on television, although there was not a single commercial message on the program. But Ford did build up a wealth of feeling in the show itself, which was transferred to the sponsor—"a warm, humanized company with much tradition"; "identified with American life"; "believing in America's future"; "progressive"; etc.

The First National Bank of Chicago has used some half-block-long outdoor signs which say nothing literally except the name of the bank and how old it is. But the grounds surrounding the boards—petunias, cannas, green lawns well watered, raised gold lettering on white background—all of this says, "Here is a quality bank, very friendly to do business with." Also, these boards always score high on memorability checks. But they depend entirely on the affective meanings, the "feeling meanings."

Even if we find it hard to accept, much communication only creates a bath of pure feeling. The content is utterly unimportant. We listen to a funeral sermon, which is usually made up of commonplace words that we don't even hear; but we are conscious of a period of emotion. Most speakers at conventions just talk talk, without conveying great ideas; but we think that they should be on the program because they add a feeling tone to the meeting. Two women talk for hours, generating friendliness, not information. We let the car radio play all day, not caring what is playing but simply enjoying the pleasure of sheer sound and pure feeling.

Undoubtedly in the great majority of advertising there will always be a balance of the affective elements and the stated, rational claims. But in multitudinous instances, the affective meanings are saying something entirely different about the product than the sales logic and not merely reinforcing it. And these meanings are far more significant for the character of the product and the success of the advertising than the product claims.

Starch studies of readership invariably show tremendous differences between the artwork and the headlines as compared to the descriptive copy of advertisements. Readership of the latter often falls to the vanishing point. An agency recently showed me extensive studies of one of its campaigns which attracted 50 per cent of the magazine readers to the artwork and the provocative but not commercial headline; yet the reading of the descriptive copy of the product benefits was absolutely zero. The advertiser was highly pleased with the impact of the campaign, although the commercial message was contributing nothing to it—not with zero readership.

Isn't it true that the affective meanings of the art, the color, the layout are carrying the biggest part of the load when such differentials in reading exist regularly between the affective components and the descriptive copy? In our copy research, when we try to determine audience involvement with specific advertisements, people talk and talk about the art subject—far more than they do about the copy claims about mechanics or economics. They are involved with the advertisement because of its affective meanings—the color, the mood, the pictorial symbols, what the people in the illustrations are doing. Why should we therefore overlook such evidence and meekly agree with the professional word worshipers who insist that every element in the advertisement should be subordinated to and support the rational and functional product claims?

I imagine that the sponsors of many TV and radio broadcasts believe that they are reaping a far greater harvest of feeling and unspoken meanings from the character of the program itself than from the recitation of the commercials. The program character of the United States Steel Hour, the General Electric Theater, the Firestone Hour, the General Motors institutional programs generally communicates far more significant meanings about these companies than the announcers' messages. Certainly the sponsors of the daytime serials and the children's shows with emotional effects like Lassie must think that the feelings generated by the program are transferred in part to their products.

Any issue of *Fortune* makes it self-evident that even the industrial advertisers believe that the intangible elements of their print copy are saying volumes about the character of their companies. Very solid corporations use the most ultramodern devices of abstract and nonobjective painting: the emotion of surfaces, the strife of line, multiple perspectives, dynamic impact created by form and color alone. The art and the over-all tone of their advertising are communicating very clearly that these are extremely progressive organizations—imaginative, resourceful, capable, years ahead in their thinking. This is what they want reflected about themselves to top-level management, to stockholders, to investment bankers. They convey this character by leaning far more on the feeling and the esthetic weight of their advertising than on the few paltry spoken statements tagging at the end of the descriptive copy. This is to say that they believe this feeling is communicating, and it certainly is not dependent on any rationality to crystallize its meanings. The free feeling has its own meanings.

And, remember, this is industrial advertising, which is always putting itself on record as being only rugged selling—just product facts for extremely rational buyers. Unlike consumer advertising, you can't waste time in this field with anything but information. Yet, contrary to this lugubrious hair shirt, here in the flesh is industrial advertising with high affectivity content and free feeling.

Outdoor advertising is "ten-second selling." How does it sell? By product identification and a splash of affectivity. By color, by art, by plays on words, it generates a quick spurt of free feeling which the advertiser hopes will be haloed around his product, as a part of its psychological label.

While I have singled out some obvious instances, it wouldn't be hard to prove that this transfer of unrelated feeling goes on all the time in varying degree. Putting it in reverse, no thinking advertiser would sponsor a program in obvious bad taste. Why? Because it would reflect on the sponsor, regardless of how lyrical the commercials were. One product sponsoring prize fights, which had a huge audience, lost sales badly, according to researchers, because the program's connotations splashed back to the product, taking it right out of the quality class.

Human beings very consistently develop feeling meanings which are associated with objects and persons and which even have a tendency to spread contrary to all the logic of the situation. Most of our likes and dislikes of stores, railroads, hotels, banks, and what have you stem from tiny incidents of feeling—possibly involving one sales clerk, one porter, one elevator operator, one clerk—which then become magnified on a broad scale.

One psychological consultant always looks for the critical incident as the key to attitudes. In the case of chain grocery stores, a woman forms long-lasting preferences or dislikes as the result of what happened when she dropped a bottle of strawberry jam or when her child knocked over an aisle display of canned peaches.

It has not been my intention in this chapter to depreciate product statements nor to suggest that they be lessened in any degree. My objective has been to clarify beyond any doubt the force, the motive power, and the memorability of the affective components of advertising, which in many cases actually say far more about the product and the advertiser than the claims and benefits. Every successful advertisement must have affective meanings. The more powerful these affective, evocative, emotive, or esthetic meanings are, the better chance the advertisement will have to establish desirability, persuasion, conviction, and product loyalty. And frequently this is the most important direction to emphasize.

Three very successful Young and Rubicam campaigns use a total of only twelve words combined: Life Saver—six words ("Life Savers—still only 5¢"), Hunt Foods—four words ("Hunt for the best") and Modess—two words ("Modess Because—"). These are great art campaigns generating esthetic meanings, desirability, and distinction.

The people who want the color, the atmosphere of Don the Beachcomber's Restaurant, the Pump Room, and El Morocco; who buy Nomad and Royal Lancer car models; who thrill to flying the "Golden Falcon"; who rush to buy homes in exciting new subdivisions transformed from dull cornfields by such descriptives as Brigadoon, Strawberry Hill, Normandy Manor; who want the extra something added by the name to Revlon's "Cherries à la Mode" lipstick; who feel that a beautiful girl has all the qualities of an angel; who think Pepsodent tooth paste is fresh because the package appears "fresh;—these are the very same people we are trying to persuade with advertising.

CHAPTER X

Passkey to Believability

Competent advertising practitioners from time to time express their concern that one of the most bothersome questions they struggle with is whether or not their advertising is *believable*.

Now, how do we set about making any human communication more believable? How do you attain a belief in anything? What does a belief rest upon—this firm, unshakable conviction that something is true? From the training given us by our society, we will immediately point to the fact involved, as if conviction depends on how firm is its buttress of logic. This is one of our myths—a naïve illusion that all adults, including ourselves, arrive at their beliefs and their conclusions after an orderly and careful examination of sets of facts. In popular mythology, the secret of greater believability is a better presentation, a more convincing presentation of facts.

But in absolute contradiction of this old wives' tale, conviction often springs from a different source. Conviction is inextricably bound up with feeling. It comes from our viscera, from within us—not from our intellect. We say, "In your heart, you know that isn't true" or "Deep down within you, you know that *is* true." Truth is a feeling, not a fact. We "know" that something is true because inside of us, our feelings "tell" us that it is true. Afterwards we may accept factual reasons to support our convictions. But the inner conviction from feeling came first and is the supremely important factor in belief. Without this inner sense of feeling, any belief rests on very insecure grounds, no matter how glittering or how overwhelming is the parade of facts and reasons.

The most logical figure in our society is presumably the judge. After listening impartially to both sides of a legal dispute, he weighs the facts and the law, and then hands down a decision. But studies of penalties given by judges reveal that the penalty could be better predicted from knowing the judge than from knowing the crime. The personal make-up of the judge, his inner feelings—tend to determine the sentence. We know how a conservative judge hands down pre-

119

dominantly conservative opinions, how a liberal judge appraises the same facts differently. Each arrives at a conclusion first based on his own inner feelings and then finds the legal argument to support this inner conviction. I believe that it was Justice Holmes who said that experience, not logic, is the spirit of the law. The very fact that the vast majority of Supreme Court decisions are split decisions, that the higher courts often reverse lower-court decisions, indicates that the law is no absolute, ironclad verity but rather something dependent for interpretation on the viewpoints, the intuitions, the feelings of the judges.

The entire personality of every individual is built around basic emotional needs, and the whole system of his thinking is determined by these needs, even though superficially the individual defends his point of view on purely rational grounds. Experiments repeatedly show that this rationality is a highly selective rationality (or in other words, not rational at all). For example, memory tests show that if Democrats and Republicans are given arguments pro and con for candidates representing each party, Democrats retain arguments favorable to their candidate and Republicans arguments positive to theirs, each group forgetting the negatives. Their memory is selective and emotionally (rather than rationally) determined.

Every enduring belief, every real conviction is set in a matrix of feeling. We rarely change people's beliefs by logical argument. The human individual accepts what is consistent with his emotionally based beliefs and rejects that which runs counter to them. This is why it is insufficient merely to convince a person on intellectual grounds. The premises must also be acceptable emotionally. Often our logical reasoning does seem to change another person's mind. But don't overlook that emotional persuasion is also occurring. Both processes may arrive at the point of conviction simultaneously. But until the "emotional conviction" is achieved, the "rational conviction" is resting on foundations of sand.

Social scientists have long since demonstrated how impossible it is to change fixed beliefs or popular superstitions merely by stating the "truths" in the case. We have no business sharing the pious illusion that factual argument or the spread of information is going to change many deep-seated attitudes.

In this day and age, hotels still avoid having a thirteenth floor. They have a 12A or a 14A, so that the guests, who are well-educated, cynical businessmen, won't be exposed to the "bad luck" associated with 13. This is a medieval, childish superstition. Logically we know that it is nonsense. But we still observe it because it is an emotional conviction.

The businessman in effect is saying, "I am completely logical but don't put me on the thirteenth floor."

Even when we would expect judgment to be highly objective, irrational distortions occur—as in the classic experiment on judging the size of coins, wherein lower-class children consistently exaggerate the size of dimes, nickels, and half dollars, in comparison with the more accurate judgment of middle-class children.

Along with the individual's emotions, another irrational determinant of what one thinks is "true" is the effect of group standards. Our beliefs and convictions are related to social influences, without our necessarily being aware of them. Nobody could sell me on wearing a pince-nez or lavender slacks, because these are contrary to my group habits. We could argue endlessly and demonstrate by irrefutable facts and yet never change a Mississippi Democrat's political beliefs. Everyone he knows is a Democrat; his beliefs are hitched to traditions and emotions. His inner self wouldn't even hear someone else's logic.

Studies of voting behavior show that people almost exclusively listen to speeches of candidates whom they have already decided to support. We read the publications with whose viewpoints we agree; we listen to the commentators who "think the way we do." We refuse to expose ourselves to contrary views. When we do encounter them, it's very disturbing. But we emerge with our own convictions intact.

This applies with equal force to our religious beliefs, our tastes, our style of living, and whether we are savers or spenders, strivers or non-mobiles, or what have you. Somebody's mere words by themselves are rarely going to alter our habits and ways of handling the world. And neither in advertising are we going to secure greater believability—or any believability—if we depend solely, or even principally, on the intellectual presentations of facts about our products.

In a discussion of the failure of institutional advertising to sell the free-enterprise system, *Fortune* pointed out that the advertisers were futilely trying to cure misinformation by information. Misinformation is resistant to information. Curiously, whenever an advertiser discovers that the consumer thinks poorly of one of his progeny for various reasons, his first impulse is to rush into action and demonstrate by facts that the public beliefs are wrong. In headlong attack he says exactly the opposite of this public feeling. Some people believe that aspirin makes them sick. Ergo, say the opposite: "Aspirin does not make you sick." The advertiser hopes to change deep convictions by proving via words that soft drinks do not harm children's teeth, that sugar is not really fattening. Can we convince people through advertising by saying exactly the opposite of what they believe?

A tremendous amount of misunderstanding about the very nature of advertising probably emanates from the classic definition that advertising is just salesmanship in print. This implies that there is an identity of method between face-to-face salesmanship and the process of persuasion through advertising, that both involve a battering down of the consumer's defenses by logical argument involving economic yardsticks and technical superlatives. This misconception, of course, completely overlooks the key element in persuasion, which is feeling.

For years the railroads have been whining in advertising about unfair treatment from excessive regulation and taxation. What happens? Nothing. With lumbering logic the electric utilities protest various government power projects. Do they change anybody's mind? I don't think so. They don't appraise the problem rightly. The public yawns off their elephantine arguments about "investor ownership."

All human interaction, all conversation, all communication is an interaction, not of logic but of feeling. In conversation both sets of attitudes occur simultaneously. The informative uses of language are closely fused with the much earlier function—expression of feeling. Only a small part of conversation is entirely informative. Much conversation starts with the expression of pure feeling and then goes on to information ("Good heavens! It's hot!"). The feeling and the logic in our conversation may get to the point of conviction simultaneously. But beneath the logic, we are basically trying to achieve an alteration in the other person's feelings.

In advertising we are in like manner contending with the other person's feelings, not his intellect. If we can change his feelings, then we can change his conviction and buying choice. If the conviction occurs, no matter how, the person will always find arguments to justify his change of choice.

A realization that we are coping with another person's feelings should be clear to many men in the frequency with which they encounter a woman's "Because—" whether from wife, secretary, or daughter. Woman's intuition is an ability to go right to the heart of the meaning by grasping the feeling, regardless of the clouds of reason.

When two people are talking, most of the sentences are grammatically incomplete, because completion isn't necessary. We sense the direction of the other person's feelings, his meanings, even though he cannot completely articulate them. "You know what I mean—" he waves his hands, and we think we do grasp what he feels and then go on. In the experience of talking out a situation, we become sensitive to the meaning of our own impulses, and both of us grope ahead toward an articulation of these feelings which are gradually becoming clearer.

The import of all that I have indicated necessitates a radical change in the very focus of advertising. We have to chart a course for the other person's feelings and emotions, not his logical defenses. To get off the dead-end street that current advertising theory and the businessman's "common sense" have led to, the creative people have to turn their eyes in an entirely different direction.

As illustration of the subtleties and the nuances of expression which are involved over and above the production of words, consider how much believability is added or subtracted by the timbre of the announcer's voice, the completely intangible elements of his personality. Quality of voice all by itself has the ability to convey believability, conviction, and feelings, entirely apart from what is being said. We make judgments of another person's real meanings from the tone of his voice, from countless inexpressible subtleties—not from his words. When a person says, "I could murder you!" it is the tone of his voice that conveys whether he is joking or serious—or really serious. The difference between a poor announcer and a top TV personality lies entirely in this ability to reach the feelings of the audience, even though both use the same identical words. The subtlety of intonation, the expression of meaning far, far beneath the words carries the real conviction.

In this chapter I want to explore two highly important approaches which are a part of this other direction—trying to alter the feelings of the reader. Both of these methods—indirection and identification— are far more effective in most cases than the sledge-hammer approach. As basic techniques in successful and persuasive communication, they deserve to be spelled out.

2

Because we are so irrational about the dominance of rationality, let me try to dig out the essence of communication. Every human being is trained from birth in this process of searching for the feelings of the other person so that he can respond properly. If the other person's manner is hostile, we are on guard. If we think that he will take advantage of us, we set up certain defenses. If he is good-naturedly friendly, we relax. In everything he says, we probe through his words for his real feelings.

As the sociologist Park pointed out, individuals communicate their sentiments, attitudes, and organic excitements to one another; and in so doing, they necessarily react not merely to what each individual does and says but to what he intends, desires, and hopes to do. The fact that we often betray sentiments and attitudes to others of which we are only dimly conscious makes it possible for the other person to act on our motives and tensions as soon as we are able to.

This ability to sense the feelings of other persons is a part of our human biology, as much as our ears are. Scientists have commented on how some of the most primitive tribes on the face of the earth possess in remarkable degree this sensitive ability to perceive feeling in others. My dog doesn't understand language, but from the tone of my voice as well as from my general manner, he knows whether I am affectionate or angry, playful or in a hurry. When I am in some mood of disappointment or indifference or frustration, no matter how much I try to conceal it, my family can sense my feeling. Consider how often in literature a character professes to discern someone's real purposes by the expression in his eyes.

Until he is two, a baby can't understand what his parents are saying; but he adjusts his behavior by means of a sensitive awareness of their exact moods from their intonation, their expressions, and their manner. And by his gurgles and cries, we can sense what he wants and how he feels. We forget that this earlier use of conversation, the preintellectual conveyance of feeling, is fused into every communication.

This is the compass guiding our intuition as we unerringly grasp the real portent of any situation. We can cut right through extravagant flattery. We can sense boredom and lack of interest. We turn inwardly skeptical when a salesman becomes too oily. We are uneasy when some superior is coldly polite. The saying, "Never overestimate a person's information, but never underestimate his intelligence" conveys that any human has this ability to perceive the real intentions, the feelings, the inner attitudes of other humans, no matter what the extent of his formal education.

This is extremely relevant, because these same people exercise this same sensitivity when the advertiser attempts to communicate with them through his media. They are still searching for the feeling behind the words. Obviously the advertiser wants to sell something; that's evident and not objectionable. But what is his tone? What does he think I am? How does he adjust to my convictions? How can I fit his wares into my life—the life of the real me? What are the symbols that reveal his real purpose?

Paraphrasing Hayakawa, the method of the novelist in conveying his propositions, either the symbolic content of his message, as in great art, or any social axes he may have to grind, is not to tell us what he is driving at but to put us through a whole sequence of experiences so that we shall feel exactly as the author wants us to. When we feel that way, we say that his message is true.

The dramatist is successful when he involves the reader's feelings by the mechanism of identification. We can project ourselves into literature and feel about the great crises of human existence just as if we lived all over the globe and in all time because we identify ourselves with the characters. Their feelings become our feelings momentarily.

3

Identification means "feeling oneself into another"—transferring one's own purposes, ideals, emotions, one's actual self into the situation. If we can make identification, then our feelings are involved. Unless this happens, then our feelings are not touched. We become emotionally excited when our college football team is playing, or the teams of our city schools or even of our region, as in intersectional games. But watching strange teams, with no players we are familiar with and where there are no ties of identification, is thoroughly dull and uninteresting.

Local news always achieves highest readership in a newspaper because it discusses people we know, places we are acquainted with, our private world. By contrast, apathy toward voting in big cities today stems from the fact that we don't know the candidates nor the issues. In spite of exhortations about our civic responsibilities, we are too uninvolved to take the trouble to vote.

Identification is an extremely important avenue for persuasion and teaching in advertising. If the reader or viewer can identify with the users of the product, if he can see himself in the situation, then his feelings become involved and the process works toward conviction and believability. Otherwise it remains dull and impersonal, and nothing happens. It is identification which makes it "for me."

For years, during my storytelling to my youngster, she would ask me to make up a boy and girl and inject them into the story. And always she wanted them at approximately her age. She enjoyed the story when it was possible to identify herself with someone not older, not younger, but an easy transfer of herself.

It should be pointed out that people can make identification in two ways:

1. Recognizing oneself in the character or scene.
2. Fulfilling a wish to be somebody else.

Imitation is a most powerful form of learning. As we notice other persons trying out new types of lawnmower, wearing new styles of casual costume, serving new dishes in new buffet ways of entertaining, we unconsciously make mental notes to try these things. We would deny vehemently that we are imitating anyone, because the process does mostly occur unconsciously. But we closely observe for cues to proper behavior. We say that a person is out of place when he doesn't recognize the proper cues. The individuals from whom we take our signals may be different for different fields. No one tells us how to adjust our actions and our tastes. We decide that from observation.

The model person has to be

1. Someone like me or ourselves, so that I can see myself in the same setting.

2. Someone I admire—someone I wish I were.

This principle of identification is extremely relevant for the teaching of new habits. Without it, the entire burden is placed on the buyer to imagine without assistance the role that the product will play in his life. Just to show a can or a package or an automobile by itself with no people and no recognizable setting is simply to reinforce whatever notions I may already have about them in a dull way, but there is little possibility for new learning. An analogy could be drawn by citing the relatively plain store windows in rural areas in contrast to the richly involving displays at Christmastime or during winter vacations in today's metropolitan department stores. The modern store window creates a richly involving scene which literally invites the passer-by to participate in an Easter parade or a cocktail party. On a subconscious level, the benefits of the product are displayed and fitted into the buyer's own life.

Demonstration is a form of identification. It helps us to project ourselves into the advertising. So does a recognizable table setting with a new food dish. The reader is much less likely to try to understand the ad which does not put its point across in personal terms. No advertiser would use scenes of South American Indians or Laplanders using his product. Why not? Because the reader does not project himself into any setting with such people. He isn't going to be influenced by anything they do, and so the ad is not personalized. On the contrary, the advertiser uses Americans of like situation to the audience or ideal types that we secretly hope or think ourselves to be. But at least we have to believe that we can realistically be in such a setting.

In a study of beer advertising, there was a vastly different reaction to the kind of people and situations portrayed in the copy. The primary beer market is the "mass-audience" man. In their attempts to cast a halo of quality and high status around their brands, some breweries used high-status characters and settings—people at formal weddings quaffing their beer, people at yacht-club dances in summer formals, people on mountaintops in ski regalia standing in the snow drinking beer, movie actors at luxury-hotel swimming pools.

These were completely unbelievable. They had no power of persuasion for the mass-audience man because he could not project himself into such settings. He had never been to a wedding where people wore full-dress suits; he never expected to in his life; and he knew that he would be completely out of place and uncomfortable if by chance he did land in such a setting. There was no identification whatever with such advertising. As a matter of fact, it aroused much open hostility, because beer was his drink and he resented the implication that he should be influenced by such extremely high-status persons who he felt seldom drank beer.

Typical reactions to such advertising were

> So those ritzy swells drink beer? I don't believe it.
> Movie actors drink cocktails? I don't know, I never saw a place like that.
> Why do they always have to show rich people drinking beer? Why can't they just use people like us?

People do look up, of course. But they have to be able to see themselves in the situation. They do admire group leaders, successful athletes, movie stars in believable situations. But if the jump is too big for their imagination, if they can never see themselves either in fantasy or in fact in such a role, then there is no identification. The use of social leaders, the snob appeal, is effective with a certain personality type that in fantasy sees itself leading such a life, as in the play *The Glass Menagerie*. However, this is a relatively thin slice of the population.

If a factory worker turned up in a socialite's garb copied from some ad, he would be ridiculed by his work associates. If his wife patterned her household after the "charming member of Long Island Society," she would be scorned by her neighbors for "putting on airs." Many products, of course, have been extremely successful using a high-status appeal. But almost never are they appealing to a wide audience. The greatest part of the population can make no identification whatever with such settings and such people.

In our studies, there is a very notable difference between the audience involvement in copy using recognizable backgrounds and people as opposed to involvement in bare illustrations of the product, especially if it is only shown in a bottle or carton. Automobile advertising which only showed the car achieved no such involvement as that with people in familiar settings or in situations where the person would like to be and where by some stretch of the imagination he can picture himself. Advertising which does achieve such identification becomes personalized. It can give the reader a fantasied satisfaction; it can reach his feelings; it can teach him.

The technique of identification is far more effective for teaching new habits—showing people with whom I am involved via my feelings, using new brands or new-type products—than a direct, argumentative, rational approach. The rational approach brings all a person's critical abilities into action. Where there are strong negative meanings and the advertiser says the opposite of the stereotype attitudes, he is worse off for having brought the issue out into the open.

When the instant coffee advertiser proclaims, "Tastes better than real coffee," the reader not only is not convinced, but she becomes irritated. The whole problem of taste is on the table to reinforce her present negative attitudes.

By contrast, Pall Mall has been successfully changing the earlier feminine character of the brand by using identification. It did not argue openly with this attitude. Rather, it consistently showed admirable men smoking Pall Malls—men with whom the reader could identify. Any open clash with the reader's preconceptions was avoided.

The Tea Bureau was faced with the same problem, since hot tea has been considered by most American males a sissy drink, a beverage for old maids and intellectuals. It wouldn't convince anybody if the industry coldly stated, "He-men now drink tea." It is far better to let the sleeping dogs keep on sleeping. But the illustrations consistently show men drinking tea—believable men. Because the advertising does slide around the expressed attitude instead of openly quareling with it, working on the reader's feelings by identification, it has a far better chance of success.

4

This leads squarely to the other technique: the ability, the art of conveying our real meanings by indirection.

Advertising is suggestion, and the adult responds very differently to direct and indirect suggestion. Almost all adults, especially equals, resent direct suggestion. Actually, it is an attack on their ego integrity, telling them to do this and that, shattering their beliefs and prejudices. If I were to prove to someone that each and every one of his cherished beliefs was fallacious, I would be "disintegrating" his personality. The self cannot allow this to happen. It simply fends off a direct approach to its integrity, which is its structure of convictions and habits and sentiments. We resent any domination and encroachment on our pride and personality. "Man must be taught as though you taught him naught." Indirect suggestion avoids clashing with the other individual's system of beliefs, which is his self.

Children will accept direct suggestion. And there are circumstances when adults deliberately put themselves into a situation where they ask for it, as when they request professional advice from a lawyer or architect or doctor, or when they ask street directions. By and large, however, direct advice is resented from equals. All of us have had the experience of seeing an idea of ours violently rejected by another only to find that some time later the person had adopted our idea as if it had come from his own thinking. By this time he has probably honestly forgotten that the idea came from somebody else. He doesn't have to admit to himself that anyone has changed his mind. When he can feel that the idea came from his own thinking, he is far more likely to follow it. When indirect suggestion is operative, we do not bother to track down the source of our impulses. We unhesitatingly pay heed to them and act.

Almost every man has to get his independence of mind off his chest. He wants to make it perfectly clear that advertising does not influence him, because he makes up his own mind about things. This is also true of upper-middle-class women. Advertising does influence them, of course, but they want to get this independence of mind on record. Indirect suggestion, however, is not only far more acceptable, but it has far more possibility of getting through to people, of changing behavior, of becoming embedded in some feeling.

When we formulate our objectives for any advertising campaign, it is immediately apparent that there are multitudinous issues which can never be openly discussed, any more than I could tell people in seriousness that I am handsome or honest or a brilliant thinker. By common consent we just don't talk about these areas. People are going to find out these things for themselves via feeling, or intuitive perception—some avenue other than intellectual discussion. The mere fact of my having said any of these things about myself—"I am friendly," "I am sincere," "I am believable," "I am trustworthy"—would be held against me. Not only would I not convince anyone with my proclamations about myself, but others would dislike me and distrust me for opening up these areas for intellectual analysis. It represents very poor taste—like trying to talk business at a funeral. Once I received a Christmas card from a struggling independent butcher which created all kinds of warm feeling, until I saw his telephone number at the bottom of the card. He spoiled it all by being too obvious.

Friendliness is probably an attribute every store would like to radiate. But nobody is convinced by an open expression. "You're always welcome at Walgreen's" is empty protestation to me. My native power of intuition tells me I am only welcome if I have money in my pocket and if I behave myself; and under these circumstances, I am welcome in any store. The advertising manager of an extremely successful savings and loan association in Chicago told me that he never used the word "friendly" in his advertising because he considered it hypocritical and unconvincing. On the other hand, he wanted everything about his advertising and everything about the atmosphere of the institution to radiate friendliness. His advertising copy is overly verbose, it is not slick and professional; but its entire tone breathes sincerity of purpose, arousing such responses as, "Here is some amateur struggling very hard to tell us about his company; he believes in it; he likes people; I think I would probably feel at home there."

By contrast, the open forays into institutional advertising in which various department stores and manufacturers indulge occasionally are generally unconvincing, because lyrical prose about ourselves falls flat. It's like dressing before an open window with the lights on. Our purposes are just too transparent. This brings us squarely back to the problem of believability. What are the directions to take here to acquire greater believability? At this point the traditionalists end up with stale platitudes about clear prose, having real sincerity, believing in your own proposition, knowing it so well that you are just steeped in it. All of this is childish and empty.

People are going to form their judgments of me, not from what I say about myself, but by a subtle, intuitive process compounding their feelings and the symbolic meanings that they read into multitudinous little things about myself—my tone of voice, my clothes, my manner. The same factors operating slightly differently are the channels to greater believability in advertising. Humans will form their own intuitive judgments by melding the tone, the affective content, and the meanings they derive from the various symbols in the advertising. By indirection as often as directly, certainly by identification, we marshal our appeals to reach out for their feelings. We cannot violate their rationality—any known facts. But the important thing is how to get at their feelings most acceptably.

5

To return to the importance of indirection, there are any number of motive areas that are difficult to even approach except with velvet gloves. For instance, there is a very evident latent masculine interest in toiletries; but to handle this touchy issue is difficult. Even though men spend millions for aftershave lotions which give strictly perfume and sensual satisfaction, the same men would angrily reject advertising discussing these appeals.

Attention getting, competitiveness, sex, hunger for praise, power drives: these are just typically important motives which can scarcely be approached except by indirection. This is why the most effective advertising, like successful public relations, is the art of saying one thing while the important meaning is often sailing out in another direction to appeal to the real motive areas.

Advertising has very successfully learned how to invest a product with a high-status aura by the use of indirection. A certain cigarette ostensibly talks about filters. But the entire tone of the advertising and of the art exudes class, sophistication. The symbolism projects the reader squarely into a high status identification in perfectly acceptable fashion, with tremendous believability that here is a prestige cigarette, if this is what he wants.

6

I am being very analytical about processes in which the creative man proceeds most effectively on an intuitive basis. Whenever an artist or novelist becomes too conscious of his symbols and analogies, they appear contrived and hence are not convincing. This is why intensely logical people are generally poor creators. As they rely more on intellect, their sensitivity to feeling and intuition becomes dulled. Eventually rationality is the only area where the ordinary man in our society feels secure. He becomes afraid to explore human feeling. And he justifies his timidity to all under the banner of reason and common sense.

Every society forces its members into molds of behavior which they come to accept without question, as if there were no other scheme of things. This is why the marginal man, living on the edges of conformity, has far greater insight into the human passional system, because he still lifts up rocks and asks questions. Nearly all great creators are just such marginal men who still retain their keen insight and sensitivity, who trust their intuition sufficiently to allow their creative power to flow from their unconscious, their nonrational minds, generated and guided essentially by their own inner selves. When their imaginations are no longer receptive, when they live by rules and formulas, then they no longer create.

The primary task facing the creative man in advertising is how to get at people's feelings. How can he communicate convincingly with the third ear, with the levels of intuition far beyond reason—where the scales of judgment are weighted by feeling and primitive perceptions. This is the "open sesame" to believability and persuasion. The intellectual elements—the facts and the arguments—are just a superstructure on the process of achieving conviction.

CHAPTER XI

Men Live by Symbols—Not Sense

In mid-December my youngster observed that our Christmas would be most unsatisfying this year, inasmuch as there would be no snow and no bubble lights for the tree. Festivities, presents, visitors no matter, the holiday would be incomplete without *all* of the symbols which to her signified Christmas. This is simply an illustration of how we think by symbolization and how we communicate by symbols.

The retail advertiser or the school child can convey the whole notion of Christmas by sketching in the crudest sort of a fir tree with a few sparkles to suggest lights or candles. A gasoline poster says "Power and Economy" and then symbolically presents these two ideas with pictures of a bulldog and a Scotch terrier. An office reception room equipped with fluorescent lights and pots of philodendron and sansevieria says that this place is ultramodern, sophisticated. When I am driving my car, I have to watch carefully for traffic lights, arterial signs, hand signals, the motions of the policemen, all of which constitute a set of symbols regulating my behavior.

Man lives in an environment of symbols, and it is extremely important to understand something about the symbol-making process because symbols are the raw material of human thought and all communication. Superficially we think that words are the only form of communication, because we live in such a highly verbal atmosphere. Yet in actuality there is a far greater amount of nonverbal communication going on all the time through the use of other symbols than words. And though we believe that all thinking must be logical and intellectual, there is an entirely different mode of thinking also used by the brain, which has a different order and a different way of conveying meaning than intellection, hinging on a different kind of symbol.

Communication is the act of conveying meaning to others. We do this by symbols. I might want to express my ideas, my feelings, my moods. Or I simply might want to convey my identity, just to say to the world at large who I am so that others will know how to communicate with me. By my manner, by clothing, hair style, the way I smoke, I am consciously or unconsciously expressing my identity. All

133

this expression will have meaning for others only if they correctly interpret the symbols I am using.

Although language is perhaps the crowning accomplishment of the human race, it is nevertheless hopelessly inadequate to express man's emotional nature. Language barely touches the world of feeling at certain marginal points with names for some vague and crude states, and that is all. There are just no words to express the various nuances of sensation and feeling, to express such things as mood and esthetic impression. Try to describe to a child how a strawberry tastes as compared to a raspberry, how a carnation smells, why it is pleasurable to dance, what a pretty girl looks like.

There are countless areas where the precise meanings and definitions have to be conveyed by nonverbal, nonrational symbols. A drawing, a photograph, a pantomime of gestures, such as the traffic policeman or the orchestra conductor uses—these are everyday obvious examples of nonverbal symbols. We determine the feelings and inner thinking of other people almost entirely from facial expressions; from movements of the body, such as the hands; from the general state of excitement such as weeping, blushing, or anger; from tone of voice; and from involuntary exclamations and sounds such as whistling or singing.

But the nonverbal symbols are not necessarily expressions of feeling. We use them endlessly for just plain information. Physical objects are carriers of endless information about people and events, for instance, that we are anxious to know. We size up strangers by the kind of glasses they wear, by whether they smoke cigars or pipes, by the gadgets on their desks, by whether they have pencils or a handkerchief or nothing in their breast pockets. Actions also can be interpreted for information alone. If a man is taking off his coat, we infer that he is going to relax or do some serious work. If many people are running in the same direction or looking in the same direction, we decide that something important is happening. If a man scratches his head slowly, we assume that he is puzzled.

All these illogical symbols develop their own logic. We use such a logic when we identify a person's mood, his personality, how well off he is, and what is his broad occupational category from his clothing. We don't talk about status in our society; we merely express it by the logic of these nonverbal symbols—by cars, by the clubs we belong to, by where we live. We evaluate an executive's place in his company's scheme of things by such symbols as the grooming and competence of his secretary, how big his office is, if it has carpet and drapes, if he has a private washroom and useless furniture like a davenport. Such completely illogical trivia as shoeshines, waxed floors, and simonized cars become "logical" symbols for good grooming, affluence, careful housekeeping, responsibility.

Realization of the extent of nonverbal communication is highly relevant for advertising. Because there are so many areas where humans customarily communicate this way, because these nonrational symbols often are far more believable and effective carriers of meaning than words, the creative person has to use them in conjunction with the logical symbols. And yet, in creating these nonrational symbols, he has to use his intuitive powers rather than intellectual reasoning, which ordinarily is quite fruitless for producing these other types of symbols. This is why it is almost impossible to assess creative work expressed in these nonrational symbols by the canons of common sense and ordinary logic. Their meaning will never fit intellectual logic. The creative person "knows" that he is right because he "feels" that he is right, but he can never explain his symbol making and his meanings to someone who is using a different mode of thinking.

The creative writer senses this just as much as the illustrator. Hal Stebbins told me that he is not interested in words as words or pictures as pictures. He wants to know what is the connotative image meaning behind the surface meaning of words and pictures. William Tyler stresses the importance of creating an "instinctive, subconscious, almost emotional feeling about an advertising idea which is the strongest force advertising has to offer—the power that sells your services emotionally, without argument, without conscious thought or rationalization."

The scientific mind, the mathematical mind, the common-sense, rational mind are utilizing a different process of communication and thought than the literary mind, the artistic mind, the religious mind, the intuitive mind. The creative mind in advertising has to work with *both* logical and nonrational symbols.

As I have said repeatedly, there are whole areas of human activity that our society just never discusses openly, including almost the entire gamut of emotions. Watch a football game and note how often the players slap each other on the back as perfectly acceptable signs of closeness, support, encouragement. But try to discuss friendship in words with any man. It just isn't done. When a certain consultant persistently says flattering things to me, I become very uncomfortable. His flattery is acceptable, but I don't want it bluntly articulated. Yet almost any situation, any emotion, any mood can be very acceptably approached with illustration, style, or music.

Furthermore, in general, words lack the wealth of association and emotional freighting that nonverbal symbols can have. Certainly words can and do have the power to create associations. Even hackneyed words and phraseologies can be manipulated by the creative writer to give impressions of freshness. But for the most part, the "rules" governing the use of words are quite rigid. They must be defined within narrow limits to preserve the mutual intelligibility of language. New uses of a word are discouraged, leaving the user open to charges of ignorance or sloppiness. We are taught from an early age to consider words as rigid building blocks with confined meanings. Creative people like James Joyce or Gertrude Stein who experiment with words face considerable hostility.

By contrast, the meaning of a picture is not hedged in and embalmed, as the teachers insist we do with words. We read whatever meaning we want to read into a picture, and we do it with complete freedom. No schoolmarm or other superior person has ever embarrassed us for "misusing" a picture, let alone mispronouncing or misspelling it. The question of whether nonverbal symbolic communication loses power because of its lack of specific (embalmed) meaning is easily answered by pointing to the inarticulate quality of two of the most moving types of human communication—the arts and religion. The problem is really one of evaluating the meanings of nonverbal symbols to maximize their advertising utility.

This is why it is so important to give study to and to use a research approach to what the nonrational symbols are saying. We always overexpress ourselves. When we speak, we are unconsciously saying many, many things about ourselves, both positive and negative, that we don't realize in this overexpression. Similarly, an advertisement is a totality of many symbols, some of which may be expressing entirely different meanings about the product than the advertiser suspects. Often these unsuspected meanings are drowning out his message.

One of the primary values of motivation research, even though it has been too little used, is to discover what symbolic associations are being created by advertising. Just because symbols may have many meanings, even contradictory meanings, it is important to ascertain what they are communicating to the audience. The advertiser may think of lamb as merely meat, whereas its strong symbolic associations with innocence and purity may actually inhibit its general use as meat. Without research it is difficult to tell whether the old craftsman who is supposed to illustrate careful workmanship will give that meaning to a product or instead the negative meaning of old age, decrepitude, and lack of style—or whether symbols which are perfectly clear to the advertising agency have any meaning at all for a mass audience.

2

First of all, a symbol is anything which stands for something else. The flowers that I send to a hospitalized friend are only flowers, but they express my concern for him, my sympathy. A flag is a dyed piece of cloth, but we attach deep patriotic significance to it because it symbolizes all our national aspirations and traditions. An engagement ring is simply a metal band on a girl's left hand, but it immediately evokes concepts of young love, happiness, virginity. Any word is a symbol. The sound of the word "fire" not only calls out the bare notion of burning, but it has the power to stir us emotionally, arousing feelings of warmth, danger, fascination just by its color imagery. Mathematics is an area of pure symbols. The little pencil marks on paper are not the quantities; we are simply manipulating symbols for the quantities.

A gesture like a handshake or an arm around the shoulder conveys friendship with much greater force and believability than words. Our national holidays operate as symbols whereby the whole society conveys things to us which it constantly wants reinforced. On Thanksgiving we rekindle our family ties, strengthening our relationships with our in-laws and our children through the ritual of a festive dinner and a mummery involving turkeys, Puritans, pumpkin pie. Such an art form as the western movie symbolizes the same theme as the old morality plays—the timeless conflict between good and evil. Because this is folk art, the cast of characters has to symbolize folk characters. The villain is the crooked banker, the too-slick gambler, something of an intellectual. By contrast, the hero is the plain, honest man of action; no intellectual he, but rather the folk man who is guided by his feelings and his fists, who loves animals, and who is shy with women.

A symbol is the expression of some idea. As pointed out by Dr. Susanne Langer, the symbol-making function is one of man's primary activities, like eating. It goes on all the time, because it is the fundamental process of the mind. This is the way we give meaning to our experiences, this is how we understand the world about us: we abstract out of the experience or stimulus its essential meaning and then we fasten this in our minds with a symbol—generally with a word, often with a picture, but also sometimes with a ceremony or a sound.

We can communicate with another human because although we never see the total experience in exactly the same way, yet both of us can abstract the same essential meaning. Easter undoubtedly means something different for the next person than it does for me, but both of us can abstract the notion of this holiday either from the word, from the pictures of Easter lilies, rabbits, eggs, Easter-style parades, or from the Easter religious services.

This is the basic process of all thought: disregarding everything about a sense experience except the skeleton form that gives the clue to its meaning as a concept. But by the ability to use symbols, we can hold on to the idea in our memory, we can manipulate it in our thinking, and we can exchange thinking about it with others. The symbols become our vehicles of thought.

The two kinds of symbols are variously termed "logical," "rational," or "discursive" on the one hand as opposed to "nonrational," "nonverbal," "evocative," "presentational," or "affective" on the other hand. They are essentially different in the way in which they take meaning. Words and logical thinking are consecutive, strung out one after the other in serial fashion. You can't say a mouthful of words at once. They have to fit in a succession, following a definite order. This is also true of mathematical symbols.

But in the nonrational symbols, in all the forms of symbolic expression used in painting, in pantomime, in religion, in formal rituals such as graduation and funeral ceremonies, in daily rituals such as greeting friends or saying grace at meals, the meaning comes all at once. A photograph has a certain relationship of parts, but whatever the total picture says comes across as soon as I look at it. The visual forms of art—lines, colors, and masses—convey equally as complex ideas as language and logic. But the whole visual structure is stated in just one single glance. A gesture expresses some feeling in one instantaneous flash. It is impossible to dissect the component parts of these symbols for logical analysis, because the parts do not have independent meanings.

The meaning of the total symbol either comes across through the simultaneous impression of the parts, or it doesn't come across at all. A wedding ring instantaneously says that the girl is married. A song in a minor key conveys a sorrowful, tragic effect. A note of boredom in my voice is a symbol comprehended immediately, without any reflection. And, of course, it is apparent that these symbols are expressing their meaning mostly below the threshold of conscious awareness. We don't stop to assemble them, to study them—we just sense what they are conveying.

No individual can untangle in any systematic manner what he has experienced from a great work of music or painting, from a great play like *Macbeth*, or from a first-rate novel. It has caused some alterations in his unconscious. We want our children to be exposed to all these things because we sense that they will undergo a spiritual experience which will make them better people. We haven't the slightest intellectual idea how or why, but we have every reason to feel that it does happen.

In exactly this fashion, the same kind of communication occurs below the threshold of conscious awareness from the various non-verbal symbols in our advertising—from the art, for instance. No one could explain precisely what the famous man with the patch over his eye in the Hathaway shirt advertising communicated—not even the people who created it.

Most great painters were relatively illiterate men. Early artists, whether creating Peruvian Inca figurines or Greek architecture, were achieving very real meaning for their audiences which they could never intellectualize. A dance band doesn't know why a sharp key produces a gay, festive mood while a flat key creates a sadder vein. While it makes no difference in the sound of piano, brass, or reed instruments—since E flat and D sharp are played exactly the same way—there are subtle differences in the tune on stringed instruments which achieve a notable difference in mood. Hoagy Carmichael's "Stardust" was not popular as a "jump tune," but when the tempo was slowed down, it became the most popular sentimental ballad of its time. These are all effects on the unconscious which are very obvious, very powerful, communicable to other persons—a different set of symbols from any used in logical thought.

The very success of package design, the fact that any cartons at all are used, the considerable experimentation with pastel colors and vivid colors ("Pink Camay," "Rinso Blue," "Schick Razors in 5 exciting colors") document how much other subtleties which are completely outside of reason or consciousness enter into sales desirability.

3

It is extremely important for any person in advertising to realize that meaning is being communicated simultaneously at several levels. Advertising combines the forces of both logical thought and emotive, esthetic thought. Because it is communication from one set of humans to another set of humans, part of the meaning will be rational; but also there will be much meaning conveyed by nonrational symbols.

Besides expressing logical thought, our words and our actions are also indicative of the emotions, attitudes, moods, and intention of the speaker. Whenever we speak, we are offering two different kinds of clues. One is manifested by the thought content. The other is at the level where intuition operates, where the speaker conveys his feelings, his intentions, his motives. In written language any attitudes such as warmth and forcefulness have to be expressed differently than in conversation. Metaphor, imagery, underlining, and tone of writing are the symbols which the reader looks for rather than gestures or tone of voice. Since advertising also utilizes art, layout, music, and the live personalities of announcers and show people, all of these develop their own symbols of meaning.

Whereas the rational part of communication is concerned with some logical thought, the affective aspect of communication is trying to create attitudes, feeling meanings, moods. Analogous sets of symbols develop for each purpose. Operating in different ways, each with a different potential ability to express meanings, nevertheless both sets of symbols are tangible, real, and communicative.

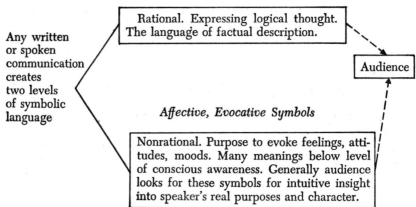

Factual, Logical Symbols

Any written or spoken communication creates two levels of symbolic language

Rational. Expressing logical thought. The language of factual description.

Audience

Affective, Evocative Symbols

Nonrational. Purpose to evoke feelings, attitudes, moods. Many meanings below level of conscious awareness. Generally audience looks for these symbols for intuitive insight into speaker's real purposes and character.

Thus it can be seen that illustration, layout, and color are much more than merely devices to attract attention. Just as it is possible for the direct emotional impact of music to reach us, so can these other nonrational symbols of form, of line and mass, of tone and mood and imagery all contribute in a language of their own to the total meaning of the advertisement, to the image of the product or institution.

We are vaguely aware that a painting or a photograph is making an emotional impact on us through its color qualities and form qualities. Just as we sense that there are distinctly felt emotional effects from the components of music, from the sound qualities and the stresses, so are we experiencing at some level distinguishably different feeling-meanings from the color and forms and masses in art and layout. Even the bric-a-brac in the advertisements—the symbols in minor key such as slogans, emblems, illustrations of the package—all of these may be adding informative meanings to the total character of the institution or the product which will vastly outweigh any stated claims.

Women refused to identify with a certain margarine ad because some thumbnail sketches—only a tiny part of the total—showed a housewife using the product who wore earrings and a dressy scarf; the audience said that no real housewife waves margarine around in such party regalia. A hand-lotion ad in a before-and-after situation showed the left hand with the wedding ring as the rough, red hand. This wedding ring shouted to women that marriage caused the rough, red hands; drudgery; loss of feminine charm. It also evoked guilt feelings in them for even having such thoughts as sighing for the free life. All of this made for hostile associations.

4

I want to point to several strategies in which the use of these non-rational symbols has produced results, building rich product character that was translated into intense consumer desirability and sales success.

The Marlboro cigarette had been typed in the public mind as a feminine high-style cigarette until it was decided to change the product personality completely by an entire about-face. I doubt if this could have been accomplished for a widely known product or if the product and the packaging had not been radically changed. But they were, and the advertising set out to establish the product as a very masculine cigarette, a cut above Camel in status. This was the strategy used to create such a product image:

1. No women were shown in the advertising.

2. All the models were very virile men. In pretests of the advertising, a regular professional model was shown as a cowboy. Typical of the fashion in which an audience scrutinizes advertising for tiny clues to hidden character, numerous people wrote in to point out that this cowboy had a manicure, and whoever heard of that? Thereafter non-professionals were used, and they were really smoking their cigarettes.

3. The models were also chosen as successful, forceful personalities to inspire emulation, identification with an admirable figure.

4. To reinforce the notion of virility and also to hint of a romantic past, each man had a plainly visible tattoo on his hand. These were

all standard U.S. Navy tattoos, and very eloquently—far more eloquently than any words could say—this symbol gave a richness to the
product image, bringing it all into focus:

—Here is a successful, achieving, virile man.

—In his youth he slipped and had a romance, although he obviously
wouldn't do it today.

The tattoo and the highly individualistic personalities in the artwork were symbols of meanings that could never be captured in words,
that would never be acceptable if the motive areas being appealed
to were nakedly exposed. They built a unique product character, completely set apart from the welter of cigarette claims. Actually, because
these symbols are so image-rich, they give the cigarette much more
than just a manhood appeal. These are powerful, vigorous emblems
of sex that appeal to women as well as men. The tattoo has the appeal
of license, freedom, love affairs. The men have a feminine appeal in
the sense that they are egocentric and confidently aware of their charm.

Hamm's beer advertising has been enormously successful through
its use of indirect symbols which invested the product with a halo of
appealing associations. Instead of the stereotyped patter prevalent in
much beer advertising about tradition, better brewmasters, caloric
control, and high status, Hamm used as a central theme "From the
Land of Sky Blue Waters."

Our motivation studies have indicated that refreshment is a primary motive force in the desirability of beer. The theme "From the
Land of Sky Blue Waters," reinforced by art scenes of blue lakes,
pine trees, and frosty glasses emerging from the snow piles up a
powerful symbolic effect of indescribably wonderful refreshment. It is
infinitely more forceful than any stated claims on the subject, proclaiming the words in big type, could be.

Furthermore, because this is an "open-end" symbol, the way is left
open for the audience to read many more meanings into the product
image than mere refreshment. If the copy stated, "Because Hamm's
beer is from the land of sky-blue waters, therefore it is refreshing,"
the symbol would have been too concrete and restrictive. It would
have closed out any other meanings.

By using posters which merely say, "From the Land of Sky Blue
Waters—Hamm's," not even indicating that this is a beer being advertised, the ad allows the reader to make his own closures. The symbol
will therefore be much richer, appealing to such motive forces as
escape to the North Woods, camping trips, and swimming in cool
waters, as well as bearing various esthetic values connected with
snow, blue lakes, pine trees, etc. There is a wealth of force in this

metaphorical symbolism reaching out for the reader's feelings. And just as is true of the Marlboro symbol, there is undoubtedly a considerable amount of meaning being communicated below the threshold of conscious awareness which is adding to the product desirability.

In this type of symbolism, it is difficult to grasp with any exactness all that is being said just because so much *is* being addressed to the unconscious mind. It is readily apparent that band music has a stirring effect on an audience, but no one can say exactly why this is, in the sense of exact meanings. We can do little except to sense that it is an observable cause-and-effect situation. In the case of symphony music or modern abstract art, we can barely guess what is happening. Because the largest proportion of the population does not share the artist's symbol system, there is little communication.

It would be completely misleading to imply that there is any research which can do much more than scratch the surface of the unconscious mind. Advertising addresses itself to the widest possible audience, and it is important to ascertain whether the creative person's symbols on this level are meaningful, whether they are positive or negative in their effect, whether the audience is reading in a different set of broad meanings from the symbols than was intended. Too often there is a tremendous gap between what we *think* we are saying and what we are *really* saying.

In one campaign addressed to the mass-audience housewife, the print advertising attempted to create a warm personality for the product by using an emotionalized art style—shadowy close-up photographs of younger models. When we asked housewives to tell stories about the situations of the photograph, completely dissociating the art from the advertising, a widespread rejection was clearly apparent. The audience saw only the emotional potentialities of the model's femaleness thrown into sharp relief, suggesting license and depravity; and while this might seem clever to an avant-garde creative artist, it only elicited sharp disapproval from housewives.

Again, a liquor advertiser attempting to express conviviality portrayed a younger man warmly addressing a group of older men. But where the artist intended to show friendliness, the audience saw a conflict situation, the younger man attempting to dominate his elders. Neither older nor younger men in the audience would identify with this power-hungry schemer.

We have repeatedly studied advertising where the effect was only dullness, lack of involvement, a "so-what?" attitude. Often the audience would fasten on some too fancy dish or ash tray, used merely as incidental background, as an indication that the product itself was

too fancy for general tastes. A soap advertisement which promised
to get clothes "immaculate" aroused hostile feelings because the word
"immaculate" was associated with the Immaculate Conception and it
was desecrating to involve religion and soap. Another advertiser used
a little girl wearing a crown to suggest highest quality for his margarine, but the housewives in our study were very often negative,
because they saw the girl as an objectionable brat—"Shirley Temple
twenty years out of date."

On the other hand, we have often isolated some entirely unlooked-
for positive meanings which nonrational symbols were creating and
which were far more responsible for outstanding product success than
routine claims. For example, while the stereotyped soap claims about
"whiteness" and "brightness" in a Wisk detergent ad were received
with indifference, the ad was highly effective because of the blue color,
the illustration of the can, the involving, friendly picture of one woman
admiring another as she used the product, the imagery created by the
words "liquid miracle," and an almost buried claim about stain re-
moval. We found that few people actually believed the rational claims
in a Pepsodent ad; they didn't believe that any commercial dentifrice
could remove yellow discoloration. But the ad was extremely successful because there was entertainment, a happiness theme, and because
of the implication that the toothpaste had a good flavor and was
refreshing, which the audience derived from the plentiful white space
in the ad and from the illustration of the package.

5

My emphasis on nonrational communication will probably seem at
variance with the world of daily advertising, which superficially at
least exists on the level of rational product claims, effective selling
messages, mundane information. I am not minimizing these aspects
of advertising. Obviously this is what the consumer has been trained
to look for, and in themselves these selling messages may have tremendous motive appeals.

Nevertheless, it is imperative to see that advertising is communicating simultaneously with two sets of symbols, both of which are
powerful, both of which are contributory to the product personality,
both of which are creating desirability for the consumer. If one level
of language sways the consumer's economic logic, the other set of
symbols is equally important as the access to emotions and intuitive
meaning.

CHAPTER XII

Creating the Product Image

Note the ease with which the retail grocery chains elbow aside long-established national brands by introducing their own private labels. Contrary to all the tenets in our credos about the power of the advertised product, these house brands of the food chains in one instance after another have captured the lion's share of the purchases in their stores—and without advertising. How can this be so?

Granted that there are many variables in the fortunes of any product, let's narrow this down to the issue of whether the advertising can and should create a real product desirability which will secure for it a share of the consumer's mind. Certainly if I were a manufacturer who had spent 50 million dollars in the belief that I was building a real brand identity, a positive product personality, only to see my hold on the consumer collapse at the advent of a completely nonadvertised brand, I would ask some soul-searching questions. I think I would have the right to feel disappointed. What was the advertising supposed to do?

The mere fact that the grocery chains have not been uniformly successful—that countless products have not been disturbed appreciably by the competition of lower-priced house brands—proves that it very demonstrably is possible for the right kind of advertising to create such an unassailable position in the consumer's mind. An extensive study at Massachusetts Institute of Technology on brand loyalties proves that there is no such thing as a "loyal personality," no such thing as a "disloyal personality." The very person who is disloyal toward one set of products is a very loyal buyer about another kind of product. The critical factor is the brand's ability to fasten itself in a consumer's mind—to represent itself as a particularly desirable symbol for me. And this can happen anywhere—anytime.

So here is a full turn of the circle: How can advertising invest the product or institution with an especially rich aura of meaning and desirability? How can advertising build a product image appealing to the most powerful motive areas? How can it build the image into a symbol that will fit the individual's psychological goals and self-conceptions? How can it communicate this symbol acceptably so that it will activate these motive forces?

This is what a product image is—the total set of attitudes, the halo of psychological meanings, the associations of feeling, the indelibly written esthetic messages over and above the bare physical qualities. If this seems vague and too intangible, after all consider the human personality and how inexact it is. What is my "self"—which I am absolutely certain that I have? I am only what other people think I am. I am the sum total of their attitudes. They see me as a physical body and also as a symbol to which they fasten many meanings.

A product or institution similarly has such symbolic associations. I and millions of others will each in our own way see it as a symbol of something—it may be good or bad, dull or exciting.

I emphasized in the last chapter that man lives in a world of symbols. That's all a "standard of living" is—a set of symbols which we see as minimum requisites for us. The union worker will go on strike for months fighting for the means to attain certain symbols which he believes are base levels for decent living—an automobile, a refrigerator, a TV set. Literally billions of humans have gotten along without these things, but he sees them now as symbols which he must have. To me a vacation trip to colorful places is a necessity I am entitled to each year regardless of cost, but what I consider a justifiable expenditure is viewed by my brothers as sheer extravagance. Youngsters from white-collar backgrounds refuse to consider careers in much higher-paying blue-collar trades because they see them as symbolizing lower prestige—a downward movement in status. I have watched women after surgery daub on rouge and lipstick and comb their hair as their first conscious acts, disregarding pain and fright in their haste to re-assemble the symbols of their feminine charm.

The product image or product personality preselects its customer body with the same logic. When I said that, except for mere organic-species behavior, every act of human behavior is a form of self-expression, I meant that it is a symbolic representation of the inner self. I am using products that I see as symbols satisfying my motive forces and consistent with my self-conceptions.

But just as I avoid stores whose image of too cheap or too expensive price lines is inconsistent with what I think is my style of life, just as I do not buy clothes that would characterize me as an extreme eccentric or a dull plodder, so I pick and choose among the product images in advance of buying. For all of the falderal about impulse

The Olivetti Tetractys offers a new way to cut figurework costs. It provides a unique combination of high speed, remarkable versatility and simplified 10-key operation. It has two registers, a memory and an automatic constant. And since no business calculation is complete until it's on paper, the Tetractys automatically provides a printed record of every calculation. For a demonstration in your own office, on your own figurework, telephone your local Olivetti dealer Or write to Olivetti Corporation of America, 580 Fifth Avenue, New York 36, N.Y.

olivetti

Industrial advertisers often ask if the objectives of brand image and advertising style apply in their field. Yet in actuality the best industrial advertising seems to have a clearer grasp of where it should go than most consumer advertising. There is more effort dedicated to building a strong corporate image than in any other field. And this by the most daring and imaginative use of modern art.

By its advertising mannerisms—its art style, Olivetti has created its own character, which sets it completely apart from any similar products.

Hey, diddle, diddle! The cat and the fiddle!

The cow jumped over the moon.

The moon was all yellow and-yum-m-made of Jell-O,

So the cow went back for a spoon.

Of course product advantages are important. The consumer is trained to explain his behavior in rational terms. But in this era of product sameness, the intangibles can be crucial. Color, style, packaging and particularly its freight of purely psychological attributes can be the most important difference in the consumer's mind.

Other products can approach or even duplicate ingredients. Nothing, however, can infringe on the Jell-O brand image so skillfully compounded of whimsey, imagination, fantasy, and esthetic meanings.

buying which would convey that the buyer's preferences are nonexistent, the areas of choice where impulse buying can operate are rigidly defined. I never in my life have bought perfume, cut plug tobacco, or gefülte fish. Never in the past twenty years have I bought a package of the three top-selling cigarettes—Camel, Lucky Strike, or Chesterfield—because for some subtle reasons of which I am completely unaware, their product image is not appealing to me. I have often changed brands, but always within the same cluster of product meanings.

2

Here, it seems to me, is the very heart of the difference between the long-range and the short-range objectives of advertising. On a short-range basis the advertiser, whether a manufacturer or a retailer, hopes to move some goods immediately. This is the blind spot of management: to assume that here is the beginning and the end of all advertising. Without decrying the desirability of immediate sales, I submit that too often the short-term efforts utterly obscure the long-range, permanent goals of building an attractive, solid, rich, meaningful product image. The advertiser whose sales momentum depends on an onslaught of hypodermics or a drumfire of rationalistic claims about technical advantages which in fact are nonexistent and which do not involve any significant motive areas is writing in water. The brand disappears inevitably into the boneyard of characterless "products-I-tried-once," into the limbo of chain-store files—"Discontinued from insufficient turnover."

The long-range task of achieving permanent brand loyalty devolves on advertising which is capable of creating a minimum base line of acceptance, which does have an individuality in my conscious or unconscious mind. This is why advertising, instead of magnifying trivia or mumbling the same unimportant claims, should strive to construct a powerful symbol capable of lifting the brand completely out of the long, long parade of faceless products, indistinguishable in quality, package, and price. It is the psychological label, the product image which will individualize it in the vast majority of instances.

Sometimes the rational sales story represents extremely important constituent parts of the product image. But mostly, I would think, it is the overtone of affective meanings and subjective imagery which constitutes by far the most forceful elements of the symbol—the image of foreign correspondents and private detectives associated with the trench coat, the notions of status and self-expression fastened to the machinery called the automobile, the aura of strength and sociability emanating from the black liquid which is coffee.

Even in the cases where the advertiser insists that his success is due to his common-sense sales arguments, there are psychological overtones and affective meanings injected into the product image which are playing a key role. I heard a Seagram official proclaim that 7 Crown advertising was no mystery, that it came logically from their salesmen's arguments. This overlooks that the big red "7" and the yellow crowns used as illustrations have very definite esthetic impact in themselves, setting the image apart from that of any competitive brands.

There are countless instances where the nonrational elements of the symbol are apparently wholly responsible for the product's desirability, conveying their meanings almost entirely below the threshold of conscious awareness. Earlier I mentioned the Hathaway-shirt man with the patch on his eye. After his appearance product sales were tripled, although I never heard any buyer try to articulate why this part of the symbol made the product more desirable. But it did, and it is apparently all that did.

Breck shampoo has been a leading national seller because of an art style showing women with pallid yellow hair and evoking a quality of positive virginal mysticism reminiscent of a medieval saint. The copy mildly says, "Beautiful hair—Breck," which is little more than a poster's name identification. Nothing in all this explains the product's tremendous appeal to the buyer.

The bearded Englishman who became the focal point for the product image of Schweppes tonic water is a further illustration of a set of meanings hopelessly beyond the realm of cause-and-effect logic. In most other cases, people concoct a rational formula to justify their selection, even though it obviously stemmed from a rich product image compounded principally of nonrational meanings. But in these specific instances I never heard a person more than barely begin to try to explain his choice on any logical basis. Schweppes is an expensive and esoteric product, in which the buyer gets what? Schweppervescence? What's that? "But why bother trying to explain?" apparently is the buyer's attitude in these instances, so long as the product image is gratifying, even if at subconscious levels alone.

3

Customarily, when the manufacturer realizes that there are some negatives in the product images of his brands, he sets out to repair these on a rational basis. If he can ascertain in some fashion that his brand is considered poorer-quality, lower-status, too high in calorie count, not as good a value as other brands, deficient in taste, then he sets out to patch up these specific inadequacies. Busy as a beaver, he proclaims that his brand really does have all these virtues.

I am just about convinced that this open argument with the public's preconceptions seldom changes anything. The remark "Don't bother me with facts because my mind is already made up" is typically human. Most of us behave this way. I believe that the best way to overcome any weaknesses in the product personality is to inject some completely new elements in the image and go sailing off in an entirely different direction. If the image becomes exciting and full of rich, new meanings, the deficiencies are buried and forgotten. Instead of wasting time and effort in rearguard actions with the traces of negative meaning in the product image, the advertiser can quietly obscure them with an important new halo of positive overtones.

I realize that all this is much easier said than done—this task of building an attractive, positive product image—often depending far more on the creative person's ability to communicate by nonrational symbols than on any stated product claims. Yet I think that this is a very obviously indicated direction. In a subsequent chapter on the applications of this philosophy to retail advertising, there is discussion of a study on the images of department stores and how the housewife formulates her instantaneous impression of the store purely from the physical appearance of the advertising, the symbolism inherent in the style of the advertising—the tone, the type faces, the art motifs. These cues establish the scaffold for the real character attributes of the store.

Ohrbach's in New York was famous throughout the country as a low-price store. It wanted to change this impression and set for itself another objective: to persuade women that for the famous Ohrbach's prices they would get high-quality and high-fashion merchandise. How did they accomplish this change in the store image? By many and sundry proclamations telling the consumer that this was so, in the typical department store's traditional manner? By words? By logic? Not at all.

Rather, in a series of ads which must have been nightmarish compared with the pedestrian standards of retail copy, these meanings were conveyed by the physical appearance of the copy and by the sophistication of the ad ideas—believably, most effectively, and with many more corollary associations than those of a straight head-on approach. There are no prices in the ads, no pious and dull verbiage about the founder's ideals and dedication to greater and greater and greater values—the repertoire *ad nauseam* of retail institutional advertising. It was the pixie-ish and astonishing freshness, the light-fun touch that generated in completely irrelevant fashion this image of sophistication, smart style, glamour. These notions in themselves became the atmosphere of the store. The mere idea that these factors are available at Ohrbach's prices—this is the very essence of what is defined as quality and value.

Because these meanings, plus so many more associations, are perceived at the intuitive level, they achieve infinitely greater force than the tobacco auctioneer's chantings characteristic of a million retail ads daily. Marshall Field in Chicago for years has devoted a sizable proportion of its advertising to pure "atmosphere copy" as its very effective way of feeding meaning into the image of the store.

With montonous regularity the orthodox teachers announce platitudinously the importance of giving the reader news about the product. "That's what people want—news." But how do you give news about a product which uses identically the same ingredients that it did ten years ago—as Kleenex, Coca-Cola, Jell-O, Heinz ketchup, Maxwell House coffee? Do you show charts from an independent laboratory? Is it news to keep on inventing incredible uses for the product, like serving it for breakfast or for midnight snacks? I don't think so.

The really exciting news comes from changing the product image. Jell-O was a low-priced, easy-to-fix dessert which has acquired a radically different product image from one series after another of imaginative ads. It is impossible to capture in words the effect of color or illustration, because words can never do that directly; similarly, I can only guess at the full changes in the Jell-O symbol resulting from the altered style of their copy. Without the benefit of any research, I would guess that the comic animal series injected notes of gaiety and delightful childhood fantasy. The series of pastel colors and faded-off background effects builds, via these esthetic meanings, a series of notions about a quality, light, exciting dessert—not something common, not a heavy dessert like pie. Pepsi-Cola became newsy and exciting to the consumer when it changed its image—not the product itself.

When a product which is not completely new changes its advertising agency, what actually is the agency's real assignment? The ingredients of the product will rarely be changed. Pricing, packaging, and distribution probably won't be changed. It is the product image which the advertising is expected to change—its collar of purely psychological meanings. Same product, same appropriation, same physical everything—but presumably it can be invested with new desirabilities. And how will this be accomplished? Is it likely that the new agency can detect some outstanding technical or ingredient advantage which has been overlooked for years? Hardly. The perfectly obvious course for the new agency, if it is going to remold the product personality, will be to fill in the image with many other meanings besides the mere rational claims about what the product can do.

This is the real genius of creative advertising. Any neophyte just out of college can put together a description of the product which even the naked eye can see is superior in value and quality. No talent is necessary for a specification diagram. But the market place is characterized by products which are not notably different in price and function. Their sales advantage can only come from more appealing psychological attributes. While the creative people undoubtedly will use product statements, because our society has been trained to think that way, they will also have to use nonrational symbols, esthetic devices, affective meanings. They will employ the characteristically human habit of fusing psychological and emotive associations with a physical thing. The resulting subjective totality, imbued with many and diverse meanings, will be seen by the consumer as a new and richer product image.

I have purposely cited some rather extreme cases—extreme in the sense that the product images were obviously being created almost entirely on an evocative level of meaning far removed from any rational meanings. In these cases the art, the color, or the style were the symbolic avenues which gave the products an individuality, a desirability of subconscious association and depth. I would think that in any advertising, however, whether print, electronic, or outdoor, there is some proportion of meaning contributed by the elements of color, program content, and art, and even by the "bric-a-brac."

I don't think this is in any sense a sideshow effect. When radio and TV commercials are stating claims with catchy jingles, it is clearly evident that any individuality and certainly the most significant associations for the product are coming from the music, the rhythm, and the qualities of the girl's voice, not from the content of what is being said. "L & M—so good to your taste—so quick on the draw"—those words wouldn't build any individuality. But the other symbolic approaches do.

Chevrolet has very effectively been using the tone of the writing, the liveliness of the word imagery to infuse into the car personality qualities of vibrant power, getaway, and youthful fire. In 1956 Chevrolet cut into every competitor's share of the market by adding these associations to its personality. One advertisement starts: "Chevrolet's red hot hill-flatteners. See that fine fat mountain yonder. You can iron it out, flat as a flounder—and easy as whistling. Just point one of Chevrolet's special hill-flatteners at it—and pull the trigger. Barr-r-r-o-o-O-O-OM! Mister, you got a flat mountain!" The 1957 Chevrolet was introduced as "Sweet, Smooth and Sassy."

This has been the essence of the Buick strategy, which redefined this product image over a period of years so very successfully: a slangy, conversational style of writing to convey the flavor of an enthusiastic ordinary citizen bubbling about his car. "No wings—but a wing-ding take-off!" Four Roses whisky carved out a distinction for itself, a personality, with its very appealing artwork, picturing the roses in a cake of ice. Modess achieved a singularity in the consumer mind with the tone and style of its "Modess because . . ." campaign.

In spite of the fact that most lipsticks come from the same laboratory, Revlon surrounded its brand with a *femme-fatale* character. When another lipstick tried to use this approach, it simply helped Revlon sales, because the consumer assumed that it was Revlon being advertised. In other words, the mood by that time belonged to Revlon, as part of its product image.

4

These are some fairly rational, understandable ideas. But the whole point of this chapter is that the high desirability of many product images often rests on some nonrational effect which just can't be explained in any logical sense. In a study we did on soda crackers, many of the women with high brand loyalty couldn't tell the name of the product which they had been using for years; they could only describe the package or where it belonged on the grocer's shelf: "I buy the brand in the blue-bordered package with the little pixies on it."

The blueness of Cheer detergent, the very unpronounceability of Pall Mall and Schweppes are important elements in their personalities. Sometimes it is the mood of the advertising. More frequently it is some effect from the color, style, or illustration that no one could even try to explain. It might not be a recognizable quality at all.

This is the way humans make judgments about the character of others—by abstracting a few cues, which may be altogether irrelevant, and then filling in the rest. For instance, suburban home owners spend countless hours and dollars watering their lawns to keep them bright green. Why? Because the condition of the lawn may be taken to say what kind of people they are. A burned-out, brown lawn can be interpreted to mean that the owner is shiftless, eccentric, going down-hill, probably drinks too much. An ultramodern office building in New York has a uniqueness of personality because the elevator opera-tors are all redheads—some dyed and some natural. I ascribe countless associations of efficiency, modernity, smart-looking offices to this com-pletely irrelevant factor—the girl operators are attractive young red-heads.

A University of Chicago professor has recorded numerous voices of certain celebrities on tape and then scrambled the words so that they are unintelligible. Only the tone and the pitch are left. Yet students can identify not only the mood and the situation but also the person. The personalities are perfectly identifiable from this intangible fac-tor, the timbre of the voice.

All of us recognize certain voices over the telephone. As a matter of fact, we have probably all had the experience of talking to some unknown person over the phone—say, someone's secretary—and formu-lating a clear idea of what she is like entirely from the illogical fact that the sound of her voice injects certain meanings into our image of her. This is analogous to the manner in which we construct a product image so often from intangible, irrelevant symbols of which we may never be consciously aware.

This is a normal human mental process. We frequently notice it in children, who openly attribute character traits to altogether inanimate objects. A tree or a picture or a chair may be seen as friendly or omi-nous, serious or playful; words may have color and size. But although it is more openly evident in childhood—this tendency to fasten feelings onto objects—this translation of esthetic impressions and stray asso-ciations and subconscious sensitivities into meaning goes on at all ages.

In our studies to isolate product images, we always attempt to get at some of these shades of meaning. Besides the usual rationalistic approaches—comparing brands on many scales and devices for their recognizable qualities—we also try to probe for these dynamic mean-ings by providing some kinds of hitching post for the vague, unat-tached feelings about the product or institution which the individual has never tried to articulate. With the realization that we can never get at all these meanings because we can only guess at the areas to explore, we nevertheless in so many instances find the really significant elements of the product image in these never-expressed but very tangible attitudes.

In one case an extremely successful food advertiser was studied in several markets. On the rational level this company was not a particular standout. Several other competitors were considered its equal or even its superior in quality, value, and flavor. This was determined on scales wherein consumers were asked to ascribe to each line of products a long list of attributes, such as "freshness," "best quality," "best package," "best advertising," "best value," etc.

But on several other scales, people were presented with lists of dynamic meanings and quite irrelevant attributes and asked to make a choice of them just as if products, like people, had personalities. Of course, they demurred at the strangeness of the qualities, but we insisted that they make a choice. The results were very consistent. This company was far ahead of any other in such meanings as "generous," "inventive," "lively," sincere" and "heavy-set." How can any series of products be clearly established in consumer minds as having these attributes? The answer is that these were simply focal points for many feelings that people apparently like to associate with this type of food, carrying associations of fun, gaiety, a picnic in the dining room, up-to-dateness, lots of sprightly new ideas for serving. Even the quality "heavy-set" was associated with this food.

This was what was being communicated by the advertising; this was the product personality being molded by masses of color, a sprightly style of layout and art, and a pixie character. It was obvious that these facets of the image were contributing far more to its sales success than the usual, stereotyped rational attributes where the brand was not outstanding. It was very notable that this advertiser was outranked by his competitors in such converse meanings as "careful," "old-fashioned," "dignified," and "quiet," which were keys to qualities that the consumer didn't prize in this type of product.

Other studies have differentiated the brand personalities of shaving cream, instant coffee, toilet soaps, gasoline, department stores, and even newspapers along such areas of meaning as sex, age, weakness or strength, dumpy or smart, hard-working or fun-loving, ad infinitum. We ask people to say which newspaper smokes cigars or cigarettes, which ones are masculine or feminine, which ones are married or unmarried, which ones are tall or stocky, which ones are athletic or quiet. When one paper clearly is characterized as "unmarried" while all the others are "married," what are people trying to say? In this context, "unmarried" means having lots of fun forbidden to the others, going to places the others can't go to, knowing lots of inside, confidential information not known to the others. But it also means that the paper doesn't have the responsible, adult member-of-society maturity possessed by the ones seen as "married."

5

In the final analysis, advertising is a kind of primitive form of communication. It is not a highly complex exercise in reasoning; it is not comparable to a problem in mathematics. Rather, just as we go to the theater expecting to be lost in a world of fantasy, just as we expect to be entertained by pictures, so our awareness of advertising is a momentary suspension of disbelief. And what impressions are most likely to come through during this instantaneous receptivity? Word ideas, of course—whenever they are strikingly important. But just as in such images as Hathaway and Pall Mall and Marlboro, as Jell-O and Pepsi-Cola and Life Savers, very often the greatest singularity of character, the most significant elements in the brand image, the most product desirability will come from the unspoken, unformulated, intangible, nonrational meanings which are also a part of the communication.

My own belief is that when the advertiser rests his case entirely on rational approaches, not only is his product personality constricted and dull, but he always faces the danger that someone else can duplicate his product advantages—or at least duplicate his claim. Bayer aspirin built a big case on the fact that it dissolved faster than other brands. Then Bufferin says that it goes to work twice as fast as any aspirin. And Walgreen says that its aspirin dissolves faster and is less expensive. The product personality built on a claim which somebody else has surpassed is on thin ice.

But no one can duplicate the nonrational elements in the product image. No chain-store brand can duplicate "for less" the product which is rich in nonrational associations. No competitor can match the subjective overtones that belong to Cadillac or Toni or Seagram's 7 Crown simply by matching the physical product.

CHAPTER XIII

Style of Life

It has been difficult for many automobile executives to realize that the factors responsible for great sales successes in the 1930s—quality, comfort, dependability, low cost, and value—are no longer the paramount elements that people prize and seek in their cars.

It is likewise bewildering to railroad officials that Americans today are scarcely interested in the proud traditions of the railroads, their vital linkage with the history and development of their sections. Tradition bores us now. Instead of being an asset, it is virtually a liability to a people looking for the newest—the newest!—always the *newest*! Trademarks, packages, and advertising styles which are supposed to convey the dependability of tradition instead become cues that here is something old-fashioned, out of date, stodgy, and dull. Psychological obsolescence is the kiss of death.

Social observers are upsetting as they point to changes in our very life goals. Instead of accepting the middle-class ideals instilled in our society for centuries—hard work, thrift, self-reliance—now, as a nation, we lean on technological advancement and on somebody's pension plan for our individual futures.

In refashioning the editorial formula for our Sunday magazine, it was clearly apparent that the pattern of Sunday living has been radically transformed. Whereas it was formerly a day of austerity, worship, and serious thought, now, in metropolitan areas at least, it is a chaotic, lazy, planless period for relaxation, visiting relatives, working around the house, golf, and fishing.

These are merely a few of the multitudinous changes in our style of life. Every advertiser has to adjust to these shifts in emphasis, because unless his product is seen as fitting these new currents, unless the image can acquire some aspects of these changing directions in our tastes and beliefs, it can lose its desirabilities. Most of all the advertiser would like to present his product as capturing some expression of these new values, so that he can ride the crest of sales popularity. In Chapter 6, I indicated how much the automobile permits the individual to express the motives and tastes which have become paramount in our present style of life.

This concept means considerably more than a passing fad. It refers rather to the underlying social and psychological currents of our society, in so far as they become translated into a way of living for the individual. Our motive forces are not something that never changes. Social pressures on all of us bend us different ways, which can mean a constant rearrangement of our motives. In many alien societies, change is very slow. In contrast, our society has always been characterized by rapid change. And in the past decade, the tempo of change has become explosive, producing, in the opinion of some social scientists, greater transformation in our system of values since 1940 than in the previous 2,000 years of Western history.

Without trying to be completely definitive, it is important to highlight some of the most significant of these currents because our advertising has to operate within their limits. Pepsi-Cola was extremely successful in surrounding itself with an aura of gay, smart, airy sophistication by using a series of girls who epitomized the ideal woman of today, as well as a tone of copy which literally breathed lightness as opposed to high-calorie anything.

By contrast to the dismal deficits of railroad passenger operations, every airport is bulging with travelers, who see present air transportation and service as what they want in their style of living: excitement, adventure, super-up-to-dateness, efficient service from attractive, younger personnel, the company of other fashionable travelers like themselves, glamour, ultraspeed, a much smarter atmosphere around the terminals than is typical of railroad stations.

It is easy to document such obvious manifestations of change as the movement to the suburbs, bigger families, and the spread of color to many hitherto drab categories of merchandise. Now even conservative men wear sports shirts and beach clothes in gay colors and flowery patterns. We exhibit different preferences in foods, cars, furniture, and vacation spots. These are surface evidences of broad, sweeping shifts in the master motives of the society. With awareness that this social and psychological climate is not measurable, that its only documentation is its material evidence all around us, nevertheless here are some aspects of our changing style of life which are extremely revelant for advertising and merchandising.

1. *The Worship of Youthfulness.* In contrast to many societies wherein the elders and their way of life determine taste, ever since World War I Americans have held up youth as the ideal. Where

previously women had cultivated the body figures and the styles of maturity, now the teen-age-girl figure is the ideal—slight-breasted, long-legged, slim, and with a minimum of body curvature. The woman of forty or fifty dyes her hair, adopts a young-girl hair style, religiously avoids sugar and starches to retain her slimness, and in general tries to look like her teen-age daughter.

Many facets of male behavior bear the same stamp—the crew cut, going bareheaded, a certain amount of dieting—plus a great deal of youthful bravado and daring, such as penchants for sports cars and convertibles, trench coats, and so on. A very important part of Ford's image is its appeal for youngsters; so therefore older people want it. Worlds and worlds of older people in our society want to look young, to be considered young beyond the reality of their years. But few young people want to be considered old.

2. *The Trend to Casual, Informal Living as Opposed to Formality.* One observer believes that this is a consequence of the blue-collar worker's present affluence. Now that he has more money and is changing many patterns of living, he still doesn't buy a tuxedo. Informal clothes—sports shirts and slacks—are his present equivalent of his former habits of relaxing in his undershirt with no shoes on.

Regardless of origin, the trend to suburban living, the disappearance of servants, and many other drifts, such as the pressure for more leisure, have spread this casual informality all over our society. Its evidence is seen in many directions—station wagons, outdoor barbecue pits, buffet-style entertaining, home construction allowing space for game rooms by shrinking the dining room area. A study of psychological differences between downtown and neighborhood shopping showed that one of the dislikes for downtown shopping is that it is a formal situation. The woman can't go downtown in slacks or shorts as she can at a shopping center.

Extremely formal entertaining, the full-dress-suit situation, has practically disappeared from the American scene. Formal wear now includes comfortable shirts and shoes, with colorful jackets and bermuda shorts in summer. The point is that throughout modern urban America, all living has had to adjust to this desire for casual informality.

3. *The Wish for Individuation—Wanting to Be Different.* I described in Chapter 6 how throughout history, long periods of prosperity have generally permitted a flowering of self-indulgent motives. Today, as people no longer are worrying about bare-subsistence living, they look around for means to be individuals. No longer are there many distinctions in our society between the "haves" and "have-nots."

As the gap between the top and the bottom extremes of wealth has been narrowed, it is no longer possible to be different merely by exhibiting an automobile, a college education for one's children, a Florida vacation, or a home in the suburbs. Anyone can have those.

But we can be *different* in our tastes. This is the avenue now for individuation. Broadly we are still conformists; we aren't going to be driving scooters or going barefoot to be different. But within the limits of conformity, we can develop individualistic style in all areas of consumer wants to show our colorful, interesting personalities through our tastes. We look for pastel telephones, new models and new decors in our cars—some different beauty in any product, a certain luxury, a feature which can be talked about. The wish for attention which might be more repressed in hard times, is in full bloom today.

History has no record of hedonism on such a grand scale. Miles and miles of Miami Beach luxury hotels; the Las Vegas strip of desert inns, replete with nightclub-saloon atmosphere and gambling; the $200,000 private track built at Elkhart Lake, Wisconsin, by one enthusiast so that 200 starters can indulge their passion for amateur sportscar racing; the 35,000 hunters in Michigan registered for deer hunting with a bow and arrow—all these are symptomatic of this determination to buy things and go to places which might reflect individuality of taste.

4. *Much Greater Sophistication in Behavior.* Just as there is a physiological aging, so there is a sociological aging. Our society has outgrown the naïveté of the twenties and the thirties. When a South Carolina law prohibited libraries in that state from stocking books by Horatio Alger or about Tom Swift, Frank Merriwell, and the Rover Boys, a newspaper in a survey ascertained that no boy today bothers to read these fiction heroes of yesterday. The libraries didn't stock the books because youngsters snickered at them as incredibly out of date. Overviews of comic-strip readership reveal how many art treatments and thematic approaches which were successful years ago are ridiculed now. The freshly scrubbed girl in the Coca-Cola ads who reeked of hygiene and Victorian virtue has been replaced by exotic, sexy movie stars portrayed in exotic, supersophisticated settings.

There is a gulf in the levels of sophistication between generations. Where the car was treated with awe in the thirties and the radio was viewed as something which would interfere with driving, today some car radios turn on with the ignition key. Where the reader of yesterday could be impressed with advertising claims of miraculous cures, patched-up marriages, even business success from the use of some toothpaste or fountain-pen ink, now these approaches are scorned or yawned at. Much broader educational opportunities provided by, for example, the GI Bill, and world-wide travel in the wars, and the natural "growing up" in taste, accelerated by better communication facilities—these are factors leading to more sophistication in view-point. Even the mass man wants style in his furniture, style in his clothing—not just *a* pair of shoes, not just *any* car.

5. *Much Greater Interchangeability in Sex Roles.* Very definitely our notions about the concepts of masculinity have changed. For genera-tions the image of the pioneer man was predominant as the mass American man, exalting masculine strength, fighting ability, hard physical labor, and contempt for all intellectual and esthetic refine-ments. Today we put far more premium on earning a living with brains than with hands. More and more in industry, technicians are replacing the heavy labor group—a change which will be accentuated with automation.

The young wife today refuses to accept the structure of the patri-archal family, which relegated her to the role of a meek drudge and set up the husband as lord and master. The husband is no longer the head of the family; he's just another member of the family. In the typical younger family, the husband good-naturedly helps with shop-ping, baby sitting, and the difficult housecleaning. The suburban wife shovels snow, takes care of the family car, picks up lumber and paint, and pays the bills. Chicago's largest sports chain reports that one-third of all sports equipment is now bought by women. Every girl in urban society works until she gets married, and a sizable proportion permanently contribute to the family income. Consequently, there is a definite breaking down of the older masculine-feminine relationship and much more of a togetherness in the task of running a home, a certain dipping into and speaking acquaintance with each other's prerogatives.

The new generation of women borrow slacks and man-tailored shirts; cigarettes and the cocktail habit; various sports activities, like skiing and golf; and certainly more freedom and self-reliance. In our study of women's apparel habits in the suburbs, the house dress and the hausfrau are disappearing. Modern wives do their housework wearing some variety of men's pants. As co-manager of the home with a certain executive role, they act like men rather than delicate females.

With the passing of the pioneer man, men are borrowing color, which formerly was reserved for women, for their own sports clothes, their cars, their office equipment, even their furnaces. King-size cigarettes and fancy drinks are thought of as effeminate in psychological studies, but men never hesitate to use them when they want them. Men are also breaking down many other barriers to give play to various latent desires subdued in the pioneer society, where the words "dude" and "dandy" were common epithets to shame any man who used fancy clothes or toiletries. Males today are buying deodorants, hair tonics, scented shaving lotions, talcum powder. Toothpaste is partly a mouth freshener and breath sweetener.

6. *Leisure Activities as Opportunities for More Self-expression.* Money for money's sake is no longer the only goal for Americans. Time is becoming an important criterion—time for leisure, for off-job pursuits which now permit people greater measures with which to express themselves. We no longer make a god out of work. Union contracts press for longer vacations and holidays, for shorter work weeks as much as for income increases, giving even the mass man time to develop his hobbies and his urges to be creative. Actually, the person with the most time for leisure is the union-card holder, not the executive. One reason for the enormous spread of do-it-yourself activities is the fact that here is an outlet for creativity. When we asked amateurs about the motives in their purchases of lumber, paint, and tile, many of them said, "I like to work with my hands" or "I just like to make things."

Hobbies gratify the desire for individuation, but they also are channels for creativity. There is an overlapping of motive satisfactions, obviously. Because of the increased standardization of job performance, man does turn to hobbies as a means of preserving his individuality. High-fidelity record playing, photography, working with home power tools are ways of being different, of being *somebody*, of being more than just a face in the crowd. But they also gratify the inner drives to create.

The huge rise in participation sports while the spectator sports are declining is another evidence of this seeking for more self-expression. Such vogues as power boating, skiing, bowling, and pheasant shooting are merely different manifestations of the age-old desire of man to express his own inner surgings—the same impulses that make people draw pictures, sing, write things that will never sell, grow flowers, make speeches, work arduously for trade associations and luncheon clubs, and cultivate avocations.

7. *Seeking of New Adventure.* In every list of primary, elemental human motives, man's restlessness, his looking for new experiences, his curiosity is always included. The old habits, the routine patterns of living become boring. Listen to a tune three times, and you dislike it. Today, with his new resources and leisure, man goes looking for

adventure. Who cares for statistics on the safety of train travel? It's more fun to live dangerously. Buy yourself $60,000 of life insurance and travel by plane. Go to new places, look for new thrills, buy a faster car. Find adventure. Just don't live like a dull clod.

8. *Being Modern versus Being Old-fashioned.* The word "new" becomes ever more important as an attribute of things and places. I have elaborated this value previously: our passionate desire to have the very, very latest, just off the drawing boards. The newest must be the most exciting; and to a generation steeped in the never-ceasing marvels of technology, the newest somehow must be better. Nostalgia, looking backward, is a subtle mark of approaching retirement—for the people who scan obituaries to keep up with the doings of their friends. We have institutionalized change and innovation as part of our American way of life.

These drifts that I have sketched briefly are just some of the most evident changes in our present-day urban style of life; and in so far as I can see, they have a bearing on advertising. They are intangible, they are difficult to study concretely; but clearly they exert tremendous influence on our behavior, including our buying behavior. As we build associations for the images of our brands, our products, our stores, our organizations, our symbols have to be reconcilable with the currents acting as master motives in American life today.

CHAPTER XIV

Class Is Open for Discussion

When observers of the American scene speak of the tremendous effects of the social revolution experienced by our society since the 1940s, I think that they should mention that these are coincidental with and partly following in the wake of the huge economic gains of the American worker classes. Previously national advertising had often ignored the existence of the Mass Man, bemusing itself with vari-colored charts proving that he lived in a virtual vacuum of no purchases. But now the evidence of the blue-collar worker's buying ability is overwhelmingly apparent, and advertising is consciously aware that here is an exciting potential which in many areas requires an education of taste, a definite steering of wants and preferences into new directions.

As we assume the responsibility of bringing the power of advertising to bear on this problem, there are many traditional beliefs that call for reexamination in the light of social science findings.

1. The "snob-appeal" theory says that if you sell the top of society, your task is complete. Inasmuch as all the other echelons are eager to copy the tastes and the foibles of the elite, the use of your product will quickly trickle down to all classes. But now there is a considerable body of research which indicates that infinitely the most influence spreads horizontally, not vertically. While there may be a trickling down in some areas, such as fashion, this is a very slow process. And many products and habits will never trickle down.

2. Advertising proceeds on the thesis that once an exposure has been achieved, there are no intervening factors between the individual and the message. But people are linked into groups. They seldom act in an atomistic sense, without regard for the standards of their friends, their job associates, their social class. I wouldn't suddenly decide as an individual to wear a monocle or to go to work in a top hat, because then I would not be conforming to the habits and tastes of my class.

So there *is* an intervening factor between the mass communication and the audience—one's group, or class, and its standards.

3. We assume that we can make judgments about the best appeals and methods to reach the working-class family in the light of our own outlook on the world, because "after all, aren't all men basically alike?" But any probing on the subject reveals that there very often are sharp differences in attitudes and motive forces, in codes, and even in communication abilities between social classes. An awareness that there is a definite social-class system operating in America is important for the advertiser so that he doesn't forget that he himself is generally looking at the world from a middle- or upper-class standpoint.

On the basis of a three-year study of the social structure of metropolitan Chicago, under the guidance of Lloyd Warner of the University of Chicago, a population breakdown of Chicago today, which is probably typical of a big industrial city, was derived:

1. *Upper Class—0.9 Per Cent.* These are the old families and the socially prominent new rich. These have been the traditional leaders in the American community. This is the group to which most manufacturers and top advertising-agency executives belong. But they represent less than 1 per cent of the population.

2. *Upper Middle Class—7.2 Per Cent.* These are the successful businessmen and professionals and the best salesmen. These two groups constitute the "quality market." Every advertising professional speaks from the viewpoint and the tastes and the codes of these groups. And yet, combined, groups 1 and 2 are only 8.1 per cent of the population.

3. *Lower Middle Class—28.4 Per Cent.* This is the white-collar class—small tradesmen, office workers, teachers, technicians, most salesmen. The American moral code and aspirational system has come from this class. This is the most conforming, churchgoing, morally serious part of the society.

We speak of America as a middle-class society; but the middle-class value system stops here. Two-thirds of the society are *not* middle-class.

4. *Upper Lower Class—44.0 Per Cent.* These are the factory production workers, the union-labor groups, the skilled workers, the service workers—and also the politicians and union leaders who would lose their power if they moved out of their class.

5. *Lower Lower Class—19.5 Per Cent.* This group includes the unskilled laborers, racial immigrants from other parts of the country, and people in nonrespectable occupations.

This awareness of social structure in a typical metropolitan area is highly significant. It is only human nature that we should exaggerate the importance of our own class viewpoint. But we account for such a small part of the total population. We must realize that between us and the vast majority of the market there are differences in communication skills, differences in moral viewpoint, differences in what constitutes humor, differences in sophistication, differences in the very reception of advertising itself. The symbols we use for communication are often completely meaningless to the class we are trying to sell.

In our study of beer advertising, we researched one campaign which was built around a fox hunter associated with the name of the product. This character appeared in every ad, clad in full costume: red coat, tiny patent-leather boots, velvet cap. But the audience representing the predominant market for the product had no idea what this symbol was supposed to mean. Never having seen his like even in illustration, they reacted to him as simply a repugnant unknown. Testimonials by intellectuals and Broadway stage stars similarly had no meaning to the social classes who had utterly no acquaintance with the legitimate theater or the fine arts.

Earlier I mentioned the department store study wherein women correctly and instantly assessed store personality from the physical appearance and the style of newspaper advertising. In this case the symbols were familiar to all classes. But from these nonrational cues, the women made intuitive judgments as to whether they would fit or be out of place in such an atmosphere. Regardless of her ability to pay, each individual wants to feel that she will be "comfortable." If the store is too high-style, the blue-collar worker's wife's sixth sense tells her that she will be subtly humiliated by the clerks and other customers because she is out of her depth classwise. "The kind of people you would see in that store are ritzy and wear furs" is her comment, expressive of her tone of uneasiness and defensive hostility.

Frequently I have heard brilliant advertising women speak on the subject of how to appeal to women. I question seriously how well these women, all of them with at least an upper-middle-class background, are really qualified to speak for the factory worker's wife. On some things, of course, they will have similar viewpoints. But on countless other issues they are poles apart because they just express different worlds. I don't think that any man is qualified to speak for all classes of men, even though, as a result of army or navy experience, sports, and job contacts, the average man does have far more opportunity than a woman to brush shoulders with people up and down the social scale. A woman is much more sheltered classwise.

I heard one copy director state that she wrote every ad as if it were addressed to herself. The question she always asked was, "Will this really appeal to me?" But every woman does not have her Vassar background, her daily association with a highly sophisticated atmosphere, her upper-class value system. In one of the classic studies in symbolic analysis of mass communication, Warner and Henry explored the daytime radio serial, scornfully ridiculed by the sophisticated as "soap opera." Yet the study clearly pointed up the tremendous appeal which these serials have for the mass-audience woman, embodying as they do many of her basic beliefs about the scheme of things.

In our motivation study on soaps and detergents, we asked women to state the first thing which came into their minds when we said the word "baby." Middle-class women said "darling," "sweet," or "mother," which I would have thought was typical for all women. But the bottom half of the market, which does not use diaper services and extra help, turned up with such reactions as "pain in the neck," "more work," "a darling but a bother."

2

Each human is motivated by various compulsive forces within him—certain biological urges and certain acquired wants—to realize numerous goals. But the yardsticks for evaluating the worth of these goals are supplied by group pressures. Other people have to validate our choices. The things we buy and do that offer the most satisfaction are those which are also valued by our friends, our groups, our class. Very rarely do our actions, our attitudes, or our purchases run counter to the approved tastes of those around us. The penalty for nonconformity is literally ostracism. An imposing list of studies points out that those who do not accept group standards have few friends, little influence, and much anxiety. After all, what is the essence of society's punishment through imprisonment? It means solitary confinement—separation from other people.

Conformity has far deeper significance than good-natured acquiescence. The group and the class literally demand conformity of their members. Social scientists point out that what society does when it shapes the individual is to insist most of all that he learn how to look at life with the set of glasses that it prescribes. And as a psychological necessity he has to anchor himself to some group setting up demanding measures of conformity.

Social class is the modern world's substitute for the medieval feudal system. While America is a political democracy and while theoretically all men are equal in the eyes of the law, yet realistically we observe a very definite social-class order. The friends we choose, the neighborhoods we live in, the way we spend and save our money, the educational plans we have for our children are determined in large degree along social-class lines. A rich man is not just a poor man with more money. He probably has different ideals, different personality forces, different church membership, and many different notions of right and wrong, all largely stemming from social-class differentials. With its disciplinary pressures of approval and disapproval, belonging versus ostracism, social class is a major factor shaping the individual's style of life. Inevitably it is a powerful determinant of economic behavior.

The American is uncomfortable in discussions of status expression, because our system very definitely is contradictory in this area. Our ideology insists that we stress equality and the similarity of everyone on the one hand; yet without ever bringing it out in the open, we sense that there are people above us and below us on some kind of a scale. It is extremely important to the individual that he be identified correctly where he belongs. However, rather than face up to the existence of this contradiction between the ideal of equality and the concrete fact of social difference, we prefer to look the other way.

While we sneer at the "social climber," mostly this is because he is too openly employing symbols of a class in which he doesn't really belong yet. "Snob appeal" is another derogatory term, which implies that one class is buying and behaving in a way which will recognizably set it off from the rest of the population. But actually every class level is doing exactly the same thing with its own habits of consumption. Certainly we all need food and shelter and clothes; but a very important quality in the things we select to fulfill our wants is the symbolic meaning of the products in regard to status expression.

Every class in America today indulges in conspicuous consumption. Precisely because our system to a certain extent is fluid, we are anxious to use ways and means that will say where we fit on the ladder. As stated by Barber and Lobel, the primary index of a man's social class (and also that of his wife and dependent children) is his occupation. One of the most important ways, although not the only way, to rate occupations is by money income. In general we make this quick evaluation: spending equals income; income equals occupational position; occupational position equals social-class position; so therefore, habits of spending and consumption equal social-class position.

Women take their position from men: wives from husbands, unmarried girls from their fathers. So the things that a woman buys put on the record her household's ability to pay, and accordingly the family's class position. However, while we in advertising are an extremely mobile group and though we do everywhere see cases of successful upward movement, nevertheless it should be stated that the vast majority of people live and die within the boundaries and the tastes of their own class.

Our research would seem to indicate that only about 15 per cent of metropolitan Chicago families could be called "upward-mobile"— that is, notably trying to break their class ties and move upward. This factor of social mobility is doubled in the upper middle class (31 per cent), but this is all it amounts to in the total population—15 per cent.

3

I hesitate to labor this subject of social class, except to emphasize that highly significant differences can exist in product areas within this dimension which can block any real communication. Most people of our background cherish the happy illusion that all segments of society are hungrily anxious to copy our patterns of living. This isn't true at all. Studies that we have done in Chicago show that other classes in one area after another have different tastes than we do, different preferences—that our likes and dislikes may be no straws in the wind at all in their own choice making.

In a very broad exploration of lamp styles, furniture styles, and home styles, it came out that the lower half of the market selected completely different styles than the top half did. They did not want the modern ranch homes and the two-story colonial homes. They didn't want the severely plain, functional styling of furniture preferred by the top segment of the market. They have different ways of saving, different ideas about life insurance, different grocery-food chains for shopping.

The study by Barber and Lobel that I mentioned previously delineates how social-class differences determine the definition of women's fashions, based on very clear distinctions in the phrasing of the fashion themes that are used in fashion copy, both editorially and in advertising.

1. In the "old-money" families at the top of the system, women may even maintain a certain independence of current changeful fashion. Their clothes can remain roughly the same for several years. The taste of these women is more British than French, running to tweeds and woolens and avoiding the "daring" which is characteristic of French styling. Ads appealing to this taste stress adjectives like "aristocratic," "well-bred," and "distinguished."

2. In the class just below—the women of newer but often greater fortunes, the level of "high fashion," the Paris-conscious style leaders—

clothes symbols are related to wealth and high living rather than to family background. These women seek to combine opulence with quiet elegance. They must spend a great deal on clothes but must appear not to have done so. Fashion copy for them stresses the pose of inbred superiority, and the adjectives revolve around "chic" and "sophistication." But the word "glamour" is never used, because "glamour" is cheap.

3. In the middle and lower classes, fashion has a different meaning. There is distaste for high style, for the daring. Paris styles are characterized as too extreme. Respectability is the standard, not breeding or effect. "Smart" is the right word, and "smart" means what everyone in the same social class is wearing. Hollywood stars are appropriate models rather than socially prominent, sophisticated style leaders, because they exemplify "glamour," which actually boils down to "femininely pretty."

The lack of growth of the perfume industry has been attributed to the fact that most of the advertising shows no awareness that such antithetical views can exist classwise. Not only are the French associations altogether meaningless to the "mass-audience" housewife, but the openly suggestive allusions to sex are repugnant to her moral codes—even though the same advertising may be amusing and appealing to a more sophisticated audience. I merely cite this as a concrete illustration of why we in advertising should constantly remind ourselves that our own individual beliefs and insights are reflective of *one* class viewpoint—a viewpoint which may not be typical of the total population at all.

4

Let us next consider a few studies which have no direct relation to advertising but which show how far these social-class cleavages can extend.

1. Part of the American ideology is that important occupational positions are not only inherited through the wealth of one's parents but can be achieved. But achievement depends on two factors: the motivation to reach the goal, and the possession of abilities. Achievement of most higher positions today requires a certain amount of formal education. One can't be a doctor or a lawyer or an engineer without advanced education.

But from a number of studies on occupational goals, Hyman shows that the lower-class individual actually is lacking in the motivation both to advance to higher position and to obtain the training which is necessary for and instrumental to economic advancement. He just doesn't put the same value on higher education. He doesn't aspire to the same dollar level. When he thinks of higher positions, he singles out such careers as politics and entertainment—and even distasteful but lucrative occupations like undertaking, offering less competition and therefore better opportunity for success. He doesn't correctly appraise the dynamics of upward movement. Rather than education, his formula for advancement mistakenly includes such courses as changing religion or moving to another city.

2. In one study of communication abilities between the lower and middle classes, Schatzman and Strauss found striking differences in their very modes of thinking. This study is based on lengthy interview documents sampling the population in several Arkansas communities struck by storms and reveals how people in different classes described what happened.

a. They differed in the number and kinds of perspectives. Whereas the middle-class individual, in relating the story of what happened to someone else, is like a movie director, controlling several cameras as he shoots a scene, the lower-class individual is a single camera, seeing a scene only through his own eyes.

b. The middle-class individual connects and explains his background to the listener to be sure that he is understood. But the lower-class person doesn't bother, so that various interviews were baffling and unintelligible because of the dreamlike sets of disconnected images.

c. In classifying events and people, the lower-class individual is rudimentary and concrete, whereas middle-class thought and speech readily falls into abstract categories.

d. The lower-class person does not give well-organized or tightly knit pictures of events. Some literally cannot tell a straight story or describe a simple incident coherently. By contrast, the middle-class individual can elaborate a theme by departing from it while yet holding it in mind, incorporating multiple perspectives.

e. Whereas the lower-class individual can only describe motives of people within a narrow range, middle-class richness of thinking shows familiarity with a host of distinct reasons for performing particular acts, allowing activities to be defined and described in a great variety of ways.

3. On the basis of research carried on by the division of psychiatry of the University of California Medical School, Dr. Jurgen Ruesch points out that class membership as such seems to be related to disease. Because the middle class characteristically follows be-

havior patterns of excessive conformity and repressive tendencies, the only possible solution for unsolved psychological conflicts seems to be in physical-symptom formation, which means the standard physiological diseases and psychosomatic reactions (ulcers, hypertension, allergies, etc., and a long list of physical disturbances which often are definitely related to emotional problems).

In the lower classes, where expression of anger is permitted and where there is much less conformity to the dominant American value system (which essentially is the lower-middle-class value system), the disease patterns are of a different shape. They are connected with exposure to machines and conduct disorders, as shown in a much higher per cent of fractures and other accidents and diseases resulting therefrom.

On the other hand, in upper-class families, with their overbearing consciences and dedication to family traditions, there is a relatively large incidence of insanity and neurotic conditions. Dr. Ruesch also states that there is a predictable relationship between the people who are moving up or down the social scale and various disease frequencies. The terrific need for achievement among the climbers often leads them into situations which their emotional make-up cannot master, so that there is an unusually high frequency of psychosomatic conditions. The socially declining individual, on the other hand, seldom shows these reactions. He takes out his bitterness over what is happening to him very often in alcoholism.

4. In addition to the wealth of research pointing to distinctions between the middle and lower classes, McArthur has made discerning contrasts between the middle- and upper-class personalities and values.

The middle-class family is steeped in the classic American success story, teaching its sons that they must surpass the father. It is the hopes of the mother that these sons must realize in order to feel successful. They are naturally drawn close to their mother, and it is her teachings that they absorb—so much so that there is a danger that the son may doubt his own manhood. Our "sissy complex" surprises foreign observers. But the American family has so consistently devalued the father that the son often has difficulty learning to be a male. After college, the son is automatically expected to leave the family, establish a new family, and move upward.

But upper-class life, as exemplified by the old New England families, creates none of these situations. The son accepts the father as his model, and any notion of surpassing the father is quite meaningless. He knows that he can't. He often has inferiority feelings as a result. There is no pressure on him to break away and establish his own, independent family. He isn't going to get independence by achieving success, because his family already has it. If he dreams of running off, it is to be happy or to find spiritual fulfillment—not to be successful or rich, because he already has these goals.

The middle-class boy sees college as a road to success, whereas to the upper-class individual it is a gentleman's club, wherein his grades have nothing to do with his future. Such avenues to the top as law, medicine, and engineering hold no allure for him because he has no incentive for the long, arduous study required. The incentives are success and position, and he already has them. In contrast to the great middle-class drive for achievement, the upper-class son thinks of management of family business affairs or of such activities as philanthropy.

In various tests which required stories, middle-class boys at some point invariably talked about work. The heroes they described worked for three reasons—ambition, desire for independence, and desire for self-realization. This last reason was the only meaning of work for the upper-class boy. His thinking was uninvolved with work. More often he wrote stories in which nobody worked at all.

5

These diverse areas of study demonstrate how striking the implications of social class can be, although it rarely occurs to any individual that they exist. Each of us absorbs the ideology and morality of his background so thoroughly that it never dawns on him that somebody else has a different system of standards. But we in advertising have to be aware of the possibility of different standards if we expect to communicate across classes.

The worker classes have become not only the center of political power but a center of purchasing power—probably, from sheer weight of numbers, *the* center of purchasing power. This is one of the problem areas of advertising—learning how to communicate more effectively with this Mass Man. The failure of such institutional efforts as the business-inspired campaign to sell the free-enterprise system would seem to indicate that advertising has much to learn on this score. It is simply class egotism to think that the Mass Man is eager to ape our tastes and preferences. He certainly follows his own mind politically.

It is important to grasp that there are profound psychological differences and therefore motivational differences between lower status and middle-class individuals.

CHAPTER XV

A Store Is More than a Store

In previous chapters I have emphasized the problems and the basic advertising goals of the brand advertisers. But here I would like to show the application to retailing—and to any institution, like a bank or service firm, for that matter—of many of these principles that come from a different understanding of advertising. Without trying to lay down any set of finalities or laws, I merely wish to indicate how many of these concepts very definitely do have fruitful meaning for the retailer—the notion of the store personality or image as a critical factor in the buyer's mind; advertising as a symbolic message which is saying many more things about the store than the literal meaning of the words; the importance of an awareness of the consumer as a dynamic organism, responsive to infinitely more appeals and pressures than bargains alone.

Immersed in the hurly-burly of day-to-day expediencies and driven by an obsessive compulsion to surpass last year's same-day-same-month sales figures, the retailer feels that he does not have the luxury of time for introspection and intellection. He sees himself only as a merchant whose success depends on his intuitive ability to detect buying trends and to supply this wanted merchandise at the lowest price. Even though it is perfectly clear that all people are not shopping all the time for just the cheapest things available, by far the greatest bulk of retail advertising trumpets, "Values!" "Bargains!" "Savings!" "Sale!" "Discounts!" as if this were the only function of advertising.

Most merchants do virtually nothing creative to materialize or accelerate buying currents, whether for casual clothes, wrought-iron furniture, or low-calorie foods. The demand either exists, or it doesn't as far as they are concerned—even though in many instances the categories of goods which they sell are severely affected. When the consumer spends more of his dollar on automobiles and homes and vacation travel, then he spends less on many other items like jewelry, apparel, chinaware.

173

Some observers argue that when the retailer does not fulfill any creative function, he must give up part of his margins. If the manufacturer has to carry the entire burden of educating the public, then the retailer performs no more function than the discount house or the supermarket. But if the retailer does intend to fulfill any creative merchandising, a better understanding of consumer motivations is just as useful as it would be to the manufacturer.

The men's-apparel industry has been actively trying to promote greater sales for its field by creating more awareness of style changes among men. But it is confronting a powerful symbolism involved with clothes which cannot be altered merely by wishful thinking and energetic words. A large proportion of home-improvement and home-decoration projects are initiated by the woman, but the traditional retailers who sell building materials haven't the slightest idea how to interest the woman or how to invest their stores with any of the rich associations that people have for their homes.

In another sense it should be important for any retailer to establish a better "feedback" with his customer body. In communication this means the return flow of ideas and opinions. What do your customers actually think of you? Are you merely offering bargains, without any consideration of the total picture of the store? What about the store personality? In virtually every area we have studied, we find the biggest discrepancies imaginable between what the company thinks of itself—the image it believes it is presenting to the public—and the way the consumer actually sees it. Very much advertising and merchandising are merely projections of the store executives. The final result has minimum relationship to the way the customer sees the store.

We have made several studies of these retail-store images, and besides the sharp differences in rational attributes which emerge, there are also crucial differences in the subtle but nonetheless tangible colorations and associations attached to the stores. One of the major mail-order chains talks about expanding its market upward, attracting the middle-class customer. Yet when the ads from stores of this chain were tested in three different cities where women did not know their actual identity, in every case the stores were seen as having strictly a lower-class appeal. Regardless of executive aspirations, the advertising symbols very clearly said, "This is a lower-class store." In other cases where the store owners described their market as being simply good, solid, middle-class people, the advertising style created an impression of dullness, lack of excitement, stodginess, no glamour, no fun in shopping.

Conversely, at the top extreme a store can convey an impression of itself as being so extremely upper-class as to frighten away even the middle-class housewife. If the store is cultivating an atmosphere of exclusiveness, this is well and good. But if it ever does hope to broaden its base, it should recognize that its symbols of extremely high fashion and upper-class atmosphere are literally warning the middle-income and lower-income woman that she will be out of place here, that the other customers and certainly the clerks will make her feel altogether uncomfortable.

For all of the retailer's remarks that his advertising is measured strictly in terms of immediate sales, that he has no intention of wasting his expenditures in high-sounding institutional advertising which convinces nobody, it is perfectly clear that every ad he runs is an institutional ad. Whether he realizes it consciously or not, all of his advertising is creating an image of his store. One of the most important functions in the housewife's role is to know the stores. She learns to single out certain cues in the advertising which will tell her about the store's status, its sense of styling, its policies on returns and credit, its general atmosphere, its customer body, even its physical qualities; and then she decides intuitively whether this is where she fits in. Far more than by any explicit claims about the store by the store, her intuitive judgments are formulated by the nonrational symbols: the type, the whiteness or fullness of the ad, the general tone, the sophistication of the art—in other words, by the totality of advertising style.

To show the almost fantastic sensitivity of the urban woman to these cues in the advertising, here is a comparison from the study by Social Research, Inc., of a leading Kansas City store's copy which was tested both in Kansas City and in Atlanta (see page 176). The evaluations by women who had no idea of the identity of the store and who were making their judgments entirely from the physical appearance of the copy provides an almost perfect match with the evaluations of women who did know the store personally.

Purely from the symbolic cues in the newspaper advertising of other stores, women made these penetrating comments about the various facets of store personality:

"I am not averse to bargains, but I wouldn't trust that store."

"I imagine if you took something back, they would want to give you something in exchange and not give you the cash. You would have to fight for the cash."

"The clerk standing there would be an immigrant, not enjoying selling. She probably could just barely speak English. You would go there and stand in front of the pile, and she would have a blank look. Then I would give her $5 and it would take her hours to make the change.

Half the time she would give the wrong change. It would be impossible."

"You would need to be careful and shop for bargains carefully. Maybe it would be better to get it at a quality store anyway. I am afraid a store like this would take advantage of my ignorance on some things."

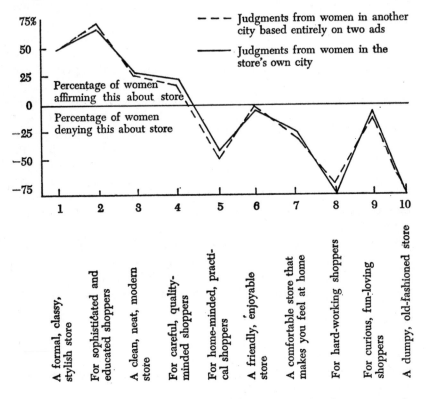

"This kind of store doesn't give people credit for knowing style. They would have the same kind of junk they tried to pass off ten years ago."

Sometimes the big retailer feels that he is presenting different facets of himself because he runs different kinds of copy—sale ads, high-fashion ads, institutional ads. But his individual style comes through in every ad. Just as writers and artists point out that the style is the man, that certain consistent elements are present in all his work to make it recognizable as peculiarly his own, so is this true about retail advertising. I am the same person whether I wear a blue suit or a gray suit or pajamas. Just so is the store's character distinguishable, whether it is running a traffic ad on housewares or an apparel ad testing the reception of certain new fashions.

I know of a mass department store which decided that it would have to "tone up" its copy to keep up with its market. Now that the "bottom" of the market has more income and can afford better things, this store felt that its advertising should be dressed up also to give a different impression of the store. But even the new, toned-up copy gave precisely the same image.

Of course, the import of all this is that the image preselects the customer body. By far the most part of any store's volume comes not from the advertised specials but rather from day-to-day buying, where the customer goes to the store whose over-all personality seems most appropriate to her. She isn't going to risk having the labels of stores which are completely antithetical to her self-conceptions and style of life. If she is a middle-class woman, she isn't going to patronize stores that her friends consider cheap and gaudy—even though the store offers tempting savings in its advertising. And on the other hand, she isn't going to reach too high either, for then she will be open to criticism of being extravagant and putting on airs. And furthermore, within herself, she senses that she will probably be embarrassed and subtly humiliated by the clerks, who will realize that she is out of her depth.

It is also important to realize that the store's advertising has to correspond roughly to its actual personality as shoppers know it to be in reality—or it isn't effective. Curiously, this works both ways. It is easy to see that if a promotion store started high-style advertising completely out of character, it would be ridiculed.

But here is a documented case study on the other side of the problem—when the style of advertising didn't measure up to the customer image of the better store. The furniture buyer in one of Chicago's top department stores clipped a mattress ad from some "borax store" and insisted that it be run just as it was—"Factory warehouse clearance! Fourteen carload special purchase drives prices to new lows for this quality bedding!" The illustration showed flatcars piled up with mattresses; the type effect was black and overpowering. Yet the ad did very poorly—although the same promotion the previous year in the store's own advertising style had done very well. Although the furniture buyer himself was mystified, the heads of the store felt that this was a very concrete demonstration that the phraseology and style associated with "borax operators" and promotion stores were completely ineffective for their own customer body. The advertising was altogether out of character with the store personality.

2

In no sense am I saying that a store cannot change its image, that it must always be stuck with the same tag. Not at all. But just as in brand advertising, this image has to be changed *gradually*. The advertising has to be within believable limits. And I think that the elements of change will be conveyed far more effectively by nonrational symbols than they ever will be by direct claims. Retailers have sensed the ineffectiveness of orthodox institutional advertising, realizing that a hollow parade of words about friendliness, courtesy, service, quality, and value is just that—hollow. Retailers are so bound to price-and-item thinking that they have not become facile enough with nonrational effects so that they can use them consciously in their advertising. Yet even as the customer is reading the ad on luggage or leather-top tables, she is unconsciously scrutinizing the copy for the deeper cues about the store itself—tiny illustrations of clothing racks, words about "discount," store hours, how much white space is used, how much fantasy is in the art.

There are uneven viewpoints about different kinds of merchandise, as a matter of fact. The woman who is perfectly satisfied to buy children's clothes or a girdle for herself in one store might never think of buying a dress or a coat there. The Sears label may be perfectly acceptable for some things and not acceptable for others at all.

Let me mention the case of Chicago's second-largest department store, which used advertising so very successfully as the instrument for changing the store personality as well as for selling merchandise. As part of changing the store's basic directions, the Carson, Pirie, Scott management realized it had to change the store personality— not by saying out loud what it hoped to convey, but by using indirection and symbolic approaches. The advertising managers consciously set about establishing new psychological overtones for the store by art, tone, copy, layout, character of items featured, and livelier public relations events, such as a dairy show. Instead of subdued, discreetly quiet art, the store now uses stronger black, white, and gray contrasts. There is more humor, more conversational flavor in the copy itself. By these indirect methods the advertising has conveyed that the store is 100 years *young*; that it has broadened its price base but is still a high-style store; that it is friendly and humanized; that it is a leader and not a follower; that it is active, busy, exciting; that its future is integrated with the future of Chicago. In just about three years, without spending any larger per cent for advertising, this approach very sharply changed the store's sales directions and share of

European poster art is nonverbal communication at its best. The meaning, the impact, the over-all effect of the communication comes thru without words. Furthermore, in contrast to our habitual seriousness and caution, this advertising is casual and enjoyable. It is not self-consciously and earnestly seeking for acceptance as is so much American advertising art.

Delightful and imaginative, this poster tradition epitomizes the fact that other avenues to human persuasion do exist besides our American emphasis on verbalism and functional qualities. (*Printed in Italy by ENIT, Courtesy Italian State Tourist Office*)

In addition to merchandise offerings, each retail ad is actually an institutional ad. The mere physical appearance—art, style, typography, layout—are saying very eloquently what kind of store it is. The shopper doesn't heed the values unless the store intangibles are also attractive to him.

This Chicago department store very successfully changed its sales and profit picture by changing its store image. By style of advertising, it molded a different personality.

This New York retailer doesn't use any price offerings. It relies entirely on an off-beat style of advertising to create a very attractive set of store meanings. By combining bizarre situations and sophisticated tone, the advertising conveys smartness and value. These elements say everything. They invest lower-price merchandise with a Park Avenue atmosphere.

department store sales by infusing these different meanings into the store's public image.

I mentioned how Ohrbach's in New York used sophistication of ad ideas and the physical appearance of its copy to alter its store personality. Marshall Field in Chicago for years has made certain that a definite share of its advertising effort is not item-and-price but rather goes entirely in the direction of building character and atmosphere for the store.

Jewel Food Stores in Chicago do a volume of well over 200 million dollars annually, and they also consciously devote part of their advertising to conveying character. Jewel for years has maintained psychologists as staff consultants, who pointed out that a big food store is much more than merely a place to pick up carrots and soap. Over the years the store has formulated a management policy that a definite share of the advertising should try consciously to say that Jewel stores are friendly places to shop; that the people in the stores are personable, helpful, interested human beings; that the stores are doing their best to offer the finest produce and meat and frozen foods; that they want to help the woman in her job as a housewife; that the stores are "clean and white."

3

By no means is price the core of every woman's definition of the shopping situation. A study of typical grocery advertising revealed that while most shoppers do read price listings, or at least feel that they should, and that 10 per cent of them do so religiously, most women follow prices for other psychological reasons than to act on them. They want to keep posted on the market, to get ideas for menus, to convince themselves that their favorite store is the right store, to do some mental preshopping.

Another study done for Sears, Roebuck set out to explore customer receptivity in the area of one of their biggest volume stores. Women were asked, "Would you rather do business with local independent merchants or with large chain stores? Why? What other advantages or disadvantages does each kind of store have? What about the personnel? Does it make any difference to you about clerks?" Then there were a great many other questions about neighborhood versus downtown shopping, qualities expected of store people, attitudes toward various types of store for specific merchandise, etc.

It was immediately apparent that different women defined the shopper's role in altogether different dimensions. Their definitions were related to such factors as richness of the shoppers' lives, social class, frustration, ambition. Those women who represented the counterpart of the Economic Man accounted for only a third of the shopping population: those who were extremely sensitive to price, quality, and assortment of merchandise; who were deeply interested in efficient, impersonal shopping; who regarded shopping as primarily a buying situation, in which behavior was directed solely to the purchase of goods. These were mostly younger, active, ambitious women who clearly expected their families to move upward in the world.

But almost as big a group—28 per cent—were women who defined the shopping situation as fundamentally social. They personalized and individualized the customer role in the store—"I shop where they know my name." Strong personal attachments were formed with store clerks and managers, and this personal relationship was far more important than purely economic factors. This type shopped least in the downtown area, least in the department store, least in the chain store. They were women who had moved to this area from other parts of Chicago, so that their close friends were not immediately available, and store personal fulfilled an important substitutive role. Even though we think of food chains as quite impersonal, these women do make friends with butchers, checkout girls, and managers.

In spite of the drift toward automatic retailing and the devaluation of sales clerks, it is important to note that personalization is just exactly what many customers want. Batten, Barton, Durstine and Osborn advertising agency did a national study in which 3,000 men and women were asked to complete the sentence, "If I were a department store owner . . ." 62 per cent of these people talked about personnel—far more than talked about appearance of the store, merchandise, or service. 50 per cent mentioned courtesy and friendliness.

We did a pilot study exploring attitudes between department stores and specialty stores, whence the depersonalization of the department store emerged as the primary finding. From a variety of psychological approaches, people clearly reveal that they believe department stores far superior in reliability, better prices, better selection, better bargains. Yet they overwhelmingly characterize them as giving little personal attention (82 per cent) and unfriendly (59 per cent). Paradoxically, customers say that department stores have more liberal return policies, easier credit, and far greater willingness to make adjustments—and yet they are more unfriendly. Apparently the department store has so institutionalized these policies which are supposed to make friends that they only achieve a dutiful respect and not any personalized feeling.

Department stores were seen as big, crowded places with poor service, in large part because of the clerks. For example, when we asked people to finish the incomplete sentence, "Department store clerks . . . ," too often they said, literally or in effect, ". . . act as if they're doing you a favor to wait on you." To another incomplete sentence, "Department stores would be better places to shop . . . ," the completions repeatly said, ". . . if their clerks were friendlier."

In trying to determine why one of Chicago's quality department stores had been so very successful in attracting Negro customers, our research invariably came up with the same answer: "X store is friendlier." No one ever mentioned bargains or savings. The store did not challenge their very shaky self-concepts.

These psychological factors also turn up in the question of neighborhood and suburban shopping versus downtown shopping. There are many other elements involved besides just transportation. The neighborhood center emerges far ahead of the downtown area in friendliness (74 per cent versus 26 per cent) and informality (95 per cent versus 5 per cent). The women overwhelmingly see downtown shopping as a formal situation, as demanding much more from them psychologically. The demands begin with preparations to be made, clothing to be worn, the institutional atmosphere to be matched, unfriendly clerks to cope with.

Inasmuch as the pronounced trend to informality and casual wear is so evident, these evaluations of downtown department store shopping as too formal and unfriendly become important in a negative sense. The housewife who has become accustomed to doing her neighborhood shopping in comfortable glamour pants and loafers can't go downtown this way. The woman in the more evident stages of pregnancy who feels no embarrassment in her local shops would think twice about being "on exhibition" in the formal downtown situation.

On the other hand, there are psychological attractions in the downtown area which have not been exploited properly. In our studies, going downtown stands for a glamorous day on the town, an exciting break in the shopping routine, meeting the girls, having lunch and perhaps a theater date or a cocktail—as well as wider selections and better buys. We used a cartoon balloon in which the husband asks his wife, "Why do you shop downtown when there are branch stores in the shopping center out here?" A third of the women mentioned wider selection, but an equal number indicated such reasons as a day on the town and a change of environment. They gave such answers as, "It's more fun, and it gives me a lift"; "I get a kick out of the day off"; "I can combine meeting friends, having lunch, and taking in a movie."

My point is that this very obvious cluster of meanings can be tapped and amplified instead of merely arranging to save streetcar fares, as merchant groups have hopefully tried in numerous cities. When the equation is entirely economic, how can a saving of 20 cents in street-car fares possibly balance out baby-sitter fees and the fatigue of a long ride and sore feet, plus all the psychological negatives of down-town shopping? The power and the scope of advertising lie in its ability to appeal to many, many motive areas that activate the con-sumer; it must not merely consider her an economic automaton who responds like a moth to a light at the mere mention of saving a few pennies. Yet the typical retailer puts on this strait jacket of thinking when he uses advertising.

The shopping experience holds a wealth of rich meanings for the woman. One sociologist says that shopping is a woman's equivalent of a man's hunting trip. It's a spree or binge when she can let herself go and be herself. It's a vicarious enjoyment of higher status. It's the woman's way to wield power which is denied her in the typical husband-wife relationship, where she is forced into the subordinate role. In shopping, she can order people about, be waited on, be courted. She is literally "queen for a day"—flattered and imperious. A retail sales clerk describes his plight as one of serving masses of unreasonable women making unreasonable demands. No matter if she is petty, haughty, mean, deliberately showing hateful and churlish aspects of herself, the oldest platitude in retailing assures her that "the customer is always right."

Shopping for apparel is an especially full area of self-expression for the woman. To quote the sociologist Gregory Stone, clothing is the woman's equivalent of heraldry, a colorful means of telling the world about herself as a person. Clothing is a symbolic statement of her social position, of her mood, and especially of her individual identity. Men in their clothing are more interested in aligning themselves with some category—their professional group, their class, etc.—so that male costuming becomes a uniform. But the woman goes in exactly the opposite direction in order to emphasize her personal identity—she tries *not* to wear the same dress as anyone else.

4

I have been trying to emphasize how little the retailer utilizes the potentialities of advertising when he uses it almost entirely for price promotion, ignoring the multitude of other buying motivations. In a previous chapter I indicated some of the basic drifts in our present national style of life. Saving and security are overshadowed by a new philosophy of spending and enjoying life—now. Even the masses have acquired a taste for taste in what they buy. Style and taste have become the criteria for goods, rather than price and mere utility. Hobbies, travel, sailboats, station wagons, patio furniture, high-fidelity phonographs—a society which wants these things from life is certainly not in a subsistence economy.

But instead of capitalizing on these everywhere-evident desires for better things, the typical retailer still concentrates on price appeal. Almost all food- and drug-chain advertising is simply listings of price. At the very time when the consuming public is raising its standards of taste, looking for something "nicer"—"more quality, more color, more style"—the retailer clings to his fixed pattern of featuring price-promotion items in price-promotion advertising. "Warehouse Sale!" "Prices slashed to ribbons!" "Incredible Savings!"

This is not to imply that price will not always be an important trigger for buying. But not all our buying, not all our desires revolve around this one appeal. I think retailers could very profitably do a certain amount of educational advertising, creative advertising, taste counseling—particularly in this day and age, when there is so much breaking with the past, reaching upward for new ways of living, seeking for guidance in taste. The most effective selling in life insurance, in investments, in the industrial field is accomplished by offering advice. Some stores now offer bridal counseling and advice on sporting goods, cameras, formal wear, travel clothes; and there undoubtedly are many other areas where the retailer could engage in taste counseling and creative advertising.

One of the basic reasons for the high readership of retail advertising is that the housewife hopefully looks to it for information. Most of what she gets is an awareness of current economics and a sense of the trends and styles from the items featured. But inasmuch as the same woman will not only accept but actually look for the advertising in women's service magazines and home magazines, which sets out to be purely informative, I would think that the retailer could do much more open and extended informational advertising.

For instance, from a study we did to explore some of the motives underlying the do-it-yourself trend in home improvement, it was easy to see an enormously powerful area of satisfactions which this activity provided. It offers an outlet for creative expression. Men enjoy a chance to do physical work with their hands, which is other-

wise denied them: they can be effective, with a masculine competence. Home improvement is a perfectly acceptable manifestation of
status striving. The home itself has a powerful set of associations. And
yet the advertising in this field was tapping none of these latent
motive areas. It was boards and ladders and tools on sale—nothing
to reassure the amateur that he could tackle many things that he
hesitated to try, nothing in the way of instruction, no awareness whatever of all the motives responsible for his interest in home carpentry
instead of golf or gardening.

5

If it be objected that creative advertising and taste counseling is a
vague luxury which won't pay off the next day at the cash register, in
the final analysis, why does the retailer use price promotion? When he
has any kind of a sale, it means that he has cut his margins of profit.
When the big retailer has a store-wide sale, its success depends on how
many price cuts he has taken. But he deliberately sacrifices his profit
to create an over-all impression for the store, to attract traffic which
will return on the days when there is no sale to buy items for which
he can get his full profit. In other words, the price promotion is his
obvious way of building a store image. That's mostly what he is
achieving—he is adding meanings to the store personality rather than
doing business at a profit.

But the shopper makes her store choice from a wide range of impressions, going far, far beyond price policy in every direction. If
she in her imagination can think of some store only in terms of pennies
saved on wastebaskets and facial tissue and bean soup, then her
loyalties necessarily will be almost nil. In essence, I think that this
is the most significant single meaning of what I have been saying.
Because my argument directly contradicts the advertising policy of
mass retailing, which depends almost entirely on price promotion,
let me restate it:

1. Any store has a larger personality, a total image of many more
meanings in the consumer's mind than that of a place for day-to-day
transactions. Prices and savings only represent one area of what the
customer thinks and feels about the store. Far more than any bargain
triggers, this over-all store atmosphere (or personality, or image) is
the determinant of regular buying, of the preselection of the customer
body.

2. Whether the retailer realizes it or not, every ad that he runs is
an institutional ad. Besides any items featured, the ad presents a set

of symbols creating meanings about the store. Even if the ad is strictly a listing of prices, it is communicating a picture of the store which the customer very clearly sees.

3. The big, modern department store uses richly involving windows, attractive store interiors, fixtures and displays, and various special events like fashion shows and travel bazaars to add to the total character of the store. But all of this character building depends on actual store traffic. Advertising is capable of reaching a far greater audience than just store traffic. Today is an era of movement to the suburbs, more phone shopping, diminishing physical contact with the downtown store, even weekly shopping at food supermarkets. Proportionately more of the consumer's impressions of any store will probably come from the advertising.

4. The manufacturer uses advertising to create a wealth of meaning and association about his product. He appeals to many motive areas besides the economic. He is skillful in the use of nonrational symbols. He often uses institutional advertising to create an atmosphere about his company itself.

5. Advertising presents the retailer with the same avenues for communicating many kinds of meaning about his store. The mere posting of prices is a rudimentary use of advertising. Advertising is literally a vast storehouse of unused potentialities for the retailer.

By contrast to the sterile, repetitious windmilling ("You save every day!" "Never in your lifetime will you see such price cuts!") to which the average retailer is addicted, the stated philosophy of the fabulously successful Nieman-Marcus store in Dallas shows a refreshing awareness that the shopper is a human being. Stanley Marcus explicitly says that all of his advertising, all of his public relations, is trying to convey that Nieman-Marcus is a "magic wonderland." Although it is strange to hear a retailer use such imaginative terminology, Nieman-Marcus has become, in Mr. Marcus's words, a "state of mind, not just a store."

The best minds in retailing more and more think of "store personalities." They are aware how much the intangibles contribute to the store success—notions of friendliness, cleanliness, style, buying excitement. It is just too bad that the typical retailer so seldom consciously uses his advertising for adding atmosphere and richness to his store personality.

CHAPTER XVI

The Art of Advertising

This book should help to establish a different time perspective for advertising by making perfectly clear that it is a dynamic, ongoing process. If we just reflect on the dazzling evolution of techniques in one short generation, the explosive development of one new medium after another that we learned to use quickly and skillfully—radio, Sunday supplements, chain-store magazines, and now television—we should sense that this human-communication force, like a powerful river, is moving, ceaselessly pushing in new directions. The final word on advertising theory and method has not yet been said—nor will it ever be, any more than it will ever be said in the arts and sciences. And quite apart from the growth of new media, advertising itself will change as there are evolutions in its functions and purposes, in its responsibilities in our economy. And it will change as there are new insights and understandings of its basic nature which can lead to greater effectiveness.

This dynamic, ever-changing character should be written in red letters so that we never find our creative powers hampered by any dead hands from the past nor by any false prophets of the present who insist we adhere to somebody's immutable rules, somebody's mechanical formula. Freshness, imagination, originality, creativity do not come from "playing it safe," following the "tried and true."

Modern advertising is a very complicated process of communication. It involves far more than any simple rules and checklists, far more than a potpourri of words that falls apart when one looks at it—tired words; often meaningless, dull, too technical words; much too often unconvincing words which are overexaggerations or rhapsodies about trivia. The routine of hopefully throwing pails of words at the consumer is something very different from the process of attaining real conviction and motivation to act.

In its essence, advertising is a form of communication. I have shown how, in addition to rational argument and language, modern advertising also uses many modes of symbolic communication, any of which is capable of infusing its own meanings into the product image entirely independently of language.

Whereas the mind can only grasp logical meanings by proceeding from one syllogism to the next, the meanings from presentational symbols in art and music come through instantaneously in flashes of intuition. You don't study them to discover what they mean. You feel their meaning either right now or never. This is why, in the greater profusion of advertising messages being showered on the consumer all the time so that he has less and less time for individual advertising, more and more meaning will undoubtedly come from the presentational symbols rather than from the copy.

It is highly essential also to realize that no matter how convincing may be our argument, successful communication involves more than rationality. There are two levels of attitude in communication. Besides the rational level, there is always the level of feeling and intuition; and it is on this level that the critical decision of acceptance or rejection will probably be made. It is generally insufficient to convince a person on intellectual grounds. His feelings must be involved. And this we achieve by affective or esthetic suggestion and imagery, by the meanings behind the words and pictures.

This is why advertising in its objectives and its techniques must lift its sights much higher than the mere formulation of product claims and economic advantages.

2

If we explore advertising as communication, we shall arrive at a completely different understanding of its place in our society. As matters stand now, there probably has never been so powerful and so pervasive a force in any society of whose real function there was so little realization as advertising in present-day America. From intellectuals, from string-tie politicians, from middle-class sophisticates, from teachers generally, there is the same sneering about hucksters: "Advertising is manipulating people, making them buy things they don't need." Even the business school economists are barely tolerating it, with their explanation that mass production needs mass advertising to lower the price of goods. This is to regard advertising as an unpleasant sufferance which has to be put up with.

And yet it should be obvious that no force could be so influential or have so widespread an effect on society if it did not fulfill some highly desirable functions for the consumer. In contrast to these irritated intellectuals, the average American doesn't think that he is being manipulated by advertising. Instead of turning away from it, he wants advertising.

Communication is a two-way process. Everyone has been concerned with the advertiser—with his purposes, with his responsibilities and his foibles, and with his techniques. But what about the other party to this communication—the audience to which it is addressed? What function does it serve for the consumer that he responds to it as he does? There is a difference between the purpose of advertising and the function of advertising. "Purpose" has to do with the advertiser's intention, which is generally to sell something. This is why he spends money. But "function" has to do with the results of the communication. Obviously advertising doesn't have the same purpose for the consumer as it does for the advertiser.

For instance, one of the Chicago department stores staged an outdoor square dance at its newest shopping center. Hundreds of people came to dance. A pre-Halloween judging contest for children's costumes attracted crowds of parents with their youngsters in full holiday regalia. The Marshall Field window displays at Christmastime depicting Nativity scenes or popular legends have become a Chicago tradition. The purpose of any such expense ultimately has to do with sales and profits. It can only be justified by management on such grounds. But the *function* of these events for the public is entirely different from their purpose. Even if their purpose is commercial, they function for the public as a source of considerable pleasure.

What about the functions of advertising? In every newspaper-readership study I ever saw, department store ads always received materially greater female readership than the average front-page news story or the average editorial. In other words, advertising has far greater significance to her than news of public affairs. In dealing with the realities of her life, it is bringing her something which is much closer, much more important to her.

During several recent newspaper strikes, people were asked what was the most important thing they missed about not having a newspaper. Again and again they reported that the *advertising* was what they missed most. Even though their buying patterns were not appreciably altered, they still wanted the advertising. In every study we make of the component elements of the newspaper, women invariably speak of the advertising as practical, sensible, helpful—one of the most valuable circulation components.

From numerous motivation studies, I could mention a wealth of functions which advertising fulfills for the woman. It relates her and guides her to the economic life of the community. There is a tremendous amount of unconscious learning going on—how to behave in various situations, what are the new styles, what are the latest wonders of our technological world. Our society offers little formal training in being a housewife. Literature and history courses in school are not much help to the young bride. Advertising is consequently a very acceptable and much-wanted impersonal source of instruction for the woman who doesn't care to reveal her inexperience to her in-laws or her husband. We always find that women constantly read price advertising to reassure themselves that they are careful and competent homemakers. Advertising permits preshopping and planning without the intimidation of sales clerks.

Advertising helps us to define products by filling in the nuances and subtle distinctions. We don't want just any toothpaste, any cigarette. We want the brand which expresses our identity—our status, sex, personality, age group.

In another direction, the art in advertising serves as the folk art of our society. Serious painting lost contact with society. It became so intellectualized and cultish that it completely lost the power to convey feeling to common understanding. Yet art is the universal human language. Its very universality indicates that it offers something man wants. Throughout history, in every country, children and plain people alike enjoy the picture, the decoration of baskets and pottery and cathedral windows, the pleasure of color and design rhythm. In modern America, advertising supplies the average man with art into which he can project himself. Completely apart from its commercial purposes, it communicates with him, and he enjoys it as art. It affords him the pleasure of the drawing and the color and the decoration that he cannot get anywhere else.

Advertising art is also comparable to folk art in the sense that its esthetic meaning is created unconsciously and perceived unconsciously. Whereas the serious painter thinks that he has a message, the advertising artist is basically concerned with the aims of advertising. The people who wear caps and gowns can only see that advertising art is not a fine art. It isn't supposed to be. It is a practical art, exactly like any folk art. But just like the temple sculptor, the weaver, and the potter, the artist in advertising is unconsciously creating esthetic meanings which are communicable and enjoyable to his audience, meanings with which they want to identify.

I would say that the better animated commercials on television are rapidly becoming another folk-art form, conveying humor and fantasy as much as any comic strip does. By far the most of the music which the ordinary individual hears is inextricably set in the framework of advertising. Advertising is primarily the source of his music. The motorist who drives for hours listening to his car radio, the housewife who works all day with her radio turned on—these people are aware that advertising is responsible for this long bath of musical pleasure.

The daytime serial was created by advertising and doesn't exist apart from advertising. The sports broadcasts, the drama, the adult games like quiz shows, and now the tremendous spectaculars on television are thoroughly fused with advertising. The function of advertising here in the public mind is to provide entertainment on a scale never remotely approximated by any other source. There is also a certain kind of advertising which is regarded as much-wanted information, such as the movie and help-wanted advertising in a newspaper, the advertising in home magazines such as *House Beautiful* and *Better Homes and Gardens,* and very much industrial advertising.

All of these are functions that advertising performs for the consumer. The primary purpose of advertising may be to sell goods and services, and the advertiser measures its effectiveness in such terms. Yet at the same time advertising has flourished because it is fulfilling so many useful and highly enjoyable functions for the consumer.

3

Perhaps advertising's most important social function is to integrate the individual into our present-day American high-speed-consumption economy. As social scientists have pointed out, ours is no longer a production economy. The average individual doesn't make anything, in the sense that he doesn't make furniture, he doesn't grow his own vegetables, he doesn't weave, make toys, or bake bread. He buys everything, and our economy is geared to the faster and faster tempo of his buying, based on wants which are created by advertising in large degree.

Standard of living is what people want. *Level of living* is what people now have. Our American level of living is the highest of any people in the world because our standard of living is the highest, meaning that our wants are the highest. In spite of those intellectuals who deplore the restlessness and the dissatisfaction in the wake of these new wants created by advertising and who actually therefore propose to restrict the process, it must be clear that the well-being of our entire system depends on how much motivation is supplied the consumer to make him continue wanting.

Perhaps this can best be illustrated by an American military experience during World War II, where native labor had to be used in Panama to build certain vital projects. But the schedules were always behind because the natives refused to work more than a few days a week. That was all the wage they needed for their wants. Why should they work any more? Arguments and pleas were useless. Finally the American commander changed tactics. He imported a supply of Sears, Roebuck catalogues and saw to it that his workers received them. The absentee problem vanished immediately. The natives had acquired wants and were willing to work for their fulfillment. Advertising portrayed for them in concrete and desirable form what wages and work could be transformed into.

In the interchange of industrial groups from various countries who have been brought over to study American production methods in recent years, the British teams themselves have observed that not only is the productivity of the individual American worker higher than that of the British worker, but his spirit is better. Almost every country is anxious to raise its level of living by copying our industrial-production system. What they fail to comprehend, what our own do-gooders cannot realize is that the production system by itself isn't sufficient. Unless the desire is created for the fruits of mass production, they simply rust in warehouses.

Two California scientists have flatly stated, after study of this effort, that a standard of living cannot be exported. It has to come from within. A desire has to be created, wants have to be planted and concretized so that a people is willing to put forth the work needed to earn a higher standard of living.

America has developed a new kind of society, a society that the world had never dreamed was possible—mass prosperity, the abolition of poverty, savings accounts and suburban-home ownership for factory workers, week-end leisure and paid vacations for the masses, the best-dressed, best-fed, best-educated people that has ever existed. But this society wouldn't have been possible without advertising. Besides just moving goods, it has operated at deeper levels to make people work toward the attainment of these material things that constitute our standard of living. The American doesn't work as a slave or a sullen peon. He works with high productivity, because he understands from advertising why he is working. Now he is clear about the goals which his work will bring him: not only the material things, but our whole way of life. Our new society is built squarely on mass media and mass advertising, which have resulted in mass participation in the good things. When advertising is seen as a communication process and evaluated in terms of its effect rather than its purpose, then, from the viewpoint of the social scientist, its primary function is that it integrates the individual into our kind of society. Its secondary function is to sell goods. But its primary function is to relate people to our American system, helping them to feel that they are participating in the best that the society has to offer, causing them to aspire and to work with willingness and high productivity. Just as the training of its formative years socializes the child, so advertising continuously socializes the adult.

4

If advertising is appraised from the viewpoint of its role for the consumer, then there is no reason why we should have to be defensive about its place in society.

It is important to realize that there has been a considerable shift in the consumer's view of the buyer-seller relationship today. The consumer doesn't feel that he is being victimized or cheated by the retailer and the producer. On the contrary, he loves his stores and the mechanical triumphs of his age—the colorful automobiles, the pink washing machines, the garage doors with electric eyes. He is far, far more interested in the people who make Polaroid cameras and power tools, color TV sets and low-cost air conditioners than he is in what the intellectuals and politicians have to offer. This is what he works for; this is what he wants from life—not the frustrated pouting of some university hermit.

As for the angry charge of the late Bernard De Voto that the capitalist system makes goods to sell rather than for their utility—this is Rip Van Winkle ranting. Of course it does! Because this is precisely what the buyer wants—exciting, colorful, and also efficient goods. If they are not efficient and not priced right, he has more choice than anywhere else in the world to buy something else. But he also wants style and buying excitement. And he welcomes the advertising, which serves as his bigger shop window in the market place.

Yet I think that of more concern than the intellectual's misunderstanding of advertising is the failure of so much business management to grasp the significance of advertising as a communication force. There is precious little management that really comprehends how necessary advertising is in the light of the changes that have happened to business itself. Far too much advertising is management-dominated by production men who have no sense of what it is, who still think of business from a refinery conception rather than from a promotion and marketing viewpoint.

A tremendous shift has occurred in the very character of business which they don't grasp. They are still obsessed with operation and engineering problems, whereas the crucial battle is now being fought out in the consumer's mind. Virtually every automobile is on a par in engineering. Every refrigerator, every television set, every loaf of bread is far more standard than ever before. The production problems have mostly been solved. And so also is marketing, in a mechanistic sense, mostly solved: the warehousing, transportation, and physical aspects of selling—branch offices, division offices, etc.

The critical problem now is: What does the consumer think of the brand? How badly does he want it? The arena of competition has largely been transferred from the drawing boards and laboratories to the consumer's mind. The fortunes of the company hinge on the answer to these questions: What kind of brand image is there? What are the meanings which the product symbol has in the buyer's mind? How much psychological desirability does it have? How much buying excitement does it have?

This is the key responsibility that advertising can assume: the task of molding a highly desirable brand image that will set it completely apart in the buyer's mind as "my brand—I just know it's better." Now it becomes far more than just a physical object. Brimming with feeling associations, carrying an aura of rich psychological meanings and desirabilities as a definite part of its totality, it is transmuted into a much-wanted thing. Over and above its use functions, it has symbolic meanings which the buyer desires for self-expression, which satisfy important motives. These subjective meanings created by good advertising convey a very tangible reality to the buyer. They give him the pleasure in buying; these are what he wants most.

Yet there are far too many people in management who completely fail to sense the necessity for the shift from production and operations to imaginative marketing and advertising. There are whole industries which do not see advertising for what it is—a builder of meanings in the consumer mind. The railroads are a prime example. Any number of individual railroads can be included among the largest capital investments in the country, yet their advertising budgets are just a token pittance compared to that of the typical consumer-goods company. Railroad management is mostly dominated by financial and operating minds whose conception of advertising is still that of the "haunch, paunch, and jowl," Jim Brady era of business thinking.

In spite of the fact that railroad service and equipment undoubtedly are at their highest level of efficiency at least in railroad history, the deficits from their passenger operations are more alarming and astonishing every year. Yet they can only think of further mechanical elements as the way out of the wilderness—new-type trains, vista-dome cars. Never does it dawn on them that the core of the problem has to do with the public image of the railroads—an area where advertising can help them more than any other force, since it is capable of altering the sets of psychological meanings which operate against them and in favor of the airplane and private automobile.

Yet they do not use the most potent tool for molding attitudes in the armory of modern business. For physical equipment is only a thing of steel until some force outside of it infuses it with meaning. It does not have desirabilities in itself. The desirabilities have to be created in the consumer mind. To a layman a Van Gogh painting is worthless. The same painting to an art connoisseur is worth $200,000. The value doesn't lie in the painting itself. It is subjective; it is in the individual's mind. Railroad management does so little to generate any desirabilities in an active promotional sense.

This is too often the thinking of the investment banker, the lawyer, and the accountant in management. Essentially it is the negative approach of the caretaker mentality which merely views advertising as a cost item affecting the profit-and-loss statement. Completely lacking is the big dream to see it as a positive, constructive force capable of unfolding new horizons, new markets because it is capable of building, on a mass basis, powerful and rich desirabilities in people's minds.

5

Further disappointing is the management habit in certain areas of overruling the creative people who are trying to influence the consumer with humanized appeals, restricting them instead to management's viewpoint—not the consumer's. The advertising ends up as arid, narrowly appealing, the sort of talk that only another professional feels at home with.

For instance, management level in the petroleum industry is primarily concerned with chemical, technical, refinery achievements and insists on communicating with the motorist in this set of values. Management feels that it is very important that the company has spent 100 million dollars to raise the octane level three points, that the gasoline now offers "supersuperpower," that another mysterious additive is in the picture. The dominant impression in typical petroleum advertising is that the refiners are talking to other refiners, not to the individual motorist who is technically uninformed and baffled by the jargon:

Controlled volatility (What in the world is that?)
Power X with the new X chemical (Excitement? Imagination? No)
Clean-burning, carbon-free Miracle Ethyl with EXA.

This tendency on the part of management to hold advertising to its most rudimentary function, that of name identification and uninvolving claims, is curious, too, because in so many other sectors business *is* completely aware of the importance of affective and motivating appeals.

In the naming of its products—"Thunderbird," "Super-Chief," "Frigidaire"; in the very concept of colorful, modern packaging conceived by industrial designers; in the styling and product design, which are completely extraneous to functional use and technical excellence; in the color motifs of gasoline stations; in an infinity of extra touches, ranging from red-headed elevator operators to piped-in music—in all these things, management senses the value of symbolic and affective communication which will generate tremendous desirabilities over and above the use meanings.

The book publisher makes his manuscript more attractive with a colorful dust jacket. The record manufacturer offers his wares in a beautifully illustrated cover, as if the picture had anything earthly to do with the music. The cardboard containers packaging beer in cans and hi-fi sets and frozen foods are dressed up to add selling appeal and desirability, which are no part whatever of the ingredients. Yet when it turns to advertising, management too often wants to revert to the wholly logical approach.

Because of the very way in which our society has been trained to think, possibly we shall always come to advertising looking first for a convincing and logical demonstration of product superiority. Certainly this approach is effective. Certainly it will be the primary approach in many instances. Probably in most cases the consumer will feel more secure about his purchases and his loyalties if advertising does provide him with some "reasons why." But my entire thesis has been that there is so much more than this going on in the process of communication and persuasion and that advertising therefore has to go so much further than a recitation of ingredients and claims. It is clipping the wings of the creative people to restrict them to this narrow framework.

We have to raise our sights to be infinitely more than mere word-smiths. In actual practice, the creative people of modern advertising are looking at much broader horizons of effectiveness and meaning. The really competent ones can build rich product personalities; they can infuse desirabilities just because they do communicate on many levels. They are not "claim-bound" and "copy-bound." On the contrary, they are searching for symbols which will be significant to the consumer's intuitive judgments and his feelings, to his self-conceptions and his unconscious motive forces as well as his logic.

Very clearly this is the indicated road for all advertising. For this is an understanding of people and of how they behave as human beings. This is an awareness of what should be happening if advertising is to achieve successful and meaningful communication. Advertising must be more than information and reasoning. Above everything else, it must develop the power to move people.

Summary

Virtually all human behavior is some form of self-expression. Everything we buy helps us to convey to others the kind of people we are, helps us to identify ourselves to the world at large. Besides the practical qualities of any product or service, what does it help people to say about themselves? How does it satisfy their psychological goals and their self-concepts? The product which only has use meanings is narrow and static. A primary task of the advertiser is to invest his product or his institution with rich psychological overtones.

Any product is defined partly by its functional qualities and partly by the attitudes which people have toward it. In many instances the product desirability lies wholly in the realm of these subjective attitudes. A cigarette, a necktie, a home permanent have no physiological function whatever. When products and services are far more alike than they are dissimilar, the real buying appeals and distinctiveness will have to come from attitudinal, subjective associations and meanings.

Certainly the consumer is interested in quality and value. All of the training of our society has taught him to look for rational reasons as justification to himself and to others for his purchase. He wants to believe that the objects of his choice do have functional and economic advantages. Nevertheless the psychological overtones have to be desirable, also. Even when he cites logic as the reason for his choice, the real buying force may have come from the psychological overtones attached to the product. This is why the ideal advertisement effectively combines both approaches. It is a blend in varying degree of both logic and emotion, of both realism and fantasy.

There is a vast difference in potential motive power, however, between reason and feeling, between an intellectual attitude and an emotional experience. Human communication is essentially an exchange of feeling, not of information. Advertising which merely supplies information is barely a first step in the process of persuasion. The advertiser must also involve the consumer's feelings. He may do this with obvious emotional appeals. But esthetic approaches, such as art and color in print and outdoor advertising, music and the

197

modulations of the announcer's voice in electronic advertising, also supply powerful feeling associations. Affectivity will create far more motive power for advertising than dull, uninvolving information about technical features.

We live so much in the world of verbalism that we overlook the tremendous amount of meaning which humans convey to one another by nonverbal symbols. Actually there are countless areas (friendship, status striving, masculinity, sincerity, etc.) that are rarely discussed in words. But the other party to the communication is always looking for clues to the speaker's deeper meanings, his real intentions. The advertiser may be unwittingly saying something with these nonverbal symbols entirely at variance with what he thinks he is saying.

Always in communication there is an emotive level of meaning occurring simultaneously with the rational meaning. By gesture, facial expression, tone of voice, manner, etc., we talk to the "third ear" of the hearer in spoken communication—the intuitive "organ" which plays such a dominant part in any judgment. Similarly in advertising, the creative people, besides putting together a sales story about the product, are trying to reach the levels of intuitive judgment in the audience with other kinds of symbolic meaning than mere claims. By emotive associations and/or esthetic meanings, or simply by nonverbal symbols, which may be far more expressive than words, the advertiser hopes to create a prelogical preference for his product, a deep inner conviction that "this is the best."

Successful persuasion through advertising consists of far more than doing clever tricks with words. The consumer has developed a protective husk against mere word claims. Words generally are too shopworn, too commonplace. Words have to create an image of some kind in the individual's mind before he can act. But other kinds of symbols, such as those in illustration, communicate images so much faster, with far less resistance, with much greater persuasiveness. The visual symbols are not just a support for the word claims. They can contribute meanings and associations entirely apart and of much greater significance. The physical appearance of department store advertising—the layout, the art, the style—operates as a language all its own to communicate the character of the store.

One of the primary functions of advertising is to help people articulate their convictions. It does put words in their mouths which will be acceptable reasons. People are looking for confirmation of their judgments. But very often the words they use are merely emotional symbols for much more powerful attitudes. In virtually every product area there exists a certain jargon of acceptable attributes—"taste," "convenience," "economy," etc.—which the consumer wants to believe are the qualities of his choice. Often this jargon is a playback from the advertising. Of course, the advertiser will supply such acceptable supports. But at the same time he has to appeal to the really important motive forces which are underlying these words.

We are accustomed to think that a product is a physical thing with an absolute set of advantages and that the function of advertising is essentially to call attention to these advantages. But nothing is an absolute. Rather, it is what people think that it is. A product or an institution is a symbol whose shades of meaning lie mostly in people's minds rather than in the product itself. Beauty and taste, for instance, are learned. What is attractive to one person may be entirely unattractive to the next. There is no such thing as the taste of margarine per se, existing in a vacuum—or the taste of coffee or the taste of a cigarette. In every case the physical properties act only as stimuli capable of setting off certain associations in the individual. And these may be pleasant or unpleasant associations, depending on the individual.

The objective of advertising is therefore to help mold this product image (personality, character, reputation). Product image is the sum total of all the attitudes which people have toward the product. Every product has an image. It may be good, bad, or dull. Some of these meanings will be rational and functional. But a great many of the important ones can be nonrational, nonutilitarian. A great part of the product desirability can stem from esthetic or emotive associations.

Advertising always has the short-range task of creating some immediate action. But it always has a far more important long-range goal—to create a rich, positive product image or institutional image with many desirabilities. The product must have many attributes besides its purely utilitarian meanings if it is to have real distinction in our competitive market place. Other manufacturers can match ingredients or engineering features or bargains. But they can never match the nonrational psychological overtones in the product image, the collar of subjective attitudes.

This is just as true about a retail store or an institution. In every choice, this institutional image or personality plays a key part. If it is not appealing to the consumer's self-concept, if it does not satisfy his psychological goals, he will rationalize himself right away from service or price attractions.

Certainly economics plays an important part in our purchase decisions. But economics operates largely to establish a ceiling over and probably a floor under our choice. In between these limits the consumer has a wide range of brands and product types to select from. Price is not the explanation of why a consumer chooses a Chevrolet instead of a Plymouth, why he buys a Pall Mall instead of an Old Gold, why he rides an airplane instead of a motor coach. Advertising is only performing in a rudimentary sense when it stops short with mere economics and name identification.

Because we are not living in a subsistence economy, because Americans today want more from their purchases than just utility, and because goods technically are so much alike, the primary function of advertising is changing. It has to go much further than claims and information. It has to create a psychological identity for the product. It has to freight the product image with taste meanings, symbolic attributes, and emotive associations, which are significant in almost any purchasing situation today.

This is not to rule out rationality from our lives at all. But we forget that rationality plays only a small part in our total motivational make-up. Any advertising will obviously be more effective if it can tap the underlying emotional and attitudinal concepts which are important in specific areas, as well as utilize the practical advantages of the product or service. This is an objective of motivation research—to probe for and to evaluate these underlying forces, and thereby to supply directional help to the creative people.

Another important function of research in advertising is to see what actually is being communicated by the message. Not only the logical content of the advertising must be considered, but also the affective elements. What are the emotive associations being created, if any? What are the various esthetic devices conveying, since these are present in all modern advertising? What meaning is coming through from the nonverbal symbols which humans use so much for just informative purposes? Expression becomes communication only when the audience derives the intended meanings from the advertiser's symbols. Is this taking place?

Human beings use two modes of expressing thought, not just one. The process of analytical, logical, common-sense thinking is entirely different from that used in creative imagination and intuition. One proceeds from the intellect, the other from the "underground workshop of the mind," from the emotional system, from the intuitive "organs." The creative person in advertising uses both modes of expression. But many of the symbols which he uses to convey meanings, often far more important than the rational meanings, are just not expressible in literal terms, because they are connected with a different process of thought.

The focus of much advertising should be changed. The advertiser is looking outward at the consumer from the product, whereas he should view the product from the consumer's eyes. Too often the advertiser is describing features which he feels are important but which may not be the least bit important or understandable to the consumer. Features are not benefits. They only become benefits when the consumer sees them as fitting into his life, as providing him with satisfactions, as meeting his felt needs. There are emotional needs, psychological benefits, esthetic satisfactions besides engineering and economic advantages.

People are people. The Logical Man and the Economic Man are fictional. They don't exist. Beneath the mask of rationality that our society teaches us to wear, the consumer is a living, breathing, feeling individual. He is not a technical expert. He wants far more from life than bargains. And his behavior stems more often from emotional and nonrational causes than from logic.

Suggested Bibliography

THE SOCIAL SCIENCES

BOOKS

Abt, Lawrence E., and Leopold Bellak (eds.): *Projective Psychology*, Alfred A. Knopf, Inc., New York, 1950.

Bendix, Reinhard, and Seymour M. Lipsit: *Class, Status and Power*, The Free Press, Glencoe, Ill., 1953.

Brill, A. A.: *Basic Principles of Psychoanalysis*, Doubleday & Company, Inc., New York, 1949.

———— (ed.): *The Basic Writings of Sigmund Freud*, Modern Library, Inc., New York, 1938.

Britt, Steuart Henderson: *Social Psychology of Modern Life*, Rinehart & Company, Inc., New York, 1949.

Cartwright, Dorwin, and Alvin Zander: *Group Dynamics*, Row, Peterson & Company, Evanston, Ill., 1953.

Cuber, John, and William Kenkel: *Social Stratification*, Appleton-Century-Crofts, Inc., New York, 1954.

Fromm, Erich: *Escape from Freedom*, Rinehart & Company, Inc., New York, 1941.

Henry, William E.: *The Analysis of Fantasy*, John Wiley & Sons, Inc., New York, 1956.

Katz, Elihu, and Paul Lazarsfeld: *Personal Influence*, The Free Press, Glencoe, Ill., 1955.

Kluckhohn, Clyde, and Henry Murray: *Personality in Nature, Culture and Society*, Alfred A. Knopf, Inc., New York, 1948.

Lindesmith, Alfred R., and Anselm L. Strauss: *Social Psychology*, The Dryden Press, Inc., New York, 1949.

Linton, Ralph: *The Cultural Background of Personality*, Appleton-Century-Crofts, Inc., New York, 1945.

Mullahy, Patrick: *Oedipus: Myth and Complex*, Hermitage House, Inc., New York, 1948.

————: *Study of Interpersonal Relations*, Hermitage House, Inc., New York, 1949.

Munroe, Ruth: *Schools of Psychoanalytic Thought*, The Dryden Press, Inc., New York, 1955.

Murphy, Gardner: *Introduction to Psychology*, Harper & Brothers, New York, 1951.

203

Murray, Henry: *Explorations in Personality,* Oxford Book Company, Inc., New York, 1938.

Newcomb, Theodore M., Eugene L. Hartley, et al.: *Readings in Social Psychology,* Henry Holt and Co., Inc., New York, 1947.

O'Brien, Robert, et al.: *Readings in General Sociology,* Houghton Mifflin Company, Boston, 1951.

Park, Robert: *Human Communities,* The Free Press, Glencoe, Ill., 1952.

Plant, James S.: *Personality and the Cultural Pattern,* Harvard University Press, Cambridge, Mass., 1937.

Schuler, E. A., et al.: *Outside Readings in Sociology,* Thomas Y. Crowell Company, New York, 1952.

Sherif, Muzafer: *An Outline of Social Psychology,* Harper & Brothers, New York, 1948.

Smith, George Horsley: *Motivation Research in Advertising and Marketing,* McGraw-Hill Book Company, Inc., New York, 1954.

Symonds, Percival M.: *Dynamic Psychology,* Appleton-Century-Crofts, Inc., New York, 1949.

Thompson, Clara (ed.): *An Outline of Psychoanalysis,* Modern Library, Inc., New York, 1955.

Warner, W. Lloyd: *American Life: Dream and Reality,* University of Chicago Press, Chicago, 1953.

ARTICLES

Chapple, Elliot, et al.: "Behavioral Definitions of Personality and Temperament Characteristics," *Human Organization,* winter, 1955.

Crutchfield, Richard: "Conformity and Character," *American Psychologist,* May, 1955.

Gardner, Burleigh, and Sidney Levy: "The Product and the Brand," *Harvard Business Review,* March–April, 1955.

Harding, Charles: "Anthropological View of Personality," *Human Organization,* fall, 1953.

McArthur, C.: "Personality Differences between Middle and Upper Classes," *Journal of Abnormal and Social Psychology,* vol. 50, March, 1955.

Rosenthal, David, and Jerome Frank: "Psychotherapy and the Placebo Effect," *Psychological Bulletin,* July, 1956.

Stone, Gregory: "City Shoppers and Urban Identification," *American Journal of Sociology,* vol. 60, July, 1954.

COMMUNICATION AND THE CREATIVE PROCESS

BOOKS

Berelson, Bernard, et al. (eds.): *Reader in Public Opinion and Communication,* The Free Press, Glencoe, Ill., 1953.

Boas, Franz: *Primitive Art,* Dover Publications, New York, 1955.

Cassirer, Ernst: *The Philosophy of Symbolic Forms,* Yale University Press, New Haven, Conn., 1953.

Chase, Stuart: *The Tyranny of Words,* Harcourt, Brace and Company, Inc., New York, 1938.

Ghiselin, Brewster: *The Creative Process,* University of California Press, Berkeley, 1954.

Hiler, Hilaire: *Why Abstract?* New Directions, New York, 1945.

Hayakawa, S. I.: *Language in Thought and Action,* Harcourt, Brace and Company, Inc., New York, 1940.

Hovland, Carl I., et al.: *Communication and Persuasion,* Yale University Press, New Haven, Conn., 1953.

Kepes, Gyorgy: *Language of Vision,* Paul Theobald, Chicago, 1951.

Langer, Susanne K.: *Feeling and Form,* Charles Scribner's Sons, New York, 1953.

————: *Philosophy in a New Key,* The New American Library of World Literature, Inc., New York, 1942.

Malinowski, B.: "Supplement I," in C. K. Ogden and I. A. Richards, *The Meaning of Meaning,* Harcourt, Brace and Company, Inc., New York, 1953.

Mead, George H.: *Mind, Self and Society,* University of Chicago Press, Chicago, 1934.

Mead, Hunter: *Introduction to Aesthetics,* The Ronald Press Company, New York, 1952.

Ogden, C. K., and I. A. Richards: *The Meaning of Meaning,* Harcourt, Brace and Company, Inc., New York, 1953.

Ruesch, Jurgen, and Gregory Bateson: *Communication,* W. W. Norton & Company, Inc., New York, 1951.

———— and Weldon Kees: *Non-verbal Communication,* University of California Press, Berkeley, 1956.

Schapiro, Meyer: "Style," in A. L. Kroeber (ed.), *Anthropology Today,* University of Chicago Press, Chicago, 1953.

Schramm, Wilbur: *The Process and Effects of Mass Communication,* University of Illinois Press, Urbana, Ill., 1954.

Whorf, Benjamin Lee: *Language, Thought, and Reality,* John Wiley & Sons, Inc., New York, 1956.

Whyte, William H., Jr., and the editors of *Fortune: Is Anybody Listening?* Simon & Schuster, Inc., New York, 1952.

ARTICLES

De Mille, Agnes: "Rhythm in My Blood," *The Atlantic,* February, 1956.

Feibleman, James: "Toward an Analysis of the Basic Value System," *American Anthropological Journal,* vol. 56, no. 3, June, 1954.

Schatzman, Leonard, and Anselm Strauss: "Social Class and Modes of Communication," *American Journal of Sociology,* January, 1955.

Segy, Ladislas: "Art Appreciation and Projection," *Etc, A Review of General Semantics*, Autumn, 1954.

Stein, Morris: "Creativity and Culture," *Journal of Psychology*, vol. 36, pp. 311–322, 1953.

THE CHANGING MARKET

BOOKS

Allen, Frederick Lewis: *The Big Change*, Harper & Brothers, New York, 1952.

Editors of *Fortune*: *The Changing American Market*, Garden City Books, New York, 1955.

Mazur, Paul: *The Standards We Raise*, Harper & Brothers, New York, 1953.

Index